The Evolution of Morality and Religion

Accepted codes of conduct and established religions are features of human societies throughout the world. Why should this be? In this book, biologist Donald Broom argues that these aspects of human culture have evolved as a consequence of natural selection; that morally acceptable behaviour benefits humans and other animals and that a principal function of religion is to underpin and encourage such behaviour. The author provides biological insights drawn especially from work on animal behaviour and presents ideas and information from the fields of philosophy and theology to produce a thought-provoking, interdisciplinary treatment. Scientists who read this book will gain an appreciation of the wider literature on morality and religion, and non-scientists will benefit from the author's extensive knowledge of the biological mechanisms underlying the behaviour of humans and other social animals.

DONALD M. BROOM is Colleen Macleod Professor of Animal Welfare in the Department of Clinical Veterinary Medicine at the University of Cambridge. He has a long-standing interest in the origins of moral behaviour in social species which has led to invitations to lecture in university departments of philosophy and theology. He is also interested in religions and attends a church. In addition to over 250 scientific papers, he has published seven books, including *Biology of Behaviour* (1981), *Farm Animal Behaviour and Welfare* (1990 with A. F. Fraser), *Stress and Animal Welfare* (1993 with K. G. Johnson) and *Coping with Challenge: Welfare in Animals Including Man* (2001). He is a member of national and international animal welfare committees dealing with the ethics of animal usage and related legislation and frequently appears in the media dealing with issues of animal welfare

D1452474

The Evolution of Morality and Religion

DONALD M. BROOM

Department of Clinical Veterinary Medicine and St Catharine's College, University of Cambridge

CAMBRIDGE
UNIVERSITY PRESS

PUBLISHED BY THE PRESS SYNDICATE OF THE UNIVERSITY OF CAMBRIDGE
The Pitt Building, Trumpington Street, Cambridge, United Kingdom

CAMBRIDGE UNIVERSITY PRESS
The Edinburgh Building, Cambridge, CB2 2RU, UK
40 West 20th Street, New York, NY 10011–4211, USA
477 Williamstown Road, Port Melbourne, VIC 3207, Australia
Ruiz de Alarcón 13, 28014 Madrid, Spain
Dock House, The Waterfront, Cape Town 8001, South Africa

http://www.cambridge.org

First published 2003

Printed in the United Kingdom at the University Press, Cambridge

Typefaces Trump Mediaeval 9.5/15 pt. and Times   *System* LaTeX 2_ε [TB]

A catalogue record for this book is available from the British Library

Library of Congress Cataloguing in Publication data
Broom, Donald M.
    The evolution of morality and religion / Donald M. Broom.
        p.   cm.
    Includes bibliographical references and index.
    ISBN 0 521 82192 4 – ISBN 0 521 52924 7 (paperback)
    1. Ethics, Evolutionary.   2. Sociobiology – Religious aspects.   I. Title.
BJ1311.B72   2003
171'.7 – dc22   2003055721

ISBN 0 521 82192 4 hardback
ISBN 0 521 52924 7 paperback

Contents

Preface

The principal arguments presented in this book are: firstly, that morality has a biological foundation and has evolved as a consequence of natural selection acting in various species and, secondly, that religions are essentially structures underpinning morality. It is argued that morality and the central components of religion are of great value.

Many philosophers and theologians write about morality and its origins without any reference to biological processes such as evolution. Many biologists discuss phenomena which are of great importance to human morality and religion without taking account of the ideas of those who theorise about these subjects. I find both of these omissions very disturbing. How can anyone believe that they can adequately discuss a system without any consideration of how it works or of factors which affect its functioning? How can a scientist ignore substantial and relevant areas of intellectual deliberation?

In some books and papers about morality and religion, confusion has arisen because arguments are narrowly focused according to the academic discipline perceived to be involved. An awareness of other disciplines would reduce some of that confusion. Hence it is important to attempt to integrate different approaches and sources of information. Many important gaps in human knowledge exist because there is pressure on academics and others to put most of their effort into studies considered to be central in their discipline. This has the consequence that those areas which cannot be adequately understood without reference to ideas from more than one discipline are neglected or are treated less rigorously than those which are perceived to be mainstream in the discipline. The writings of those who would consider themselves to be biologists, philosophers or theologists are referred to when introducing the general ideas in the book. My training is in biology but I have tried to explain ideas from each discipline and to present balanced judgements about them. Following this attempt at an interdisciplinary study, I hope that experts in each area will be stimulated to comment and take the arguments further.

General ideas about the concepts of morality, religion and relevant biological science, especially the origins of social living and behaviour, are discussed in Chapter 1. Morality is distinguished from sexual and other customs and the role of moral codes as a basis for religion is explained briefly.

In Chapter 2 the extent to which animals of various species, including man, cooperate and show altruistic behaviour towards kin and non-kin is described. When behaviour with each kind of function is discussed, the possibilities for it being cooperative or just competitive are considered. The genetic basis of some of the mechanisms underlying cooperative and altruistic behaviour is explained, as are possible ways in which such behaviour might have evolved.

Since the importance of the key concept of reciprocal altruism has been emphasised in the first two chapters, in Chapter 3 there is a review of the level of sophistication of brain functioning which is necessary for vertebrate animals to be able to show it. Ideas about awareness, consciousness, feelings and cognitive responses are presented with reference to morality in humans and other species.

The first part of Chapter 4 concerns the range of views about what is right or wrong, what people should do and how they should decide what to do. Problems associated with the concept of rights are presented and the idea of conscience is discussed. Questions about the inter-relationships between morality and sexual, developmental and legal matters are then explored in detail. At the end of the chapter, one of the central propositions of this book, that morality has evolved, is presented.

Religion of some kind is ubiquitous in human society. It is argued in Chapter 5 that the common aspect of religions is a moral code which in each of them is largely the same. This central aspect of religion, and some other aspects, have evolved. There are problems associated with certain divisive aspects of religions but the core of religion is of great value and will persist. Suggestions for future conduct of religions are presented.

In Chapter 6, views contrary to those expressed in the previous chapters are presented and discussed. These range from diatribes against evolution by theologians to diatribes against religion by some sociobiologists.

The final chapter, Chapter 7, concerns the social and political consequences of this biological view of morality and religion. The way in which individuals should act and the way in which governments should act is discussed. What should be our view of 'us' and 'them' in relation to other humans and individuals of other species? To what extent is there morality and religion in other species?

Acknowledgements

I thank all of those who have helped me to think, especially my late father Donald Edward Broom, Molly Beswick and my wife Sally. I am also grateful to Sally for help with data collection and to Jill Armstrong for typing the manuscript and helping me to organise my time whilst writing. I thank Tom Broom for useful proof-reading, Harry Bradshaw for helpful comments on the whole of the text and Nick Davies, Robert Hinde and Hans Kummer for advice on specific topics. I thank: the late Bill Hamilton, E.O. Wilson and my PhD supervisor Bill Thorpe for inspiration in their writings; Richard Dawkins whom I have known for forty years for encouraging scientific development and for ideas, even if I disagree with some of them; and for helpful writings, Michael Banner, Daniel Dennett, Mary Midgley, Mark Ridley, Robert Trivers and Frans de Waal. I have been able to improve the book because of the constructive advice of staff at Cambridge University Press and anonymous referees.

I Concepts and codes of living

1.1 CONCEPTS OF MORALITY AND RELIGION

Something is *moral* if it *pertains to right rather than wrong*. The question of what is right, or good, or beneficial is discussed further in Chapter 4, Section 1 but, as Midgley (1994 pp. 13–14) has emphasised, morality should not be thought of as a topic which is obscure and difficult to comprehend. We each have many clear ideas about actions which are good or not good. Planalp (1999 p. 161) states that:

> To behave morally is to judge right and wrong, good and bad, and to behave accordingly.

Hence decisions about moral issues are taken many times during every day. People 'behave morally' most of the time and often discuss questions of what is right or wrong. In doing this they express an interest in *ethics* which is *the study of moral issues*.

Most people who refer to moral acts are considering a circumstance where there is some interaction with other individuals. These individuals that are the subject of moral acts are often, but not necessarily, of the same species. They are usually alive at the time of the act but the action may affect individuals at a later time or may affect those as yet unborn. The idea that another individual is affected by a moral action is clear in Rottschaefer's (1998, p. 42) statement:

> Moral actions and intentions can be discussed either in terms of providing benefits or in terms of refraining from harming.

The benefits and harms are effects on other individuals. These may actually accrue to the individuals or they may be potential effects which would result if an intended or planned act were carried out. Individuals could have moral intentions even if the act was not followed by the expected beneficial effect on another. Actions which would never affect another individual are not moral or immoral.

Moral actions form part of moral systems within societies. Alexander (1987 p. 1) writes:

> Moral systems are societies with rules. Rules are agreements or understandings about what is permitted and what is not, about what rewards and punishments are likely for specific acts, about what is right or wrong.

He considers that moral behaviour consists of following rules and not cheating. These and many other authors are referring to actual or potential impacts on others when they consider what is moral.

In order to act in a moral way, some degree of responsibility for actions is needed. Aristotle (330 BC in Sections 1109 b30–1111 b5) proposed that the six kinds of knowledge requisite for being responsible are to know: what you are doing, who you are, what or whom you are acting on, and to what end and to what degree you are doing it. Fischer and Ravizza (1998 p. 25) extend this argument by saying:

> A person can be morally responsible for his behavior. Moral responsibility, however it is understood, appears to require some sort of control.

The question of control is explained further in Section 2 of this chapter. If individuals had no control over their actions, they would not be responsible for them, so a brain which enables them to have some degree of control is a prerequisite for moral behaviour.

An individual with the capacity to be responsible must have some ability to think and hence to behave in a rational way. Kant (1788) argued that rationality is a foundation for morality and conversely (according to Porter 1995 p. 9):

> Kant's own work is largely motivated by a desire to show that morality has a central place in rational discourse.

Bentham (1781) also drew parallels between discussions about morality and rational investigation. Some recent definitions of morality include reference to rationality; for example, Gert (1988 p. 6) states:

> Morality is a public system applying to all rational persons governing behavior which affects others and which has the minimization of evil as its end, and which includes what are commonly known as the moral rules at its core.

The reference to a 'public system' could be misleading here as it might imply that the morality would not apply in situations involving two or three individuals. Gert (1998, p. 5) also says that some people 'define morality as the code of conduct that would be adopted by all rational persons' and 'morality is a system that all rational persons advocate that other people adopt, whether or not they adopt it themselves'. As soon as there are references to control, thinking and rationality in an explanation of morality, a proportion of people will stop thinking of any individuals, except those humans who have developed such abilities, when considering moral behaviour. However, each ability is present to some extent in young children and in animals of other species.

The description and elucidation of moral problems has long been a subject of great discussion. Kant (1788) advocated analytical debate about moral issues and he thought that this could determine the uniquely correct answer to any moral question. However he did not believe that it is possible to devise moral principles, for he said:

> Who would want to introduce a new principle of morality and, as it were, be its inventor, as if the world had hitherto been ignorant of what duty is or had been thoroughly wrong about it.

Some modern philosophers have gone much further than this; for example, Williams (1985) considered that there should not be attempts to develop theories about morality. The argument that some prohibitions of actions are central tenets of moral dogma which should not be questioned is presented and discussed by many authors, e.g. Anscombe (1958).

Every major religion includes widely known positions on a variety of moral questions (see Chapter 5). However, definitions of religion often include statements about belief which are difficult to verify objectively. The following definition is more descriptive. *A religion is a system of beliefs and rules which individuals revere and respond to in their lives and which is seen as emanating directly or indirectly from some intangible power.* The power may be considered to be either an individual deity or a profound consortium of interests. These beliefs and rules form the basis for individuals' attempts to conform with their own evaluation of what the power would construe as right. There are very many statements of what particular religions are, an example being that of Sykes (1984, p.246):

> Christianity from the Christian standpoint is the response
> appropriate to the undeviating goodness of God.

If the words Islam, Muslim and Allah were substituted in this sentence, it would probably be acceptable to a further large section of the world.

1.2   THE COMPLEXITY OF BRAIN CONTROL

In every aspect of human functioning we can usefully look for parallels and origins in other species. As a biologist, it seems to me entirely normal to say that we humans are animals, to include humans as one of the animal species and to refer to 'humans and other animals', and not to 'humans and animals' as if these were fundamentally different categories. However, many people do not think in this way. In order to counteract this view Midgley (1978) felt the need to state in the introduction to *Beast and Man: the Roots of Human Nature*:

> We are not just rather like animals, we are animals.

It will be assumed, throughout this book, that humans are animals. This does not mean that humans are identical to any other animal.

The extent of similarity is explored further in Chapter 2, Section 1 and some human views of other species are discussed in Chapter 7, Section 3.

In order to be able to appreciate the extent of control exerted by individuals who may or may not act in a moral way, we have to consider the functioning of the brain in man and other social animals. When attempting to describe and understand the extent of control over their behaviour which individuals have and their interactions with their environment, including other individuals, biologists have often been afraid to postulate the existence of complex mechanisms. Many people who discuss non-human species are reticent about referring to their purposive behaviour, the cognitive ability of the individual, the existence of complex concepts in the brain, or the degree to which terms such as aware, conscious, or moral can and should be used. Theories about these aspects of the functioning of the brain and attitudes to them have been considerably affected by zealous adherence to the use of Occam's razor and Lloyd Morgan's canon. William of Occam (1285–1347) presented a principle of parsimony which commended a bias towards simplicity in the construction of theories. This principle, which was utilised specifically in relation to brain function and the control of behaviour by Lloyd Morgan (1896), has been held as an axiom by those who argue that no complex mechanism should be accepted as the explanation for observations if a simple mechanism is an alternative explanation. In several aspects of biology where the underlying mechanisms are complex, this approach can lead to false conclusions. Crick (1989, p. 138) stated that the use of Occam's razor is dangerous in biology and referred to physicists looking for the wrong kind of simple generalisations. The brain is extremely complex in its function and it is my view that progress in understanding thought processes and the control of behaviour has been slowed down considerably by an excessive desire to use simple theories. Erroneous ideas which are a consequence of this way of thinking include: animals are automata; much of behaviour is controlled by 'instincts' or by mechanisms involving only simple stimulus–response links; habituation is always a simple process; learning is an occasional event in life rather than a very frequent event; human babies and non-human animals do not feel pain; the systems controlling interaction with the environment of an individual operate exclusively by negative feedback rather than by more demanding feed-forward control; anxiety, boredom and intellectual pleasure are confined to a small proportion of gifted humans. These ideas are now refuted by many, including the author (Broom 1981 p. 13, 1998, Broom and Johnson 1993, p. 25). The investigation of more complex mechanisms has often been blocked, or not seriously contemplated, because of the pressure on scientists and others to look for and investigate the simplest explanatory mechanisms. Papers and other scientific writings have been criticised or ridiculed because serious consideration was given in them to an explanation of brain function and behaviour which was not the most parsimonious available. In some cases, the more parsimonious explanations have been found to be correct and there is a danger associated with moving too rapidly to the conclusion that an individual has some elaborate ability or controlling system. However, where complex mechanisms may exist, they should be investigated in a balanced way.

Since the writings of Sechenov (1863), most scientists have accepted that behaviour is controlled by the brain and that thoughts, decisions, hopes and beliefs are located in the brain and in no other organ. These views have been gradually accepted by others in society but it is still not uncommon to hear people referring erroneously to feelings, hopes, beliefs or even decisions as being located in the gut or heart. An underlying implication of distinguishing between brain functions and the supposed heart or other body functions is that analytical thinking is different in some fundamental way from the more important and less calculated processes in life. People may feel uncomfortable if the seat of their decisions about what should or should not be done, and of their aspirations, desires and reverences is said to be the mechanistic organ which they perceive the brain to be. Those who have moved away from referring to the heart or other body parts as being the alternative site to the brain have often found solace in making a distinction between mind and brain. The brain does not act in isolation from the body for we now know that most body control systems involve complex interactions between the brain and cells and organs in the rest of the body. Information of various kinds is stored outside the brain, for example in the cells of the immune system (Dantzer 2001), and new information comes into the brain from many sources in the body. However, the complex analysis of the available information is carried out in the brain.

There is discussion amongst philosophers about this distinction between mind and brain but whilst this discussion might occasionally raise an interesting point about brain function, I believe it to be a sterile argument. It is my view that the mind is part of the brain and all of the processes attributed to the mind are a part of brain function. It is not useful to view the brain as consisting of two separate parts, one of which is the mind (see Chapter 3, Section 4). The substantial literature on this subject is not reviewed here as I have found no need to use the word mind in the remainder of this book.

The systems in the brain involve processes which range from relatively simple to very complex. An example of a simple decision taken in the brain is that which leads to the cessation of all movement for a few seconds when a sudden loud noise is detected. This clearly involves a different complexity of processing from that which occurs when deciding what kind of communication to initiate with another individual about a delicate subject in a circumstance where several slowly changing social factors must be taken into consideration. There are many kinds of interaction with the environment of an individual which are complex and involve difficult and wide-ranging analysis in the brain. However, amongst the most complex are those which occur in a long-lasting social group. Within groups of free-living individuals, each of which can behave in a wide variety of ways, the prediction of the optimal way to act is very challenging for every group member. Chance and Mead (1953) argued that the enlargement of the neocortex of the primate brain had occurred because of the complexity of the social situation with which the individuals had to contend. Jolly

(1966) was more specific in proposing that group living would lead to selection for intelligence. The idea was taken further by Humphrey (1976) who stated, firstly, that primates have intelligence which is surplus to that required for normal daily maintenance and, secondly, that social complexity might have been the significant selection pressure promoting primate intelligence. Byrne and Whiten (1997), in a book which explores primate intelligence in social situations much further, explained (p. 2) that Humphrey referred to:

> social manipulation to achieve individual benefits at the expense of other group members, but without causing such disruption that the individual's membership of the group is put in jeopardy. Particularly useful to this end would be manipulation in which the losers are unaware of their loss, as in some kinds of deception, or in which there are compensatory gains, as in some kinds of cooperation.

Although the idea of complex intellectual processes having evolved as a result of long-lasting social living was developed by those who study primates, it is clear that these abilities are also present in socially living ungulates such as cattle, sheep and pigs, carnivores such as wolves, cetaceans such as dolphins, birds such as jays, ravens, parrots, babblers and fairy wrens and probably in some fish, bees and ants.

Attempts to relate brain size to intellectual ability in mammals and birds (e.g. Jerison 1973) have been shown to be worthwhile only when comparing rather diverse animals. Within taxonomic groups of animals, diet and ranging behaviour are not consistently related to brain size (Harvey and Pagel 1988, Harvey and Krebs 1990, Barton and Dunbar 1997). Positive correlations have been found between the size of the hippocampus, a part of the brain which is involved in learning and memory, and the practice by birds (Krebs 1990) and rodents (Jacobs *et al.* 1990) of storing food in hidden caches. There is also clear evidence that the neocortex ratio (neocortex volume divided by the volume of the rest of the brain) is larger in those group-living primate species that live in larger rather than smaller groups and hence, presumably, have more complex relationships (Sawaguchi and Kudo

1990, Dunbar 1992). Similarly, carnivores living in larger groups have a larger neocortex ratio than those living in small groups and the vampire bat, which lives in stable groups and shows reciprocal grooming and feeding (Wilkinson 1990), has a larger neocortex ratio than *Phyllostomus discolor*, a less social frugivorous bat (Barton and Dunbar 1997).

The control by individuals of their interactions with their environment during life, which is important for survival, involves motivational systems (Broom 1981, Chapter 4, Broom and Johnson 1993, Chapter 4). The effective functioning of motivational systems depends on the quality of the input to the decision-making centres in the brain. In a very complex environment, such as one which includes many social group members, adequate control requires good quality input and effective decision-making processes. One form of control is that which occurs by negative feedback; for example, when an action is taken and the consequences are monitored and have some corrective effect on the way in which that action is continued. Another form of control, which can result in greater stability of the system, is feed-forward control, in which destabilising events are predicted before they occur and actions are taken to prevent the disturbance of the stable state. The utilisation in feed-forward control of experience, memory and other information to predict and prevent possible perturbations of state requires more brain processing capability than that which is needed for most negative feedback control systems.

An ability to control is important for moral actions. Blum (1980, p. 3) states that 'morality must involve self control' and the importance of control in all aspects of moral responsibility is emphasised by Fischer and Ravizza (1998). The subject of control in social and other situations has been investigated during much ethological and psychological research. Dennett (1984, p. 51) says:

> We want to be in control, and to control both ourselves and our destinies. But what is control, and what is its relation to causation and determinism? Curiously, this important question has scarcely been addressed by philosophers.

The subject of free will and the relationship between the concept and our knowledge of brain function is one which is also worthy of discussion by neurobiologists. Even though some responses of humans and other species have a partly automatic component, there is much scope for the actions of individuals to be modified following thought and hence to involve free will. Many actions that can have a significant impact on other members of a social group, carried out by mammals, birds and probably other vertebrate animals, involve free will. Even those which are wholly or largely involuntary, such as startle responses when danger is perceived or movements required to obtain a food item, have some potential for deliberate modification and in some species can be mimicked in order to deceive a watcher.

1.3   IDEAS ABOUT THE ORIGINS OF MORALITY

For many people in the past and in recent years it has been impossible to disentangle morality from religion and hence to consider an origin for morality except as coming from a deity. This point is developed further in Chapter 5. Midgley (1994, p. 109) says:

> Until quite recently, this whole range of questions about the
> source of morals was answered in our culture by a series of
> powerful myths.

As a consequence of religious or traditional explanations, many people did not expect to think much about the basis of moral actions. Those who did think and write about the issues referred to external guidance and sometimes to intrinsic human qualities. Adam Smith did both: in 1776 (p. 423) he described human intentions and actions as being guided by an invisible hand to promote an end which is in the interests of society whilst in 1759 (p. 9) he said that Man possesses capacities:

> which interest him in the future of others, and render their
> happiness necessary to him, though he derives nothing from it,
> except the pleasure of seeing it.

For many people in the past and some now, moral guidelines have been considered to exist and to be usable without any human intellectual contribution or questioning being necessary or desirable. Such people are referred to as transcendentalists by Wilson (1998, p. 265) who contrasts them with empiricists who think of moral guidelines as contrivances of the brain. Wilson summarises the transcendentalist view and then presents his own empiricist view as if religion had little part in it. The view presented in this book follows many of Wilson's evolutionary arguments but extends them to explain that religion should be viewed as within the structure which has evolved and not outside it (Chapter 5, Section 4). Wilson's emphasis of this dichotomy impedes understanding in my opinion (Chapter 6, Section 2.2).

T. H. Huxley, the great champion of Darwin's theories, thought of morality as a weapon to be used against human nature. This view, which is quite contrary to the arguments in this book that morality has evolved, is nicely summarised by de Waal (1996, p. 2) as follows:

> Viewing nature as nasty and indifferent, he depicted morality as the sword forged by *Homo sapiens* to slay the dragon of its animal past.

Huxley (1894, p. 83) said:

> The ethical progress of society depends, not on imitating the cosmic process, still less in running away from it, but in combating it.

Some philosophers have been disturbed by any attempt to explain scientifically any aspect of morals. Indeed, the influential philosopher G. E. Moore (1903) went so far as to state that it is illegitimate to argue from the facts of nature to human values, a view which had a stifling effect on the development of this area of philosophical theory for generations (Johnson 1993, p. 140). During the first two-thirds of the twentieth century, there was a strong tendency for philosophers, psychologists and anthropologists to speak as if human culture and its moral structure was either divinely inspired or arose out of nothing. In recent years, the opinions of philosophers interested in ethics about how to use biological information concerning man and other species have often been to ignore all of it completely or to dismiss it as irrelevant. In some cases, this is because parts of the information are irrelevant and the key aspects appear not to be fully understood. Rottschaefer (1998, p. 14) states, after some mention of cognitive capacities and motivation:

> What we seem to want to know is the meaning of our lives and, perhaps most important, the meaning of ourselves as moral agents. All the biological and psychological information in the world about our moral agency and its sources doesn't seem able to give us that answer.

Some evolutionary biologists have also differentiated sharply between morality and characteristics which have evolved. In the midst of a strong argument about the importance of evolution by natural selection in social life, Dawkins (1976, p. 215) says:

> We, alone on earth, can rebel against the tyranny of the selfish replicators.

with the implication in subsequent text that morality is not a part of evolved characteristics. Alexander (1979, p. 276) presents the view that evolution has nothing to say about normative ethics, about what people ought to be doing. A rather confusing argument from Williams (1988) is:

> I account for morality as an accidental capability produced, in its boundless stupidity, by a biological process which is normally opposed to the expression of such a capability.

As explained in the next section of this chapter and in Chapter 4, Section 4, confusion between true morality and sexual customs may account for some statements of this kind by Alexander, Williams and others.

The importance of cooperative behaviour and the fundamental virtue of Man are the central themes of the writings of Kropotkin (1902). Until recent years, this book has had little influence. Some of those who sought a basis for ethics emphasised that scientific information must be taken into account. One, whose approach was called naturalistic, was Sellars whose view of what is important included connections between what he called the manifest and scientific images of humans (Sellars 1963). Such general statements did not encourage careful thought about any biological basis for morality. A much stronger, if somewhat tactless, encouragement in this direction came from Wilson (1975, p. 562):

> the time has come for ethics to be removed temporarily from the hands of philosophers and biologicized.

The idea that consideration of the biological basis of morality is at odds with the concept of humans being able to take important ethical decisions was criticised by Midgley (1978, p. xviii):

> The notion that we 'have a nature', far from threatening the concept of freedom, is absolutely essential to it. If we were genuinely plastic and indeterminate at birth, there is no reason why society should not stamp us into any shape which might suit it.

Midgley goes on (p. 174) to argue that more careful consideration of the biological basis for morality means 'philosophising better'. It was thought by Dennett (1995, p. 468) that ethics must be based on 'an appreciation of human nature' and Brandt's theory of ethics is based on 'spontaneous beliefs' (1996, p. 174). Detailed expositions of the biological basis of morality are presented by Ridley (1996) and de Waal (1996) who (p. 2) says:

> Given the universality of moral systems, the tendency to develop and enforce them must be an integral part of human nature.

The widespread occurrence of cooperative behaviour and its particular value are described in Chapter 2, Section 2 and arguments for the evolution of altruism and morality are presented in Section 7 of this Chapter, Chapter 2, Section 4 and Chapter 4, Section 7.

1.4 MORALITY DISTINGUISHED FROM SEXUAL AND OTHER CUSTOMS

The argument that is introduced in this Section and developed in Chapter 4, Section 4 is that there are some actions which might be criticised by some or many in human society but which are to do with sexual or other customs rather than with true morality. Many sexual taboos serve a mate-guarding function for males rather than being in the general interest of the members of a social group. A straightforward example is the view that it is morally wrong for women to derive pleasure from the act of copulation, and, as a consequence, the practice of clitorectomy. Once such a practice exists, there can be an argument that its continuation helps to maintain stability in the social group because women are less likely to be unfaithful to their husbands. However, there are counter arguments: one is that an individual should not be deprived of body tissue and a particular sensory capability and another is that sexual pleasure may help to strengthen pair bonds and hence social group stability (Broom 1998).

In an attempt to describe what is good for every individual, J. Griffin (1986, p. 67) lists:

(1) personal accomplishment,
(2) freedom to decide what to do, by one's own rights, without constraint,
(3) having the basic capacities (to move one's limbs, the minimum material conditions required for life, freedom from pain and anxiety),
(4) understanding of oneself and the world,
(5) enjoyment, and
(6) having deep personal relations.

This list has close parallels with the list of five freedoms which Brambell (1965) said should be provided for farm animals and which has been used by the UK Farm Animal Welfare Council. For socially living animals, including humans, Griffin's list might be augmented, or specified, to include acting in such a way as to remain in the social group and to maintain group stability. In compiling his list, Griffin did not include any reference to sexual behaviour.

Some actions are always wrong, in my view, and can never be justified by a beneficial consequence. However, in considering what is bad for every individual, the lists produced by many people would include certain kinds of sexual activities. Some of such lists would state that any kind of sexual interaction between most possible pairs of individuals in a society is wrong. However, I consider that sexual acts are not in themselves wrong and advocate the consequentialist argument that moral judgements about sexual activity should concern whether or not there are harms to individuals as a consequence of it. In any sexual interaction, it is the consequence, rather than the interaction itself, which may mean that the interaction is wrong. Sexual behaviour is wrong if it: produces offspring who will not receive adequate care, or damages a relationship, or results in abnormalities during development in the young, or creates false and damaging expectations, or causes other harms such as disease in the individuals involved. This argument can be applied when considering all sexual customs in order to determine whether or not, and how, they might be related to questions of morality.

There are other actions, or failures to act, which are really customs but might be regarded as morally wrong by some people. Conventions about ways of eating or dressing are not in themselves moral issues, as emphasised by Brandt (1996 p. 61), but the consequences of failing to abide by them do have to be considered. If the consequence of such a failure was that the person who did not carry out the appropriate act lost some esteem in the eyes of others, that is clearly no moral issue. However, if that failure caused severe distress to a third party, and this distress was predictable by the person acting, the failure would have moral connotations. Some religious practices might be considered to be customs which are not, or not necessarily, associated with moral issues. As Gert (1988, p. 256) puts it, 'people may fail to distinguish between a religious support for morality and a religious support for its own particular rules or ideals' and the latter need not be equated with morality. The religious practices may serve a useful function in helping to strengthen social bonds in the community, or in providing comfort for individuals, but failure to conform with them would not in itself be morally wrong. Again, the consequences, for individuals and the group as a whole, of not conforming need to be assessed when deciding whether there is a moral issue.

Care must be taken and all kinds of possible consequences considered when deciding whether a custom has moral consequences or not. For example, van Schaik *et al.* (1999, p. 222) describe various aspects of the behaviour and physiology of female monkeys which minimise the risk of infanticide by males. One of these is variability in the strength of signals that ovulation is occurring, such as sexual skin colour and mating calls, and another is the occurrence of sexual activity outside periods of regular ovular cycles. These are the kinds of physiological changes and behaviours which might be taken to indicate undesirable coquettishness or promiscuity and which might in human society be the subject of sexual customs, but which have a biological function in helping to increase the number of offspring which survive.

1.5 CODES OF CONDUCT

Codes and rules of conduct, which include issues of great importance, are widespread in human society. Midgley (1978, p. 298) said that: 'rule formation is a universal human characteristic' whilst Wilson (1978, p. 185) proposed:

> To counteract selfish behavior and the dissolving power of high intelligence and idiosyncracy, each society must codify itself. Within broad limits, any set of conventions works better than none at all.

Some of these codes are specified as laws, for example those to prevent murder, theft, rape and fraud. Other selfish acts are the subject of sanctions which, although social rather than legal, are important nonetheless. Indeed Ridley (1996, p. 38) refers to 'a taboo against selfishness'. Codes of conduct have been written down in many societies, for example The Ten Commandments of the Jews and Christians, in the Bible (Exodus, 20: 3–17 and Deuteronomy, 5: 7–21) and the Greek Rules of Conduct (see Brandt 1996, pp. 78–79). This moral core of religion is expanded upon in Chapter 5, Section 1. Bischof (1978, p. 50), considering a variety of human societies, presents a list of moral norms based on:

(1) those which protect against the unbounded self-interest of others, e.g. murder, theft, witchcraft, slander, adultery;
(2) marriage rules which proscribe partners who are so closely related that there would be incest or are so distantly related that a racial taboo would be involved;
(3) spiritual rules honouring gods, ancestors or totems;
(4) those which establish and corroborate personal maturity, e.g. moderation, asceticism and abstinence;
(5) rules to spare society from observing sexual intercourse, defaecation, menstruation, birth and death.

Some of these rules are customs, as discussed in Section 1.4 rather than always being morally important. A list of moral rules relating to impacts on other persons (Gert 1988, p. 98) forbids killing, causing pain, disabling, depriving of freedom and depriving of pleasure whilst enjoining others to obey the rules.

Some of these rules would seem to be relevant to any society whilst others are most relevant to societies with particular characteristics. The rules which minimise the likelihood of serious harm being caused to another individual come into the first category and, as Brandt (1996, p. 71) points out, they include a moral obligation not to cause an accident to another individual. Society condemns, albeit to different degrees, those who injure another deliberately, those who cause injury by careless contact with another such as a push which

leads to a head injury, and those who are negligent with the consequence that an injury is caused to another, for example leaving a large
hole in the ground uncovered in the dark or giving a child a dangerous
weapon. There are also rules relating to the use of important resources.
If plentiful quantities of food are occasionally obtained by individuals
in a social group, there is likely to be an expectation within the group
that it will be shared. Ridley (1996, p. 115) argues that humans were
hunter gatherers with intermittently plentiful food for a large proportion of their existence as a species so the code that windfalls of food
should be shared evolved. Even as agriculturists, there were periods of
plenty when the harvest might be shared and periods of severe need
when those with much stored food might give to those without. Such
situations still exist today and there is a parallel with the Lottery win-
ner who is expected to share with their family, with members of their
immediate social group and with the deserving in the wider community. An example of a society with particular characteristics requiring
different rules is one which encourages retribution for harmful acts
remembered from the past or favours returned after a long time-lag.
An example of this, the largely obeyed code which requires children
to care for elderly parents, is discussed by Alexander (1987, p. 89).

It is of value for individuals to abide by their society's rules and
codes because of sanctions if they do not and because of increased
stability in the society in which they live if they do. Kummer (1978,
p. 42) discusses this issue:

> In a moral society, the individual respects the norms not only in
> order to avoid sanction and to seek the reward of acceptance but
> also to weigh his value of himself by the degree to which his
> conduct during life matches the ideal which his culture has set up
> for an individual of his class. Approaching the ideal is at the same
> time a third kind of incentive for moral behaviour and a new,
> non-biological 'function' of morality: the meaning of the subject's
> life to himself.

The advantages of having some rules, codes or norms in a society
apply to all societies.

As explained in Chapter 4 there will be much variation in the customs of societies but little or no variation in true moral codes. Whilst de Waal (1996, p. 36) cautions that variability in moral codes must not be ignored, the real meaning of moral codes and the important distinction between these and sexual and other customs should be borne in mind. Gert (1988, p. 4) explains that differences between codes of conduct in different societies 'often mask essential similarities'. However, Gert appears to be considering sexual customs when stating that the work of anthropologists shows 'that there is no universal morality'. Midgley (1978, p. 37) derides the description of various peoples encountered by European explorers and colonisers as savages because they were unfitted for society. These people had different customs which were emphasised in the explorers' categorisation as savages but the similarity of the latter's true moral codes was often ignored. Indeed, such peoples were often assumed to have no moral code. To some extent, this was because the colonisers did not wish to show to them the same moral obligations that they would be obliged to show within what they regarded as their own society. Midgley (1978, p. 30) points out the savagery of the white hunter in Africa as compared not only with indigenous peoples, but with other social species there. When good quality anthropological studies of supposedly primitive peoples have been conducted, they have demonstrated the existence of moral codes as well as various customs. There have been reports of apparent contradictions to this but some were subsequently shown to be the result of calculated misinformation by the supposedly primitive subjects, in order to deceive the stupid foreigners. Others, such as Turnbull's (1972) study of the Ik people, seem likely to have been much affected by the fact that the whole world of those people was being destroyed. The extent to which there are codes of conduct in other species is discussed in Chapters 2 and 3.

1.6 CONSEQUENCES OF SOCIAL EVOLUTION

Each cell in an animal or plant is a result of collaboration in that the chloroplasts in plants and the mitochondria in both animals and plants are thought to have originated as free-living organisms which were more successful when they functioned within the cell milieu than outside it. There is also collaboration between different cells with different functions in a body. Although these cells share the same genes, they differ in that genes are expressed to different extents in different cells. The genes compete with one another for bodily resources but the functioning of most depends on effective collaboration. Multicellular individuals may also cooperate and one may remain in contact with another, sometimes living colonially. In some colonial animals, such as corals, the individuals are very similar to one another but in the complex free-swimming Siphonophora, such as the Portuguese man-of-war, different zooids have different functions in a free swimming colony. Colonial and social animals dominate much of the world. The shallower waters of the tropics are dominated by corals and the seas generally are exploited especially well by shoaling species of fish and squid. Much of the land is dominated by ants, social herbivorous ungulates, rodents and primates. The most successful birds spend part or all of their lives in social groups. The fact that the social species are so successful indicates that, although there will always be competition as well as collaboration, the latter is more important in many aspects of life.

The various functions of social behaviour are discussed in detail by Broom (1981, p. 176). Animals can create a more favourable micro-environment by grouping, and some, such as termites, ants and humans, can do this particularly effectively by building structures in which to live. Food finding is important at all times but especially so when food is scarce. Birds which roost communally at night and flock during the day may survive periods of low food availability because they use the knowledge of others to obtain some food at these times (Ward and Zahavi 1973). Animals living in groups can learn new feeding methods by watching others and may be able to collaborate in acquiring, handling and defending food.

Many of those who have considered the functions of group living in humans or other primates have described the increased chances of predator avoidance which it confers. One example of a study of monkeys which indicated that group size is affected by predation is that of van Schaik and van Noordwijk (1985), who found that long-tailed macaques lived in larger groups when there were predators such as clouded leopards, golden cats and tigers in the area than when there were no feline predators. The conclusion from such studies by van Schaik (1983) was that:

> the lower threshold to group size is set by predation, the upper limit is posed by feeding competition among group members.

Young animals are particularly vulnerable to predation and de Waal (1996, p. 171) points out that protection of the young is easier in various animals such as monkeys, elephants and dolphins, because they are in groups. The question of why humans live in groups is reviewed by Alexander (1987, p. 79). The proposed link between intelligence and complexity of social life is discussed in Chapter 1, Section 2.

Mate-finding is also much easier when living in groups than when solitary and there are various possibilities for collaboration in rearing young and helping relatives when in a group. Group-living can have various functions but this does not mean that each of these functions was concerned with the origins of group-living in any species, for this has arisen by several evolutionary routes (Broom 1981, p. 191).

When considering the possible effects of genes which promote group-living, as offspring will often be with parents after rearing, the first question should not be 'why aggregate?' but 'why separate?' (Broom 1981). Competition between parents and offspring, or between peers, forces separation but advantages such as better environment modification, food acquisition, predator avoidance or help for offspring may counteract this. Where food or hiding places are patchily distributed, as they frequently are, aggregation at a food source or a hiding place may occur. Once animals are aggregated, Broom (1981, p. 192) proposes five routes towards staying in the group and hence living socially: (1) predation risk is reduced by getting into the middle of the group (Hamilton 1971); (2) predation risk is reduced because early warnings from others in the group about danger can be used; (3) when food is depleted, an individual which knows where to find food can be followed (Ward and Zahavi 1973); (4) offspring stay with parents because they learn from them about social techniques, feeding methods and predator avoidance methods; or (5) close relatives survive better if the individual stays in the group. The possibility of advantageous collaboration in feeding and the possibility for substantial and useful modification of the environment are other possible factors promoting group-living.

1.7 COOPERATION AND MORALITY

Hans Kummer, a pioneer in demonstrating the sophistication of social organisation in monkeys, observed that (Kummer 1978, p. 43):

> The essential benefit of social life is cooperation, its essential disadvantage competition.

Social living allows various possibilities for cooperation, provided that the individuals have the abilities to exploit these. John Crook, who has studied social behaviour in humans, other primates and birds, stated (Crook 1980, p. 185):

> with a large population living under conditions of finite plenty, there will be in the ethics of the people an emphasis on collectivity, a power in the service of others, on the resolution of conflict without combat and on nepotistic values generally.

Group-living will necessarily lead to conflicts of interest between individual group members for resources such as food, resting places, positions of safety in the group, mates, opportunities for social influence, etc. Alexander (1987) and Goldsmith (1991) emphasise that concepts of what is moral or immoral exist because there are conflicts of interest and codes within social groups to resolve these.

Moral attitudes, and structures within animals which make them possible, have not persisted in populations by chance but because those individuals which had them gained selective advantage from having them. The basis for this is that certain genes would promote moral acts and those genes which interact with the environment to produce beneficial characters in the phenotype of the animal are more likely to persist in the population. Those individuals which have moral attitudes and show moral behaviour are more likely to be able to collaborate effectively with other members of their own species and, to a lesser extent, with members of other species. The genes which promote morality increase the chance of being accepted as a collaborator because morality helps in the promulgation of anti-cheating methods and in persuading other individuals that the bearer of the gene is unlikely to cheat. It is not implied here that all social behaviour in humans, or any other species, is directed towards helping others or attempting not to harm others. Some of such behaviour which is competitive, predatory or careless is damaging to other individuals. However, the extent of harm done to others within a social group is much less than that which might be caused if short-term self-interest were thoroughly pursued, and the frequency with which good is done to others is much greater than that which would be expected at the level of chance. Selfish and vindictive behaviour will sometimes be advantageous but, in the longer term, provided that the advantages of living in a group or of some intermittent collaboration are substantial and are impaired by the selfish behaviour, failure to show altruistic behaviour is dangerous.

The propositions presented above are based on a series of premises and the argument that these premises, and what follows from them, are correct is the substance of much of the remainder of this book. Philosophers refer to the argument that morals are in some way a consequence of the biological functioning or nature of the individual as 'naturalistic'. The contrary view, that moral propositions are self evident, is presented by Brandt (1996, p. 4) and then strongly criticised by him. Biologists are more likely to support the naturalistic view, for example de Waal (1996, p. 2) says:

> Given the universality of moral systems, the tendency to develop and enforce them must be an integral part of human nature.

de Waal also argues for the central role of social behaviour and the value of the social group in understanding morality, for example (de Waal 1996, p. 10):

> 'Social inclusion is absolutely central to human morality' and 'Immoral conduct makes us outcasts.'

Altruistic acts are those which, at least in the short-term, benefit one or more other individuals in that their fitness is increased and involve some cost, measured as actual or potential reduction in fitness, to the altruist. Very many people have referred to the role of altruism when attempting to explain the foundations of human society, or, more particularly, the way in which individuals should behave. Wilson (1978, p. 149) says:

> Generosity without hope of reciprocation is the most cherished of human behaviors.

and

> We sanctify true altruism in order to reward it and thus make it less than true, and by this means to promote its recurrence in others.

The altruistic act may be an isolated interaction between the two individuals, or may be directed towards a close relative, or may be to a greater or lesser extent reciprocated at some later time. However, its occurrence when noted by others can have an effect on relationships within the society. Crook (1980, p. 396) points out that altruism may:

> serve both the biological fertility and the social security of individuals,

and would be:

> a generalised rule of action, the distinction between nepotistic, reciprocal and 'real' altruism would cease to have much significance in a culturally altruistic world community.

Reciprocal altruism is more likely in long-lived species in which social contacts are prolonged (Trivers 1971). Broom (1981, p. 194) explains that reciprocal altruism is vulnerable to cheating and punishment of cheats may be costly and continues:

> It is likely that reciprocal altruism is especially important and extensive in man because of our abilities to communicate and to recognise cheats. As a consequence of these abilities, a gene which promoted some form of reciprocal altruism would have been especially likely to spread in a human population . . . Many codes of conduct based on reciprocal altruism have been devised in human societies and these have been effective in promoting cohesion within the society which utilizes them.

These ideas were also emphasised by Trivers (1985, p. 393):

> There can hardly be any doubt that reciprocal altruism has been an important force in human evolution.

and Alexander (1987, p. 77):

> Moral systems are systems of indirect reciprocity. They exist because confluences of interest within groups are used to deal with conflicts of interest between groups.

If the arguments presented briefly above are followed, are moral systems likely to have arisen in species other than man? Before proposing that they have, de Waal (1996, p. 34) presents:

> Conditions for the evolution of morality: 1 group value – dependence on the group for finding food or defense against enemies and predators; 2 mutual aid – cooperation and reciprocal exchange with the group; 3 internal conflict – individual members have disparate interests.

There are other valuable group-dependent functions in addition to those specified by de Waal. Food utilisation after it is found can be better in groups; for example, crocodiles have difficulty pulling flesh off large prey but groups of crocodiles take turns to hold the prey whilst others pull off some flesh and then acquire some of the meat themselves while others hold the carcass. Another function is better thermoregulation in huddled pigs or wrens and in termites within a nest. Examples are detailed in Chapter 2, Section 2. Where de Waal refers to 'dependence on the group' and 'mutual aid', it may be that only two individuals are involved or there may be more complex interactions. If, with these small qualifications, de Waal's conditions are accepted, it is clear that there is a potential for the evolution of some degree of morality in many social animals. Midgley (1994, p. 129) criticises the idea of:

> animality as a foreign principle inside us, alien to all admirable human qualities

and the summary of this attitude as:

> the beast within us.

Midgley's view (p. 175) is that:

> Morality . . . cannot be a thunderclap, occurring along with the instant invention of language at the moment of the sudden and final emergence of the human race.

1.8   MORALITY AND RELIGIONS

Three major arguments, presented briefly here and detailed in Chapter 5, are: firstly that moral codes are the core component of religions, secondly that some form of religion is an inevitable consequence of the necessity for moral actions and thirdly that religions are valuable to all because of their key aspects. It is important to distinguish between the fundamentals of a religion and structures or rituals which help some or many of the individuals who adhere to that religion to understand and practise the religion. The fundamentals, or central tenets, of the religion are those which promote the helping of others and minimise harm to others, for example commandments, certain parables and the concept of God, gods, or spirits reinforcing these. The idea of a common good and of something greater than the individual, a common spirit, God or gods, helps moral systems to function. An example of religious teaching which closely parallels the arguments about biologically based morality presented in Section 7 of this chapter and indicates the relevance of the concept of God, is the statement by Jesus as recorded in the Bible, Matthew, 18: 15–20:

> Moreover if thy brother shall trespass against thee, go and tell him his fault between thee and him alone: if he shall hear thee, thou hast gained thy brother. But if he will not hear thee, then take with thee one or two more, that in the mouth of two or three witnesses every word may be established. And if he shall neglect to hear them, tell it unto the church; but if he neglect to hear the church, let him be unto thee as an heathen man and a publican. Verily I say unto you, whatsoever ye shall bind on earth shall be bound in heaven: and whatsoever ye shall loose on earth shall be loosed in heaven. Again I say unto you, that if two of you shall agree on earth as touching any thing that they shall ask, it shall be done for them of my Father which is in heaven. For where two or three are gathered together in my name, there am I in the midst of them.

In this text, 'thy brother' means someone known to you, 'the church' means your community of people and it is made clear that there are very close links between earth and heaven and between people, God and Jesus.

Where moral codes are elaborate because of the variety of positive and negative effects which individuals can have upon one another, the long intervals between events which are relevant to one another for moral reasons, or the subtleties of inter-relationships within the society, a structure which is the basis of a religion is likely to develop. Moral codes have greater efficacy and universality if they are spelled out. In order that the codes will have effect, a belief that morally good or bad behaviour is monitored in some way, and that something or someone controls reward or retribution, is necessary. Religions, and other sets of beliefs relevant to human conduct which may or may not be called a religion, will arise as the structure for the moral system which encourages the promotion of cooperation and the detection and discouragement of cheating. Examples of pseudo-religions, which include some of the characteristics of religions, are those which underlie trade groups in cities, political groups, freemasons, knights templar, aristocrats, the European Union and the United Nations. Some religions and pseudo-religions are viewed as pertaining to some rather small constituency and may have customs which encourage hostility to non-members, a position which is harmful and conflicts with the fundamental codes of all major religions. Such codes are reviewed in Chapter 5, Section 1.

The argument that religion has some biological basis has been presented by several authors and a few of them make a link between the evolutionary origins of morality and the existence of religion. Thorpe (1974, p. 378) says:

> 'I consider man as essentially a religious animal' and:
> 'agree with Hobhouse that religion is progressive apprehension of the spiritual'.

Thorpe refers to a biological foundation to religion and explains his idea of the Holy Spirit and of God as all seeing but benevolent in relation to moral issues. However, he does not make the firm links which are made in this book. Many philosophers referring to moral or religious codes 'rely on intuitions or considered beliefs' (Brandt 1996, p. 5) with the underlying idea that these come from the functioning of the individual. The view of Wilson (1978, p.169) is that:

> The predisposition to religious belief is the most complex and powerful force in the human mind and in all probability an ineradicable part of human nature.

This topic is discussed further in Chapter 5, Section 4.

Are there conflicts between the evidence concerning the evolution of behaviour, the existence of religions and the beliefs encouraged by religions? Midgley (1978, p. 127) clearly finds the reconciliation of evolution and religion difficult, as does Wilson (1975, p. 120):

> When altruism is conceived of as the mechanism by which DNA multiplies itself through a network of relatives, spirituality becomes just one more Darwinian enabling device.

The serious problem with this statement is the word 'just' because the existence of a biological explanation does not devalue spirituality. It may well encourage people to be a part of a religion because they understand it and its benefits better. Writers who criticise and denigrate religion generally pick on what are actually rather peripheral structures and rituals, apparently without appreciating the central tenets. Some general statements by evolutionary biologists, see for example Dawkins (1993), such as 'religion is just like a computer virus' are bad science and indicate a failure to understand either evolutionary mechanisms or the complexities of organisation of societies.

2 Cooperation, altruism, reciprocal altruism

2.1 THE COMMONALITY OF GENES AND THE CONCEPTS OF ALTRUISM

The system controlling any behaviour develops in the individual as a consequence of interactions between the genotype and its environment. Hence it is of value to consider how genes might influence behaviour and to consider how a gene which does so might have spread in the population. Those who have sought to explain altruistic behaviour towards close relatives have found it useful to consider degrees of relatedness because these would allow estimation of the likelihood that a gene which promoted altruistic behaviour would be shared with the individual who benefitted from the act. Hamilton (1963, 1964a, b) referred to degrees of relatedness such as 0.5 between parents and offspring and between siblings and 0.25 between grandparents and grandchildren. However, other authors sometimes made the assumption that degree of relatedness could be translated directly to the number of genes in common. Alexander (1979, p. 45) said 'full siblings on average have 50% of their genes in common' and Barash (1979, p. 134) referring to bees with haploid reproductive males said 'each worker shared three quarters of its genes with its sisters'. However, as Broom (1981, p. 10) explained:

> it is not correct to say that the siblings share 50% of their genes because this depends upon the variability within the species. Many genes are the same for all individuals because they code for some essential protein which will not function if its structure is altered . . . the actual proportion of genes shared by siblings is much higher than 50%

Recent DNA sequence analysis has shown, for example, that humans share 99% of genes with chimpanzees, 97.7% with gorillas and 95% with tigers (Rolston 1999, p. 106). We also know that much of the DNA in humans and other mammals is duplicated or non-functional and the actual size of the human genome is much smaller than had been expected. What is the significance of the large proportion of genes which are shared by individuals within a species and between species for the evolution and occurrence of altruistic behaviour? Dawkins (1979) addressed this question and argued that a gene U which led to its bearers being altruistic to every other individual would lose out to a competitor gene K which led to its bearers being altruistic to kin but never to any other individual. This would be true whether K was rare or common initially. However, this argument does not allow the conclusion that genes promoting altruism would not spread in populations, or that sharing a high proportion of genes has no relevance to the spread of genes promoting altruism (see Chapter 2, Section 4). Two relevant arguments are as follows.

The first is that, in the real world, altruism is not universal but has limits. One realistic strategy U^R could involve altruistic behaviour except where information from monitoring beforehand indicates that it is inadvisable because reciprocation is unlikely. Another strategy could be $K(U^R)$ which leads to altruism to kin only, except where information indicates that altruism to others is likely to be reciprocated. Either of these might out-compete K. U^R might be relatively more successful in a population in which more of the individuals benefited also carried U^R. The actor would benefit from reciprocation and the individuals benefited would themselves produce more offspring bearing U^R. The net increase in U^R in the population could be greater than the maximal increase of K whose actions benefit only K. $K(U^R)$ might also be successful and the most successful strategy would be in the range between U^R and $K(U^R)$.

A second argument is that the U^R strategy would benefit the actor, and the individuals affected positively by the altruism, in an additional way as a consequence of the increase in stability of the social group resulting from U^R. Such a benefit might be considerable in that unstable groups might die out. This benefit would obtain if the strategy were U^*, which did not necessitate reciprocation but did avoid altruism to permanently anti-social individuals, like X, whose bearers are always competitive, or K when bearers are not interacting with kin. Hence genes promoting reciprocal altruism to some degree, such as U^R, and genes promoting altruism in general to some degree, such as U^*, might both survive in a well organised social species. In neither of these arguments is it proposed that all behaviour is altruistic, just that there is a significant amount of altruistic behaviour. It might be that some genes promoting cooperation are relatively old and hence widespread among species.

Darwin (1859) presented life for all organisms as a struggle against considerable odds to survive and reproduce. The mechanisms which have evolved within organisms which increase chances of survival and reproduction include a variety of mechanisms for reducing the risk of failure to do so. In more complex animals, these mechanisms include means of assessing risk. As mentioned in Chapter 1, Section 7 and explained further in this chapter, the minimising of risks, such as those of failing to get enough food and of predation, is very important to animals. The risks can be significantly reduced by living in groups and cooperating with others. Most individuals may go through much or all of their lives without using the potential benefits of group-living and cooperation but if the lives of the bearers of genes which promote such behaviour are saved during a period of severe food shortage or frequent predator attack, the genes will spread in the population. Occasional severe risk will result in the presence in animals of certain behavioural, physiological and anatomical characteristics such as aspects of social living and cooperation.

Individuals will compete for resources unless their fitness is increased by not doing so. Refraining from competing may sometimes occur because the direct costs of the action to the competition initiator are too great or, in social situations, because the consequent social disruption involves costs to that individual. As Bertram (1975, 1976) pointed out, if refraining from competing is later reciprocated, this is a form of cooperation. However, there are many occasions when individuals act in a way which just furthers their own ends because it increases their fitness, the spread of their genes, at the expense of the fitness of another individual. In some cases the action is truly selfish in that the individual is aware of the likely effects on itself and on the other, harmed, individual. In other cases, there is no such awareness and it would be more accurate to refer to harmful subject-benefit rather than selfishness. Rottschaefer (1998, p. 38) makes a similar distinction when he refers to ordinary selfish behaviour (straightforward selfishness) as 'doing something to benefit oneself, with the motivation of helping oneself' and to biologically selfish behaviour (directly selfish) as 'doing something which has net benefit for oneself, and thereby one's children, with the consequence of increasing one's individual fitness'. However, these definitions, especially the second one, would include almost all behaviour, feeding, grooming, reproduction, etc., as it makes no mention of a harmful effect on another individual. The terms are also confusing as the distinction between 'ordinary' and 'biological' cannot be exclusive, much of the ordinary being also biological and vice versa. In this book, the term *selfish* will be used to describe *an individual acting in a way which increases its fitness at the expense of the fitness of one or more other individuals whilst being aware of the likely effects on itself and on the harmed individual or individuals*. The word selfish is thus limited to individuals rather than groups and it could not describe a gene. A comparable act with such awareness involves *harmful subject benefit* but not selfishness.

Altruism is a word which is used by some people to refer to motivation only but it is also used to refer to the consequences of actions or to both motivation and consequences. Hamilton's (1963) concept of altruistic behaviour involved reduced fitness for the individual that is being altruistic and increased fitness for the beneficiary. There are very clear ideas of cost and benefit here but no mention of awareness or motivation. When Nagel (1970, p. 15–16) wrote on the subject he was probably unaware of Hamilton's writings in another discipline:

> The general thesis to be defended concerning altruism is that one has a direct reason to promote the interests of others – a reason which does not depend upon intermediate factors such as one's own interests or one's antecedent sentiments of sympathy and benevolence.

and

> by altruism I mean any behaviour motivated merely by the belief that someone else will benefit or avoid harm by it.

This definition includes no mention of any cost to the altruist and does not require that there should be any benefit at all, merely a belief that there would be some advantage to the other individual. Blum (1980, p. 9) says:

> By altruism I will mean a regard for the good of another person for his own sake, or conduct motivated by such a regard.

Blum later (p. 10) indicates a degree of realisation that some cost is implied in the altruistic act by saying that such an act is one which is 'not carrying the connotation of self-sacrifice or, at least, self neglect'. These definitions with no reference to the cost of the action to the altruist are insufficient and do not distinguish between altruism and benevolence. For similar reasons, Rottschaefer's (1998, pp. 37–40 etc.) definitions and distinctions between ordinary and biological altruism or between biological altruism, psychological altruism and morality (p. 34) do not seem logical or useful to me. I prefer to use a definition which is principally concerned with consequence but to consider altruistic thought as a component which may also be present. *An altruistic act by an individual is one which involves some cost to that individual in terms of reduced fitness but increases the fitness of one or more other individuals.* Altruistic thoughts are those which involve an intention to carry out an altruistic act or to reaffirm the value of an altruistic act which is being or has been carried out.

The concept of cost requires some explanation. Some actions have a cost which is easy to describe in fitness terms in that death is more likely or reproduction is less likely to occur or is less successful. Other actions may have a cost in terms of energy expended, time used during which other useful activities could have occurred, injury, loss of resource use, impairment of resistance to disease, or a slowing of growth rate. These effects may reduce individual fitness but need not do so. Hence when recognising or assessing altruism, it is necessary to consider the probability of fitness reduction and its likely magnitude. The probability, in a range from 0 to 1, that there will be any effect on fitness can be largely assessed by considering the individual itself. The magnitude of effect on fitness could range from a minute reduction of gamete production to termination of the genetic line and has to be assessed by investigating the various offspring and other relatives who bear the genes.

Some altruistic acts are directed towards kin. According to the definition given above, altruism towards kin is still altruism provided that there is a fitness cost to the altruist and there is a fitness benefit to the related individual and the two are independent individuals. Altruism is carried out by individuals and not by genes so the interests of parents and offspring, or of two sisters, are not identical and one can act altruistically towards the other. This point is misunderstood by some writers who assume that a benefit to offspring equates to a benefit to the parent. The evolution of altruism towards relatives is readily explained by considering the spread of a gene which promotes such altruism. However, not all acts of parents towards offspring, or vice versa, are altruistic. The subject of parent–offspring conflict has been explained by Trivers (1974) and others. The expected higher level of altruism towards kin depends upon an ability to discriminate between kin and non-kin and, preferably, to assess the degree of relatedness. There are various methods for doing this (Chapter 3, Section 3). Examples of altruism towards close relatives include: people who earn money during their life times and want to pass on much of it to their children, children who look after elderly parents, young female chimpanzees who collected fruit for their elderly, sick mother (Goodall 1986, p. 357) and pig-tailed macaques who, when helping group-members which were attacked, did so most readily for close relatives, less readily for more distant relatives and least readily for non-relatives (Massey 1977).

The phenomenon of reciprocal altruism has been expounded many times in many societies using various terminologies. There have been large numbers of treatises on religious principles and on moral behaviour in which it was described and it formed an important part of the writings of Kropotkin (1902). A more recent exposition of its occurrence and evolutionary origins was that of Trivers (1971). *Reciprocal altruism occurs when an altruistic act by A directed towards B is followed by some equivalent act by B directed towards A or by an act directed towards A whose occurrence is made more likely by the presence or behaviour of B.* Trivers' argument was summarised by de Waal (1996, p. 24) as follows. Reciprocal altruism occurs if:

(1) The exchanged acts, while beneficial to the recipient, are costly to the performer; (2) there is a time lag between giving and receiving; (3) giving is contingent upon receiving

The second point is made to exclude simultaneous cooperation in hunting etc. The third point is not quite correct as the first altruistic act cannot be contingent upon receiving. Trivers (1985, p. 362) makes several further points:

'In reciprocal altruism, the main problem for the altruist is making sure it receives the return benefit. This will tend to occur when frequency of interaction is high,' and 'both a long lifespan and a low dispersal rate will tend to maximise the chance that two individuals will interact repeatedly. Interdependence of members of a species (to avoid predators, for example) will tend to keep individuals near each other and increase the chance that they will encounter altruistic situations together.'

The occurrence of reciprocity of altruistic acts had been considered by Sahlins (1965) who referred to three different kinds. The first is called 'generalised' and implies a net giving on the part of the giver under consideration; the second is 'balanced', involving direct exchange of favours of equal value, and the third 'negative', such that the giver cheats and returns less than the value given. Regulation so as to prevent cheating is one of the most important aspects of the organisation of societies. However, as Noe (1986) emphasises, asymmetrical or negative, altruism can still be reciprocal and valuable, for the smaller of the two favours may still be of considerable value to the recipient.

Crook (1980, p. 185) explains the complexity of reciprocation quoting Alexander (1978):

> Personal altruism with respect to society at large is conducted in the expectation of reciprocity from the collectivity of people, either in individual responses or through contracts undertaken with representatives of the government of the people.

This 'indirect reciprocity', as Alexander calls it, might be equated with the action of Adam Smith's impartial spectator who would evaluate your behaviour as good and hence commend you to the group, elevating you in the eyes of group members (de Waal 1996, p. 33). The importance of friendship and of feelings such as gratitude and sympathy in the functioning of reciprocal altruism is emphasised by Trivers (1985, pp. 388–389) who reports:

> Psychologists have shown that human beings reciprocate more when the original act was expensive for the benefactor, even though the benefit given is the same.

The complexity of reciprocation and the subtlety of the effects of some actions make assessing the magnitude of reciprocal altruism very difficult. Alexander (1987, p. 98) asks how much effort is altruistic but is not able to answer the question. The magnitude of reciprocal altruistic behaviour would appear to increase exponentially with the complexity of the social group.

2.2   COOPERATIVE BEHAVIOUR IN ANIMALS

2.2.1   *Associations*

The evolution of social living is briefly introduced in Chapter 1, Section 6. Animals may aggregate for various reasons and, if these aggregations last for some time, relationships between individuals may form to the extent that some social organisation may be said to be present. In some fish shoals, bird flocks or mammal herds the individual members respond differentially to other group members and respond socially according to their previous experience of interactions with various individuals. Even without complex social behaviour, however, cooperation may occur. A shoal of fish is just a local concentration but a school is a coordinated, synchronised, polarised group (Pitcher 1979). Each member of a school must monitor continually the positions of the others and adjust its course and speed so that it does not become separated from them or collide with them. Some degree of cooperation is involved in the behaviour of the fish in a school or of birds flying in a tight flock or an organised formation and the individuals derive benefits from this cooperation. Such cooperation is also likely to occur in schools of squid as these animals have large brains, elaborate eyes and a complex system of communication involving rapid and sophisticated changes in colour and light polarisation patterns in the skin (Messenger 2001).

The composition of more permanent animal groups is usually described in terms of the age, sex and degrees of relatedness of the group members. Some types of groups are described here (after Broom 1981, pp. 243–244).

Monogamous family groups

The minimum number is a pair which remain together outside the breeding season and the maximum number is a pair with all of their non-breeding offspring. Examples include many monogamous birds, gibbons and marmosets.

Multiple monogamous family groups
The basic unit is the monogamous family group but brief or prolonged associations of family groups occur. Geese, swans and some seabirds form such groups outside the breeding season and wolf packs are usually family-based in this way.

Matriarchal groups of females with young
Throughout most of the year some mammals, such as cattle, sheep and red deer, form groups composed of reproductive females, their daughters and their sons of, in this last species, less than three years of age.

Single males with females and young
In the South American vicuña the male maintains his harem throughout the year. Similar groups are formed by jungle fowl or domestic fowl and by several primate species. Blue monkeys sometimes congregate at food feeding sites but separate again later. Male gorillas may tolerate the presence of their sons until they are fully grown.

Bands of males with their females and young
Baboons of various species often spend much of their time in such bands. They are sometimes aggregations of single male groups. These larger groups may form at good sleeping places or feeding sites.

Multi-male, multi-female groups
Many species of animals spend most of their lives in social groups containing adult males and females. These include species of spiders, insects, fish, birds and mammals. Amongst the most social birds are the babblers and the anis, in which groups remain together during breeding and non-breeding periods. Examples of mammals which form groups of this kind include kangaroos, wallabies, prairie dogs, dolphins, peccaries, macaque monkeys and humans.

Multi-male and multi-female groups where most females are
sterile workers or soldiers

The organisation of social wasps, bees and ants is sufficiently different
from multi-male, multi-female groups (above) to warrant a separate
category. Most males leave the colony before they reproduce and there
is usually one reproductive queen at any time.

Early studies of social interactions emphasised competitive interactions within social groups. However, across a wide range of social species, most studies show that friendly, often cooperative interactions are very much more common than aggressive, competitive
interactions. This conclusion is even more marked when account is
taken of what individuals in social groups do not do. Most altruistic
behaviour involves refraining from doing things which would be easy
to do but which would harm others, even if the perpetrator might
benefit in some way from doing this. Any short-term benefit of the
harmful behaviour is presumably outweighed by the longer-term benefits of maintaining group stability and good relationships. If individuals are in a prolonged association with others it is easier for them to
appreciate bad effects on others in the group and hence the full consequences of their own or others' actions and what could happen to
themselves.

Some of the associations among individuals can be inter-specific
rather than only intra-specific. Schools of fish and flocks of birds can
include more than one species. Even the more permanent groups can
be composed of individuals of different species. Hence cooperation
between individuals of different species in finding or acquiring food,
controlling the physical environment or defence against predators can
occur. There can also be associations between species whose capabilities are different and which involve mutually beneficial cooperation
that is more effective than what could be achieved by cooperation
within any one of the species. Mixed flocks of birds, or groupings of
mammals and birds, may differ in the sensory systems which they
use to detect predators so the likelihood of a predator approaching
close enough to be dangerous is reduced by the presence of several
species in the group. In the association between a cleaner fish and

large fish which it cleans, both derive an advantage. Similarly, when a honey guide shows a bees' nest to a stronger honey consumer, such as a human (e.g. Boran people) or ratel, both derive benefit from their cooperation. More long-term associations, like those between Sami people and reindeer, or between many different human peoples and dogs, are also mutually beneficial. In neither case, as Budiansky (1992) has pointed out, is it clear who initiated the association or who domesticated whom. Reindeer like to ingest salty human urine and this benefit might have saved reindeer lives. The wolf ancestors of dogs might well have stayed in the vicinity of human hunts or human habitations in order to glean food, especially when food was scarce. Wolves and humans could cooperate during a hunt because the wolves or dogs could detect, chase and indicate or hold at bay large prey which they could not safely kill but the slower humans could kill it and share it when they arrived.

A variety of circumstances where cooperation is valuable and the nature of organisation necessary for it to occur are discussed in the remainder of Chapter 2.

2.2.2 Grooming and preening

Relationships in which one individual grooms or preens another, allogrooming or allopreening, are widespread amongst animals. In some cases the particles or parasites removed by the groomer from the groomed animal are eaten. This is seldom of great importance as an element of diet when the animal groomed is of the same species but it is certainly of value to the ox-pecker, which removes ticks from buffalo and rhinoceroses, and to cleaner fish which remove parasites from much larger fish. Ridley (1996, pp. 63–64) reports that at least 45 species of fish and six species of shrimps living on coral reefs will act as cleaners to large fish. They are readily recognisable by colouration, behaviour and location because the large fish visit cleaning stations frequented by the cleaners, may show colour changes indicating a readiness to be cleaned, remain still while parasites are removed from skin, gills, etc. and do not injure the cleaners. The value of the cleaners to the large fish is shown by studies in which cleaners were removed from an area of reef, with the results that the large fish in the area were more likely to show sores and infections and were reduced in numbers. Cooperation is essential in these relationships but no individual recognition is needed.

Some allogrooming or allopreening leads to a benefit to the groomer because the groomed individual is being courted, is more likely to continue a sexual relationship, or is less likely to act in an aggressive way towards the groomer. The grooming or cleaning may be unidirectional, although mutual allogrooming commonly occurs in mated pairs which remain together for a long period. Unidirectional allogrooming or allopreening is also shown by parents towards offspring, with obvious benefits in terms of increased chances of offspring survival. Mutual allogrooming, between pairs of individuals who are not sexual partners, within a long-lasting social group has been described for many species of animals. Ungulates such as domestic cattle and horses often have grooming partnerships. One kind of cooperation is the prevention of fly attack, or the dislodging of flies which are on the body, by standing head to tail so that each horse or cow benefits from the tail movements of the other. Grooming with the mouth and tongue can also occur and Benham (1984) described long-lasting mutual grooming partnerships in cows. The individuals concerned, both female in each case, seldom showed any aggression towards one another, spent long periods in one another's company and groomed one another with approximately equal frequency. When lemurs, macaques and baboons groomed one another, the groomer preferentially groomed parts of the body which were more difficult to access during auto-grooming, dirt was removed from the skin and from wounds and parasites were removed (Simonds 1965, Hutchins and Barash 1976). Animals which were not allogroomed became badly infested with ticks and other parasites. Mutual grooming may help individuals to gain acceptance into a group (Struhsaker and Leland 1979) and accentuates reproductive (Box 1978) and other social bonds. Allogrooming occurs often in humans between mother and young. Individuals caring for groups of children will often help all of them to keep clean and parasite free, whether they are related or not. The much reduced amount of body hair, as compared with other primates, reduces the extent to which grooming is necessary but removal of dirt or parasites from the bodies of others is a widespread friendly act in human societies.

Some allogrooming clearly has benefit in the short-term for the groomer but its function varies through more and more long-term and uncertain potential returns. Some baboon grooming is directed towards a high ranking animal but baboons also have equal grooming partners (Kummer 1978). In vervet monkeys two-way grooming relationships were found to be quite common. In seventeen relationships where kinship could be accurately determined, ten were with close kin and seven were not (Cheney and Seyfarth 1990, p. 26). Grooming relationships are more likely to develop for mutual benefit between individuals who know one another very well and close relatives are likely to fall into this category, but allogrooming may also be directed towards unrelated individuals. In an experimental study by Stammbach (1988), low-ranking female long-tailed macaques were trained to press a series of levers to obtain a highly desirable food from a machine. Some days after return to their social group, high-ranking females were observed to increase the amount of grooming which they addressed to these 'specialist' feeders. Individuals may be recognised by other signs as desirable allies for the future, for example Cheney and Seyfarth (1190, p. 41) described female vervet monkeys directing higher levels of grooming towards other females if they were going to be high ranking in the future. The same authors reported (p. 44) that alliances were more frequent with grooming partners than with other individuals. When Seyfarth and Cheney (1984) played a tape recording of a particular female vervet monkey to another female who was a grooming partner, she was more likely to look in the direction of the sound if the tape was played up to one hour after a bout of grooming than if it was played over two hours later. Inter-male grooming partnerships also affect other social interactions; for example, Dunbar (1983) found that the likelihood that male gelada baboons would challenge another male for a female declined according to the extent of mutual grooming which had been carried out with that male.

Mutual grooming can occur in situations where the major function seems to be consolidation of friendly relationships or benefit to the groomed individual with no significant return being likely. When fights occur in social groups of monkeys, the peace which follows is often characterised by an increased frequency of mutual grooming. Reconciliation between chimpanzees which have been fighting or threatening one another often involves a kiss on the mouth but this may be followed by prolonged mutual grooming (de Waal 1982, 1996). Individuals who are weak for some reason may sometimes be groomed. A rhesus monkey studied by de Waal (1996, p. 49) had been slow developing because she was trisomal, a chromosomal abnormality. She was intellectually backward and far less well able to look after herself than the other monkeys in the group but was groomed twice as much as her peers by both non-relatives and relatives.

2.2.3 Feeding

There are many ways in which individuals benefit, in terms of obtaining food or water, from the presence of other individuals or by cooperating with them. These are reviewed by Broom (1981, pp. 179–183) and include: joining others who are likely to have found food; observing others in order to find food sources or learn how to find or acquire food; collaborating in hunting for, acquiring, handling, or defending food or avoiding depleted sources; sharing food; and giving food to others. In all of these cases, the advantage of tolerating others or collaborating with them must outweigh any disadvantage associated with disturbance or competition caused by others. The advantage may obtain at the time of feeding or may be significant only at times of high risk. In order to avoid starvation or death from lack of water, individuals may live socially and tolerate the close presence of others at times when there is little or no advantage to be gained from doing so. Relationships must be established and nurtured in times of plenty in order that the very great gain of avoiding death or failure to reproduce can be achieved at times of scarcity. Once individuals tolerate one another in a group they are more likely to cooperate in obtaining food. An older, weaker individual in a group may be tolerated because, at a time of shortage, it may remember a source of food or water which is otherwise difficult to locate.

A vulture, soaring over the plains of Africa, will join an aggregation of other vultures because their presence is likely to indicate a food source. In many species where such an event occurs, the individuals which are joined at a food source are less aggressive than might be expected. This tolerance, which might be reciprocated at a later time, can be a form of cooperation. Assemblages of animals, such as communal roosts or breeding colonies, can sometimes act as food information centres (Ward and Zahavi 1973). Recruitment of birds departing for feeding or drinking sites from roosts or colonies and the aggregation of small roosts into larger ones in adverse conditions have been described by Ward (1965, 1972), Krebs (1974) and Broom *et al.* (1976). Laboratory experiments with the weaver bird *Quelea* showed that naive individuals would follow knowledgeable birds to food (de Groot 1980). Animals which live permanently in social groups can benefit from the knowledge of group members about where to find food and those individuals with such information are often the controllers of group activity. Bees, sheep, baboons, humans and other species find food and exploit their resources more effectively because such knowledge is shared (von Frisch 1946, Kummer 1968, Favre 1975, Ridley 1996, p. 100). When Menzel (1974) showed a hidden food source to one member of a group of young chimpanzees, most of them led the group to the food by running towards the food, stopping, looking back at other members of the group and sometimes tapping them or otherwise soliciting them to follow.

Wolves, hyaenas, hunting dogs, lions, chimpanzees and humans collaborate when hunting with the result that they can collectively be much more successful in catching large, fast prey than if they hunted individually. In the same way, white pelicans catch more fish by moving forward in a U-shaped formation and synchronising scoops into the water with their large bills. Many seabirds congregate at fish shoals and catch more because fish escaping from one bird are more likely to be caught by another. A very specialist collaboration in food acquisition is that of the extinct New Zealand huia in which the male had a strong bill for breaking rotten wood and the female had a curved, slender bill for extraction of insect larvae, etc. from it. Hence collaboration results in more food being obtained than either individual could obtain alone. Handling food can also involve cooperation; for example, crocodiles cannot easily rip food from a carcass and must grip and then twist their whole body in the water in order to do it. This procedure is not very effective if the body of the prey twists as well but works well if other crocodiles hold the carcass whilst one twists. The first crocodile will later hold the carcass whilst others twist.

Methods of obtaining food can often be learned from parents or from other individuals in the social group. This may result in different food acquisition methods occurring in different regions of the world, as is the case with killer whales cooperating to catch herring off Norway, salmon off British Columbia, penguins in Antarctica or sea-lions off the Patagonian coast (Ridley 1996, p. 182). Animals also learn from others what not to do, for example, flocks of finches which avoid searching again for seeds in a recently denuded area (Cody 1971). An experimental study in which capuchin monkeys were trained to collaborate by pulling on a rope in order to obtain food was carried out by de Waal (1996, p. 148).

In some of the examples of cooperation in relation to obtaining food, the individuals involved must actively work together and in some they must be able to recognise the individuals with whom they cooperate. In other cases, however, neither of these is involved. Cooperation in defence of a food source may occur just because a large flock of birds is less likely than a small flock to be displaced from a source (Emlen 1973). On the other hand, some active defence may be a favour to other group members which is noted and reciprocated.

When food is found by an individual that is in the company of others, there may be no indication of any sharing; on the contrary, the individual may attempt to conceal the fact that food has been found and consume it all. The captive chimpanzees studied by de Waal (1996,

p. 152) 'celebrated' the arrival of food by calling and embracing one another. They were not attempting to conceal their observation of food
arrival and their actions increased the chances that all in the group
would get some food. When a group has obtained a quantity of food,
one individual may steal food from another. Such behaviour would
be expected to result in a vigorous response, including attempted re-
trieval of the food or some form of punishment if there was no cooperation or food-sharing occurring. Blurton-Jones (1987) pointed out that
in human and other primate societies, 'tolerated theft' in such a situation is a form of sharing. Parents might allow their offspring to take
a portion of their food and group members might also share food with
others in this way. The tolerance of others taking portions of food, or
feeding alongside, is likely to occur when the food source is relatively
large. A large prey animal might be shared by a group of humans, lions,
wolves or chimpanzees. Human hunters share food which must be obtained by collaboration. The Ache people of the Paraguayan rain forest
and the Yora people of Peru would share meat or fish with everybody
while on a hunting or fishing trip but on their return home, the meat
or fish was shared with family members only (Hill and Kaplan 1989,
Ridley 1996, p. 100). On the other hand, fruits or vegetables were not
shared if found, probably because the items are small and the amount
obtained depends largely on the energy expended in searching. In the
course of hunts there was some division of labour by the cooperating
individuals. Captive chimpanzees are usually fed large quantities of
food at once and de Waal (1989, 1996, p. 13) described the sharing of
food as commonplace but not universal. Ravens often live in groups
during the winter period and Heinrich (1989) describes how, when an
individual finds a carcass, he or she advertises it to the others by calling. One member of the group will check that the carcass is really
dead and is not defended by any predators and will communicate that
discovery to the others.

An impressive example of food sharing is seen in the vampire
bat (Wilkinson 1984). The bats live for up to eighteen years, stay in
the same roosting place and go out looking for a blood meal each

night. Young animals do not succeed on one in three nights and older animals on one in ten nights during favourable periods. However, if these small, rapidly metabolising animals have to go for more than sixty hours without a meal they are likely to die. Bats which have obtained a meal will regurgitate blood to their roost neighbours who have not. Experimentally deprived animals received blood more readily than those in normal conditions, i.e. with a more distended belly, and bats which had received blood reciprocated more than would be expected by chance.

The characteristics of shared foods are summarised by de Waal (1996, p. 144) as follows:

1. Highly valued and concentrated but prone to decay. 2. Too much for a single individual to consume. 3. Unpredictably available. 4. Procured through skills and strengths that made certain classes of individuals dependent on others for access. 5. Most effectively procured through collaboration.

These do not all apply to vampire bats. Ridley (1996, p. 108) emphasised the importance of food sharing in the origins of human society, suggesting that:

big game hunting introduced human kind to public goods for the first time.

This seems unlikely to be true because finding food sources, defending against predators, and modifying the local environment are all cooperative activities requiring reciprocal altruism and probably occurred as early or earlier in human evolution than big-game hunting. However, it is quite clear that many foods utilised by primates are too small to share. Cheney and Seyfarth (1990, p. 291) consider that the vervet monkeys which they studied do not often exchange objects such as food items even though they reciprocate acts.

Some cooperation in feeding will have other motives in addition to feeding. Stanford et al. (1994) describe chimpanzees hunting colobus monkeys, a necessarily cooperative behaviour which is not very common. Such a hunt is more likely to occur if the group of chimpanzees is large in number and if a sexually receptive female is present in the party. If a monkey is caught, some is usually given to the female and she is more likely to mate with the provider of meat. Some degree of mate quality assessment by females is also likely to be a part of hunting by human tribes. In some cases the hunt appears to be largely contrived for certain of the hunters to impress women who observe the hunt itself, or at least the outcome. The cooperation has a complex motivation, as does the provision of food gifts by one person to another with various expectations for response. It is also possible for individuals to learn that the sharing of food is important in human society and chimpanzees can be trained to share food. Two chimpanzees were initially given half each of every good item but later the more dominant individual would take each item, break it and give half to the other (Savage-Rumbaugh and Lewin 1994). When the chimpanzees were provided with a keyboard with which they could request items, they were usually given two portions of each. If one ate both portions, he gave both portions of the next food to the other. They could also signal to one another with food labels to request food items.

2.2.4 Control of the physical environment

The substantial constructions produced by hydroids, corals, termites, ants and humans are impressive monuments to social living, some of it long past. The individuals involved in the great branching colonies of hydroids on the sea bed or the massive reefs produced by corals in the shallow seas of tropical regions are each making a rather similar contribution to the rock-like structure. However, individual termites, ants, bees, wasps and people have various roles in the construction of their edifices. Naked mole rats are able to construct a complex burrow system in which they can live in social groups but could not produce an appropriate environment at all if not living socially. In each case, the structure provides individuals with a better physical environment than they could have had if they had not cooperated in its production.

As soon as animals aggregate they start to change the characteristics of their immediate surroundings. Allee (1938) reviewed studies of the physical and chemical changes which are consequent upon group-living. Woodlice keep their microclimate more humid by clustering, penguins keep one another warmer in the Antarctic winter by huddling, bees cool the hive by fanning (Lindauer 1961) and aggregated brittle stars can feed without being washed away (Warner 1971, Broom 1975). Termite nests and modern human dwellings have elaborate air flow systems which provide an adequate gas exchange and keep the temperature within a tolerable range (Lüscher 1961). Division of labour and some of the various forms of direct cooperation are necessary for building to occur.

2.2.5 Defence against predators

As already emphasised in relation to food finding, the minimising or avoidance of risk is a major factor affecting the organisation of behaviour in particular and aspects of physiological and anatomical adaptation as well. Even very occasional risky events may have profound effects and may counterbalance the costs of being in groups, such as greater conspicuousness and competition for resources. In some species there is a net reduction in predation-caused risks of death, or reduced or delayed reproductive output, because the individuals hide within a group or use group defence during feeding or resting, or nest in a colony. The genes which promote the behavioural or other characteristics necessary for the essential social behaviour will spread and persist in the population even if they have their useful effect for only very small periods during life. If wading birds in a high tide aggregation, or starlings in a roost, or fish in a school are very close together, most individuals are very unlikely to be caught by a predator. It is necessary for individuals to tolerate the close presence of conspecifics in these tightly packed groups, and in other groups where they derive protection from the presence of others. This toleration is cooperation in the sense that individuals have to refrain from most threats or attacks on others. Individuals in groups which are not big enough for adequate protection may also encourage others to join, as suggested for vervet monkeys by Cheney and Seyfarth (1990, p. 46), even at the expense of other groups. Some group-living birds attempt to entice young birds into their social groups, probably because of the defensive advantages conferred by larger group size. House sparrows which wish to move from a garden fence into a garden to feed will sit on the fence and chirrup until enough other sparrows join them to increase safety before flying down in a group into the garden (Elgar 1986). Cooperation amongst existing group members, in the form of toleration or concerted efforts, is necessary for such recruitment behaviour to occur.

Animals which are in groups could possibly collaborate in concealing themselves, deterring predators, exhibiting active defence or showing some forms of escape. Large groups of prey animals, especially if they are closely aggregated, may deter predators from attacking. Rapid movements, such as the aerial gyrations of some birds prior to roosting, or the rapid twisting and turning of fish shoals, may add to this deterrent effect. Animals with warning colouration, such as ladybird beetles gain more from their warning colouration by aggregating. Some camouflaged animals, such as plover chicks, are harder for predators to detect when they aggregate. The costs of cooperation in these examples are probably quite small, for example overcoming a desire to avoid contact or some increased competition for food.

Individuals in a group can often feed or rest whilst others are vigilant. Lazarus (1978) reported that time spent vigilant by geese was greater in those which were further from their neighbours. The vigilant individual, of any social species, which detects a predator may just show freezing, escape, or defence behaviour, or they may produce some kind of alarm signal. Any of these reactions is likely to have an effect on the behaviour and physiology of others but the alarm signal will often be more likely to do so. There has been considerable debate about whether or not alarm signals are altruistic because a signal may cause another individual to be more likely than the signaller to become the target of the predator. There is also discussion about whether the beneficiaries from alarm signalling are largely close relatives of the signaller. There can be no doubt that alarm signals save the lives of many group-living animals. Sherman (1977) who studied ground squirrels reported that almost 10% of predator attacks resulted in the death of a squirrel. Sherman also reported that alarm callers were often attacked, so alarm calling is risky. More alarm calls were given when close relatives were present. Whilst females, who were more likely than males to be closely related to group members, gave more alarm calls outside the breeding season, males gave as many calls as females after breeding. In many flocks of birds, alarm calling is risky and groups include individuals that are not closely related, sometimes being of different species. The alarm calls given by many small birds are different for different predators; for example, a complex, easily heard call when a ground predator is detected, and a high pitched, single note call which is difficult to locate when a bird of prey is seen. Struhsaker (1967b) and Cheney and Seyfarth (1990) have described three different alarm calls given by vervet monkeys when they detect a leopard, eagle or snake. The monkeys respond in different ways to these predators and to tape recordings of the three types of alarm calls. Young monkeys refine their signalling with experience, initially giving the eagle call for any large bird in the air but later limiting the call to eagles, which are the real aerial danger to vervet-sized monkeys. If alarm calls were solely for the benefit of the caller, a general call would suffice and there would be no need to produce different signals for different predators.

Information about danger is also given by the individual who is caught and gives distress signals. The signaller may benefit from this because the predator is distracted and releases it, or because other group members come to its aid. There will often be a benefit to the recipient of the signal. Distress calls often elicit approach and aid responses from relatives and other group members but repeated or intense distress calling is aversive. Vervet monkeys make sounds which may elicit support from other group members. When Cheney and Seyfarth (1990) played tapes of such sounds, the vervet that heard the call was more likely to respond if the caller had helped it in the past.

Communication about danger in a quite distant place is reported for a bonobo (pygmy chimpanzee) by Savage-Rumbaugh and Lewin (1994, p. 261). Sue Savage-Rumbaugh, a bonobo named Panbanisha and some dogs were walking in a familiar area of woodland when first the dogs, and then the primates, detected a large feline in a tree. On return home, Panbanisha vocalised to five other familiar bonobos which lived there. Sue Savage-Rumbaugh told these five about the event. When two of the bonobos next went to that area of woodland they showed signs of being frightened. Such behaviour is frequent and valuable in humans.

There are many examples of socially living animals collaborating in defence or of some of the individuals in a group actively defending others. Some ants, termites and aphids have soldier castes whose members hurry to the defence of the other, very closely related, members of their group. In many cases, for example when a bee stings a mammal or when the abdomen of the termite *Globitermes* explodes releasing a sticky glandular secretion, the soldier will die protecting her group. Group defence in horned animals such as buffalo, eland, bison or musk oxen can prevent completely the death of group members when there are attacks by hunting dogs, hyaenas or wolves. Colonially nesting arctic terns assault intruders such as humans or dogs and drive them off by collectively diving on them screaming and hitting them with their sharp bills, whilst fieldfares, colonially nesting thrushes, also dive on predators but pull up before collision and defecate on them. Whales will help a group member which is trapped or attacked. Monkeys collaborate in attempts to drive off predators with both males and females involved in some species, such as vervets, or largely males concerned, e.g. gorillas. Cooperation in defence against predators is likely to have been a significant factor in the development of the organisation of human society. Gorillas, like humans, defend individuals in their groups whether or not they are close relatives.

In addition to cooperating during defence, individuals can sometimes cooperate during escape by distracting or confusing the predator. In almost all of the examples given in this section, there is a substantial energetic cost and a potential reduction in life expectancy associated with the cooperative behaviour. In some cases there is direct benefit from the collaboration, in other cases there is a time delay before the return from the individual which benefits or from another individual, whilst sometimes there is never a return.

2.2.6 *High risk or high benefit altruism*

Some human altruistic acts have a very high potential cost; for example, attracting a charging bull to yourself and away from someone else, stepping in front of a person about to be shot, giving your last crust when you are starving, or risking drowning to save another. In most of these cases the potential benefit to the recipient is high. However, cost to the altruist and benefit to the recipient should not be confused as there can be acts which have great benefit to the recipient but incur little cost to the altruist. One example is that of a warning from a human in a safe place to another about to step in front of a fast-approaching car. Similarly, a concealed bird or monkey might warn an individual in the open about the approach of a predator.

There are many examples of high cost altruism in social insects. Wilson (1971) lists the following:

(1) Soldier termites which are the first to defend winged reproductives from attack by ants.
(2) Injured workers of the ant *Solenopsis* which attack more readily than do uninjured workers and leave the nest before dying.
(3) Workers of many species, which approach danger when there is a disturbance.
(4) Honeybees, some polybiine wasps and the ant *Pogonomyrmex*, which die when they sting a mammalian predator.
(5) Worker bees, fed on sugar water, which donate their own tissue proteins to the larvae which they feed.

(6) Workers of many species whose egg laying is inhibited by the presence of a laying queen.

(7) Honey ants which spend much of their lives acting as a communal stomach for others in the nest.

The social Hymnoptera are haplodiploid, i.e. the males are haploid with one set of chromosomes but females are diploid with two sets, so the workers and soldiers are more closely related to one another than diploid brothers and sisters; the degree of relatedness is 0.75 rather than 0.5. However, there are very many examples of altruistic behaviour, involving great cost to the altruist, by diploid animals towards their offspring and towards parents and siblings. Mother mammals and some fathers have a high degree of certainty that their offspring really are closely related to them. This is probably the reason why parental altruism in high risk situations is so common. In evaluating how much to sacrifice for offspring, a parent should take account of the likelihood of being able to produce more offspring. However, in emergency situations, action may be based mainly on perceived risk to offspring with little time being available to accurately estimate costs.

Where the probability of an individual being closely related is high, the likelihood that altruistic behaviour will be shown is also high. In general, individuals are more likely to accept high risks to themselves where the beneficiary is a close relative. However, many other individuals which are encountered may also share the genes which promote altruistic behaviour. Hence the taking of some risks for non-relatives may occur. In general, altruism towards non-relatives would be expected to be of a less costly kind than would be tolerated if relatives were the beneficiaries. In long-lasting social groups, individuals do defend other group members against attack by conspecifics or dangerous predators. Monkeys, wild pigs, buffalo and various bird species such as jays and babblers will do this. Several species of whales have been described as staying with trapped individuals, supporting sick or injured individuals so that they could reach the surface to breathe and also supporting humans with snorkels who might have sounded as if they had respiratory distress caused by a blocked blow-hole (de Waal 1996, p. 42).

In human society, altruistic acts which are of great benefit to the recipient earn the approbation of others in society, the more so if there is a significant risk of or an actual cost to the altruist. A person who dives into dangerous waters at considerable risk to themselves to save another who would otherwise drown is respected for that act. However, an act which has very little cost is much less noteworthy. I am a strong swimmer and once rescued a girl of about six who had been washed away from her parents and into deep water by a large wave. She was back with her mother in less than a minute and although she might otherwise have drowned the cost to me was negligible. Some of those who act as lifeguards on beaches are able to exploit their considerable swimming ability and their training in saving lives. They take some risk but may also gain benefit such as attracting a good quality mate, or furthering their career prospects, as a result of their good reputation. The successful male defenders of monkey troupes may also gain general approbation as a result of their altruistic acts and this approbation might be reflected in food sharing or mating opportunities. All those in social groups who take risks which save the lives of, or prevent injuries to, other group members may benefit from the greater group stability which occurs if individuals are not lost to the group. Where altruism may be reciprocated, in some cases the recipient returns exactly the same favour but if the recipient responds with some other act which benefits the altruist, or if another individual in the group provides that benefit, the spread of the genes which promote the altruistic act will still be furthered. Rare but risky altruistic acts are unlikely to be reciprocated exactly. The chances that an individual saved from drowning will have an opportunity to save the altruist from drowning in the future are very small. The altruist whose act is rare but valuable is not likely to receive an identical act in return but may well benefit in other ways. In the United Kingdom all people who give blood receive no payment for it. The blood often saves lives so the blood donors enjoy that thought and may also receive some credit from their acquaintances. If is of interest that the employment types that include the largest proportion of blood donors are government employees, police, or teachers while those working in advertising or as business executives are much less likely to donate blood.

2.2.7 Alliances and their furtherance

Whenever two or more individuals are close together, there is a possibility that they might act in alliance if the appropriate conditions exist, even if they do not know one another. A predator might attack and be more readily repulsed if two prey animals act in concert than if they act independently.

However, such alliances between individuals that do not know one another are likely to be rare and short term if they do occur. Within long term social groups, alliances are much more likely and may involve friendships which affect many aspects of life. Alliances can confer immediate benefits, may allow better defence or management of resources in the long term, can restrict harmful behaviour and may lead to a perception of group identity. They require some degree of cooperation, either at the time of joint action or by the return of some favour after a time delay. The alliance may be limited to one situation in life, such as defence against attack from outside the group, or it may involve different functional systems. The amount of effort put into alliance activities may differ amongst the various allies. A costly act by one ally may be reciprocated by an act by the other ally which is less costly, but still of considerable value to the first.

Most studies of alliances have concerned primates and Harcourt (1988, 1992) suggests that alliances are used much more by primates than by non-primates. However, ethologists have looked for alliances in primate societies much more than in other social species. Harcourt also states that primates choose potential allies on the basis of their competitive value. Competition need not involve any physical confrontation, for speed of action and intellectual ability may also lead to success (Broom 1981, Fraser and Broom 1990). Good allies may be effective fighters, fast movers or individuals with a good capability for thinking about how to achieve objectives. Good allies should also be trustworthy, so the value of any assistance, reciprocation or companionship has to be assessed in the course of alliance relationships and compared with one's own efforts to sustain that relationship. Allies are often close kin but may also be other individuals known during development or individuals encountered when adult (Hemelrijk *et al.* 1999).

Collaboration by social group members in fights for resources against other social groups has been described for various bird species such as jays and babblers, for wolves, hyaenas, hunting dogs, lions, pigs and many primate species. In addition to alliances amongst the members of whole groups, there may be alliances of individuals within groups. DeVore (1965) described male baboon A consorting with oestrous female B with male C nearby. During a one-hour period, male D gradually approached and finally threatened A. Males A and C then drove D away. Male A remained with female B and it was speculated that C might derive some gain at a later time. In another group of baboons, for some weeks four males prevented a fifth male from having access to any of the females in the groups even though the fifth male could beat any of the four if they were not supported. Clear evidence of reciprocal altruism in such situations in baboons was reported by Packer (1977). He described male baboons soliciting help from another and then together attacking and chasing away a male who had been consorting with an oestrous female so that one of them could mate with her. On other occasions, one male would distract the male consorting with the female whilst the other mated with her. The individual who helped the male who was successful in mating did so most if that male had previously supported him at a high rate. In general, those who gave most aid received most aid. Most of these males were not close kin. Smuts (1985) found similar reciprocity in alliances but simple, high rates of reciprocity have not always been found (Noe 1986, Bercovitch 1988). Alliances to hold receptive females have also been reported between male dolphins (Connor *et al.* 1992). The males who are defending the female against others both mate with her. There may be two or three males defending a female and sometimes another alliance helps them to steal a female, with no obvious return to themselves.

Alliances between male monkeys that are effective during fights with other males do not always have an obvious resource objective such as a receptive female. There are many reports of coalitions to defeat another male, and perhaps depose him from an influential position. For example, in vervet monkeys (Cheney and Seyfarth 1986, 1990 p. 79) and in chimpanzees (de Waal 1984). Many of these coalitions are between individuals who are also grooming partners so the relationships may be of long duration (de Waal and Luttrell 1988, Hemelrijk and Ek 1991). Cheney and Seyfarth (1991, p. 28–44) pointed out that alliances in female vervet monkeys were considerably commoner between close kin than between non-kin but that when alliances were formed between unrelated female vervets, there was a high correlation between rate of help in fights and rate of receipt of grooming. Again it seems that relationships are formed using grooming and other friendly interactions and, thereafter, assistance in competitive situations is much more likely to be provided. Large group alliances were more successful than smaller group alliances.

When another individual is helped in a competition situation, this event has to be remembered if reciprocity is to occur or to be expected. Many studies show that those who help are more likely to be helped in return. The reverse is true in that those who intervene in a fight against an individual are themselves more likely to be the subject of an assisted attack by that individual. There are memories of who has done a favour in an attack and who has assisted an enemy. The importance of reciprocity in chimpanzee society, with particular reference to alliances, is emphasised by de Waal (1989, p. 207). If the reciprocity is not provided when an opportunity has arisen, retribution can occur. de Waal (1989, p. 206) reports:

> apes can visit personal resentment afterwards on an individual who has failed to back them up during a contest.

The actual amount of benefit which is acceptable after a favour has been done varies from one beneficiary to another. Noe (1986) explains that a high ranking male savannah baboon may help a low ranking male once for every two occasions when the lower ranking male provides assistance, but the ratio of benefits to costs may be equal because the help by the high ranking male is more valuable to the recipient. The key point is whether there is a net benefit from the alliance to each.

Although the research indicating the widespread nature of co-operative relationships in primate societies started with descriptions of alliances during inter-group or intra-group fights, it is clear that many of the relationships between allies might reasonably be described as friendships. Smuts (1985) describes how adult male and anoestrous female savannah baboons form special friendships in which the partners spend much time in close proximity. Both play a role in maintaining this proximity and each grooms the other more frequently than other partners. Goodall (1986) describes friendly dyads in chimpanzees, many of which were not potential mates or mothers and offspring. Watts (1994) describes similar relationships in gorillas and there are general reviews of friendships in Dunbar (1988) and Cords (1997). The importance of friendly relationships with a partner of any kind were detailed by Kummer (1978) as allowing opportunities for close monitoring of behaviour, facilitating prediction of behaviour and raising possibilities for the modification of the partner's qualities, tendencies and availability. Cords (1997) states that allogrooming and calling to one another are indicators of friendship and that friendship can allow tolerance in feeding, warning of predator arrival, active defence against predators, support in contests with conspecifics and joint access to food patches. Allies and friends may show particular behaviour which promotes the continuation of their relationship; for example, Colmenares (1991) described how male baboons who are allies have prolonged periods of greeting each day with lipsmacking and genital touching, behaviours which require trust. Close associations and mutually beneficial behaviour such as reciprocal grooming are common in group living mammals such as ungulates, and birds, such as parrots. The relationships between some cows in a suckler herd described by Benham (1984) involved long periods of association during resting, feeding and movement and reciprocal grooming. Aggressive interactions were very rare in this stable herd and in many other stable social groups of mammals and birds. Hence the statement, based on primate studies, that there is great significance associated with the existence of more coalitions during aggression in primates than in non-primates may indicate a difference in levels of aggression or an artificially high level of aggression in some primate groups which have been observed, rather than a fundamental difference between primates and other animals.

When fights or acts of punishment occur in primate groups, the losing or injured individual may receive attention, which has been described as consolation by de Waal and Aureli (1996), from other group members. This behaviour would appear to be beneficial to the recipient and hence altruistic. Consolation behaviour was seen much more often in groups of chimpanzees than in groups of macaque monkeys. Another behaviour, which must serve to cement or restore social bonds, is reconciliation behaviour after a fight or other altercation between erstwhile allies. Reconciliation behaviour by chimpanzees includes kissing and grooming and is described by de Waal (1996, pp. 164, 176). Cords (1992) studied long-tailed macaque monkeys which lived together in a large enclosure and were put in a situation which led to aggressive food competition. After this they were likely to show reconciliation behaviour. Reconciliation was allowed by experimenters in some situations but prevented in others. When the pair of monkeys were subsequently put together in a different feeding situation in which aggression would not normally occur, after reconciliation simultaneous feeding was more likely and further aggression less likely than if there had been no reconciliation. Much reconciliation behaviour is also shown within groups of stump-tailed macaques, a rather unaggressive species. Rhesus monkeys showed little reconciliation behaviour but if they were kept with a group of stump-tailed macaques, more reconciliation and less aggression was seen. A similar result occurred when rhesus monkeys were kept with bonobos (de Waal 1996, p. 178 and pers. commun.).

The obvious parallels between the complex social interactions in groups of chimpanzees and in human groups led de Waal (1982) to refer to chimpanzee politics. Alliances between individuals within social groups against other members of the group are widespread in human society, as are inter-group conflicts. Groups of people categorise themselves and other groups according to location or personal characteristics. People with a particular skin colour, or hair colour, or accent, or smell because of the food which they eat may act as a group and there are many levels of such groups from a gang of five boys to a whole nation. The group may be the people who live in a small area, or the supporters of a football team, or the inhabitants of a large area such as Liverpool, or New York. People decide whether or not to help others, partly on the basis of whether they perceive them to be members of a group to which they themselves belong. Blum (1980, p. 87) suggests that a car owner would be more likely than a non-car owner to help another car owner to dig their car out of snow. Alliances in serious competition may also be decided by perceptions of group identity. Within groups, however, people accept the presence and actions of others in a remarkably tolerant way. Thompson (1976, p. 226) wrote:

> To an ethologist, what is surprising about people in subways [underground trains] is not their hostility; on the contrary, it is the degree of coordination and habituation which permits thousands of people to move daily through an environment so physically hostile as to stampede the herds of any sane animal

Similarly, Blum (1980, p. 16) points out how remarkable it is that people wait in a supermarket queue and sometimes allow someone to go ahead of their turn. The actions are part of an elaborate structure for perpetuating social order and gaining subtle advantages. Both the group identities and the strategies which involve a high degree of tolerance of others have clear parallels in the societies of non-human animals. Indeed it is easier to understand what happens in human society if the events in other societies are studied and considered.

2.2.8 Care for the weak

The life history strategies of most species with complex brains involve parental care. Care for the young involves a variety of adaptations of anatomy, brain function, the hormonal system, other bodily physiology and behaviour. Once there is a system for caring for others, there is a possibility that it will be more wide ranging in its effects and that some degree of toleration and care may be directed towards others. In social species, any such toleration and care may have advantages for personal advancement within the group or for enhancement of group stability. Some care for those who are not offspring may be an accidental consequence of the system for care of our offspring, but most of it is likely to be of value in itself and hence not to be just an epiphenomenon, i.e. mistaken parental behaviour. Such behaviour includes rescuing or adopting the young of other parents, accepting unrelated young individuals into a social group, and helping the sick, injured and old.

Long-lasting social groups of which offspring remain members allow the possibility for individuals to have contact with their grandchildren. In some cases, the grandchildren may not be recognised as such but there are several studies of primates in which grandparents are of clear benefit to their grandchildren. Fairbanks (1988) studied a colony of captive vervet monkeys and found that monkeys with their mother present in the group were less protective of their own infants and these infants became socially independent at an earlier age. Chimpanzee grandmothers also interact with their grandchildren (Goodall 1986). The help which is given by grandparents may sometimes be relatively inexpensive but of considerable value to the young. Hill and Hurtado (1991) point out that an individual in a long-lasting group may survive error or misfortune because of help from others; for example, if a female has too many offspring for her to rear successfully, a grandmother may help and increase the extent to which her genes survive in future generations by doing so. The benefit is greatest if the grandchild might otherwise have died. Where the grandmother is reproductively active, the cost to grandchildren of food provision is probably too great. However, Hill and Hurtado were writing principally about humans in which the menopause may well be a mechanism for promoting grandmother help of grandchildren because the inability to continue to reproduce has a net fitness advantage. Blurton-Jones et al. (1999) point out that women in societies where they have to gather their own food do often produce children faster than would be expected on the basis of their energy availability and that grandmothers allow mother humans to wean children at an earlier age than is possible without them. Juveniles who are helped by several females generally have higher quality abilities. In a discussion of why there is no menopause in other species, Blurton-Jones et al. mention human longevity but also state that the amount of food which humans can gather is greater in energy terms than that which monkeys can gather. However, humans living in the same area as chimpanzees exploit fewer staple foods so the grandmother role in chimpanzees might be expected to be considerable.

Parents and offspring will have some conflict in that it is in the interests of the offspring to prolong parental care for longer than the optimum for the interests of parents who are able to breed again (Trivers 1974). Offspring attempt to deceive parents, by pretending to be younger than they are, in order to extend the care period. Where grandparents or other social group members help young individuals, it is likely to be easier for them to decide when care is important to the individual. The behaviour of grandparents and other carers towards young individuals will usually fluctuate according to mood and other demands on resources, so failure to care for a young individual at one moment does not mean that there is no long-term concern for that individual.

Helpers at the nest who are not the parents are widely reported in birds. Trivers (1985, p. 184) estimates that they occur in more than

1% of bird species, largely tropical or subtropical, including Harris' hawk (1.3 young reared without helpers and 2.0 reared with helpers), Tasmanian native hen (1.1 : 3.1 reared if inexperienced and 5.5 : 6.5 if experienced), kookaburra (1.2 : 2.3 reared), white-fronted bee-eater (1.3 : 1.9 reared) and superb blue wren (1.5 : 2.8 reared). Most of the helpers are males of less than one year old who are helping siblings or offspring of siblings. Helpers are commoner in species and local populations where there is a male-biased sex ratio and commoner in conditions where there is not a superfluity of food. In the scrub jay 67% of the helpers were helping to rear siblings but 3% of helpers were unrelated to the young. Mammals also help in the rearing of offspring who are not their own. There are reports of orphaned chimpanzees being cared for by adult brothers and sisters (Goodall 1986) and of other primates and elephants doing the same. However, cooperative care is the norm in the painted hunting dog (Kühme 1965, Dugatkin 1997). Females nurse pups which are not their own and both male and female pack members bring back food for pups. Individuals which remain with pups are also fed by other group members. In some cases the carers are quite closely related to the young but in other cases they are not. Females allowing young which are not their own to suckle are reported for lionesses (Bertram 1975), despite the fact that the average degree of relatedness with these young was 0.075 as compared with 0.5 for her own cubs. Domestic sows will sometimes allow cross-suckling, and the provision of food for, or defence of, young which are not their own offspring is described for wolves, rhesus monkeys and other primates (Mech 1970, Spencer-Booth 1970, Clutton-Brock and Harvey 1976). The most extreme mammalian example of shared care for the young is that shown by the naked mole rat in which, like some social insects, many individuals are non-breeding workers who help to care for the offspring of a reproductive individual who is quite closely related to them. The behaviour of older young with the parent's new offspring is sometimes helpful and sometimes a hindrance; both were reported by Zahavi (1974) in a study of babblers and Zahavi pointed out that helpers obtain some useful experience when they are helping in that they may rear their own young with greater success after having helped.

Within social groups of monkeys, older unrelated individuals may act in a way which could help to improve social stability but which helps younger individuals in the same ways in which their parents might do so. DeVore (1965) describes dominant male baboons watching young baboons at play and intervening by grabbing one individual and punishing it with a bite to the neck if the other has shown distress. The behaviour seemed to be the same, whether or not the male was the father of either of the young individuals. Similarly, Hrdy (1976) described female langurs intervening on behalf of the infant of another female in the group.

Long-term studies of gorillas have shown that adult silver-back males will sometimes accept young unrelated males into their group who will later grow to become their rival (I. Redmond pers. commun.). In one group which Redmond studied, a ten-year-old adult male allowed a three-and-a-half year old male to join his group. When that young male grew up and the older male became too old to win fights, the younger one allowed him to remain in the group. There are many human parallels and those groomed for future leadership may be chosen on the basis of quality or availability rather than because of relatedness.

Elderly, sick or injured members of social groups may be helped by other group members. Painted hunting dogs feed such individuals and increase their chances of surviving and remaining useful group members by doing so. Moss (1988) describes the various efforts of members of a herd of elephants to assist an individual which had been shot and (de Waal 1996, p. 53) reports that when an old bull elephant was dying, the other group members tried to lift him, one breaking a tusk in the process. Whales and dolphins support sick and injured individuals by remaining close by, attacking aggressors, including human boats, pushing the distressed individual away from captors or attackers and pushing up from below to facilitate breathing (Trivers 1985, p. 382). Many of the helpers are not kin because the behaviour is widespread, and in so many groups most members are not close kin. In a report on the Discovery Communications web-site, a baby monkey which had been hit by a car in Assam was surrounded by a large group of monkeys and defended for some time, preventing traffic from passing. Sometimes members of one species will help another, for example a group of striated dolphins stood by when a female pilot whale was being captured. Humans help sick, injured and elderly individuals who may or may not be kin. Such behaviour in other primates is reviewed by de Waal (1996, pp. 49–59). A slow developing rhesus monkey with a chromosome abnormality was protected by her sister. An infant Japanese macaque with cerebral palsy was not punished for actions which would have elicited punishment in a normal infant. A blind rhesus monkey was defended more than normally by kin. A ring-tailed lemur which had received an electric shock was carried and cared for by others who would not normally do so. Behaviour which helps the injured seems to be expected to be returned. Several primate species will lick the wounds of other group members and a male toque macaque which did not receive wound licking in a group which he had joined left the group and returned to his former group (Dittus and Ratnayeke 1989).

The vocalisations or other behaviour of very young, sick or injured individuals elicit responses which would often be described as sympathetic. Young rhesus monkeys respond to another which is crying by contact which appears to be comforting (de Waal 1996, p. 46) and human children will do the same, responding to adults as well as children in this way. A hand-reared chimpanzee was disturbed by illness in the human carer. It would appear that sympathy is a feeling which is elicited by detecting pain or distress in others. Responses may be elicited by behaviour prior to death and may be remembered. Smuts (1985) described a baboon mother showing agitated searching behaviour when passing the place where her three-month-old infant had died one week earlier.

Brandt (1996, p. 30) suggests that some sympathetic or helpful behaviour is carried out solely in order to prevent the distress vocalisations or other behaviour of others because such behaviour is aversive. Similarly, an individual may be motivated to show sympathy because of being disturbed by the sight or smell of blood. The implication of this argument is that it is the motivation underlying sympathetic or helping behaviour which is important when deciding whether altruistic acts have occurred. However, it is my view that where there is a mechanism within humans or other animals which promotes helping behaviour, an action which has a cost to the altruist and a benefit to the recipient is altruistic, even if some of the motivation for carrying out the act is explicable in terms of response to certain stimuli.

2.2.9 Detecting and reporting cheats

An essential part of reciprocal altruism is the detection and reporting of cheats. However, cheating can be of various kinds. Some trouble-making which causes difficulties in social groups is cheating in the sense that the perpetrator knows what should be done and does not do it. Another form of cheating, exemplified in Chapter 2, Section 2.7. by chimpanzee data, is failure to support an ally in a circumstance where support was possible and, especially, where the individual concerned had been previously supported. Deception and provision of misinformation are also forms of cheating. Where an individual has been the beneficiary of an altruistic act, it may be that the cheating involves failure to reciprocate at all or that something is done in return but the benefit to the other is considerably less than that which was received. As mentioned already, although the extent of reciprocation should be based on the extent of the cost to the giver, it will often be assessed according to the magnitude of the value to the recipient. An act which is life-saving is the most likely to be remembered and reciprocated.

Assessment of the value of favours is facilitated in long-lasting, friendly relationships. If individuals meet infrequently and do not know one another well it is more difficult to remember what altruistic acts have occurred and who has been the beneficiary. There are many species, however, whose group members spend much time together and monitor one another's activities closely, so failure to share food, or assist in aggression or work which is difficult for one individual is easy to detect. Some anti-social acts, such as those of a female chimpanzee who stole, killed and ate infants in her own social group (Kummer 1978), seem not to be recognised. Humans are particularly good at recognising any form of cheating. Transgressions are remembered and their magnitude carefully assessed.

Where cheating occurs and the perpetrator is aware of it a feeling of guilt may ensue. Broom (1998) defines *guilt* as:

> *the feeling of individuals who have behaved in a way that they or their social group members would normally condemn or punish.*

The feeling of guilt continues to draw attention to the cheating action and makes it more difficult to forget or otherwise ignore. Hence Trivers (1985, p. 389) proposes that guilt is:

> selected to motivate the cheater to compensate for misdeeds and behave reciprocally in the future.

The reparation required may be great if the initial cheating has been detected. Planalp (1999, p. 162) refers to guilt as one of several emotions which:

> draw attention to, assert and celebrate whatever moral standards we hold.

Where there is failure to reciprocate an altruistic act which is relatively frequent, such as defence against an attack or the sharing of food, the simplest punishment response is to avoid the individual concerned and refuse to act in an altruistic way towards that individual again. An extension to this is to communicate disfavour to others as this will sometimes have the result that the price paid by the transgressor is high. de Waal (1996, p. 160) described differential responses to chimpanzees who regularly shared food and to those who did not when they begged for food from an individual with a large quantity. The former were normally given some of the food whilst the latter were much less likely to be successful and their begging attempts elicited loud vocal protestations. Another example from de Waal's work (p. 89) concerned a response to trouble-makers. The chimpanzees at Arnhem Zoo were not fed until they were all in the building and they were very familiar with this routine. When two young chimps delayed feeding for two hours they were housed separately overnight but when reunited with the group next morning, they were pursued and beaten. In several species the response to cheating which has been described is what Trivers (1985) calls 'moralistic aggression', the magnitude of which may be disproportionate to the extent of the cheating. As cheating is sometimes difficult to detect, punishment at a high level may occur and may act as a deterrent to other potential cheats. In some studies, such as that of Wilkinson (1984) on vampire bats, no punishment of cheats was reported but reciprocation does normally occur and it may be that cheat detection is infrequent. In human societies, Alexander (1979, p. 274) argues that the kind of individual cheated is a significant variable in the meting out of punishment:

> I suggest that parents are more likely to punish children for
> (a) cheating close relatives, (b) cheating friends with much to offer
> the family in a continuing reciprocal interaction, or (c) cheating in
> an obvious, bungling fashion sure to be detected, than they are to
> punish them for simply cheating.

He was referring to cheating in the very general sense of 'any kind of social deception or taking of advantage' so was not clearly differentiating between reciprocation of a favour to an altruist and other self-seeking acts. Punishment by the group as a whole may not be on the same basis as the punishment by parents which Alexander postulates.

2.3 COMPETITION, AGGRESSION AND WAR
Much evidence of cooperative behaviour is presented in Section 2.2 with little reference to the competitive behaviour which these same individuals show. Evidence of competition is so widely available that it will be summarised relatively briefly in this section. The lengths

of the sections in this book are not intended to reflect the amount of information which exists.

The cells in a body and the genetically identical individuals which make up certain colonial animals compete for resources to some extent but there are regulatory mechanisms such as immunological recognition and central neural and hormonal control which minimise the competition. Ridley (1996, p. 26) refers to: the amoeba-like individuals which when aggregated form slime-moulds, competing to form the reproductive spore-bearing part rather than its stalk; the ovaries as parasites of the liver in complex animals; mutant or otherwise modified cells which invade as cancers; parasitic B chromosomes which some people carry; and segregation distorter genes which get into egg or sperm cells but confer no benefit. Individuals which are not genetically identical may compete in a wide variety of ways. There is even competition between the mammalian foetus and its mother. Haig (1993) reported several ways in which the foetus acts rather like a parasite in that its effect on the mother is to increase what it gets from her to a level higher than that which the mother would have given. There are maternal responses which tend to counteract these foetal effects. One example is that foetal cells embed themselves in the walls of the artery which brings blood from the mother to the foetus, and destroy muscle cells there, thus making it more difficult for the mother's body to restrict blood supply and hence nutrient supply to the foetus. Hormones from the foetus can increase the proportion of blood going to the foetus by reducing the amounts circulating elsewhere, with the side-effects of high blood pressure and pre-eclampsia in some human mothers. The placenta, which is largely under foetal control, produces a hormone called human placental lactogen as a consequence of the action of a gene inherited from the father only. This blocks the effect of the hormone insulin produced by the mother when there is too much sugar circulating in the blood. The human placental lactogen is tending to increase the amount of sugar getting to the foetus from the maternal blood while the insulin level is being increased by the mother to reduce the levels of sugar in the blood. If the foetus is too successful in this competition, the mother gets gestational diabetes. In the same way, and as mentioned in Chapter 2, Section 2.8, there can be conflict between parents and offspring after birth or hatching, especially as the time when the offspring could live independently approaches. In both the mother–foetus and the parent–older-offspring situations the relationship is largely cooperative but an element of competition is usually present.

Both social and non-social animals may compete to the extent that one kills the other. A male langur monkey, or a male lion, joining a group and pairing with a female in it, may kill the young in the group with the likely effect of increasing his reproductive output. Animals may prey on their own species for food. In one isolated Scottish loch, the only fish species present was the predatory pike so they had to eat members of their own species. The largest pike in the loch were over a metre long and fed on middle-sized pike about 20 cm long. These in turn fed on young pike about 4 cm long. The small pike were able to feed on invertebrates. Even social animals like chimpanzees will sometimes collaborate to catch, kill and eat members of their own species.

The vast majority of competitive interactions do not result in death but in one individual gaining a resource or an opportunity at the expense of another. Competition between two individuals should occur uninhibited when the competitive act of one is not likely to have adverse consequences for it, because of the later behaviour of the disadvantaged individual or of others which become aware of the competitive act or its effects. Where the individuals have social relationships, and especially if they meet often in a group situation, there can be such advantages associated with non-competitive living that at least some competitive activity is inhibited. The balance between competitive acts and suppressed competition or active cooperation will vary according to circumstances. Individuals use a variety of strategies to achieve objectives, some involving competitive acts, and decide about which to employ after assessing the situation. In the studies of Rasa (1979) on the socially living dwarf mongooses when population density increased there were more aggressive acts but also more affiliative acts which have the effect of stabilising the group. Crowding is one of the variables which affects the sorts of coping strategies that are used by individuals.

Competitive behaviour, like altruistic behaviours, may have reciprocal aspects. If an individual is robbed of food or attacked by another, the harm may be repaid to that individual at a later time when the opportunity arises. There can also be indirect revenge, for example Aureli (1992) found that long-tailed macaque monkeys which were the victims of attack by another group member often attacked a weaker relative of their attacker, either immediately or after a delay. The occurrence of cooperation during predatory attacks and inter-group conflicts has been mentioned in this chapter in Sections 2.3 and 2.7. There may be small group alliances like the 'war parties' of about five chimpanzees which may attack other chimpanzees (Wrangham et al. 1994). Rather larger raiding groups may also be formed, such as the ants which capture and enslave individuals of their own or other species, or the wolves, hyaenas or rhesus monkeys which have been recorded as engaging in battles against other social groups. Human groups which initiate aggressive encounters may also be relatively small, such as gangs of children or young men from a localised area, or rather larger like those supporting a football team, or very large like national armies. Some of these aggressive consortia seem to be subject to rather few rules and to utilise only aggressive strategies. Others have obvious rules or employ conciliatory as well as aggressive strategies. Whilst male rhesus monkeys from rival groups are threatening and fighting one another, females from one group may groom individuals from the other. Human wars have strict codes concerning which people are acceptable subjects for attack and even at what times battle may be commenced but it is relatively unusual for alternative strategies such as appeasement to be countenanced in the course of a war. An example is the occurrence of friendly interchanges between British and German troops in the trenches at Christmas and some other times during the First World War. It would seem that some of the soldiers on both sides felt that they had more in common with soldiers on the other side than with their own officers. These actions were seen as a problem by the senior officers on both sides and Generals moved troops around to prevent it. The soldiers in wars sometimes have to be coerced or bribed to fight because their motivation is not quite the same as that of the politicians or high-ranking officers directing their actions. During the American War of Independence, many people in Britain were opposed to the war which they saw as the attempted suppression of law-abiding British people living in North America by the rich land-owners. Hence, some of those who were supposedly fighting against the rebels were rather half-hearted and it was necessary for the British authorities to use foreign mercenaries. Natural attempts to use alternative, non-aggressive strategies were suppressed by the organisers of the war.

A central theme of this book is that the idea that social behaviour is largely uninterrupted competition, in which those who seek their own immediate advantage are the most successful, is wrong. Competition occurs but does not usually proceed unchecked. Cooperative alternatives which promote group stability are more successful in many situations. Social behaviour is far from being all cooperation but competition is avoided, or its adverse effects are minimised, on very many occasions. When birds hold a territory, they do not spend time and energy defending it against neighbouring territory holders once the boundaries are established. The work of Falls and Brooks (1975) showed that territory-holding white-throated sparrows responded less aggressively to a tape recording of a neighbour's song coming from the expected direction than to that of a stranger. The known individual, even though a rival, was categorised in a different way from an intruder. The advantage of stable relationships is much greater to animals living in groups than to territory holders. Goodall (1986) described how chimpanzees who saw that a weaker group member had obtained a prized item of food would not normally take it forcibly, even though they were capable of doing so, but would beg for it. She considered that this was a means of avoiding fights which could be harmful to the perpetrator if group stability were jeopardised by so doing. Kummer *et al.* (1974) reported that a male hamadryas baboon who was capable of taking a female by force from another male did not do so if he had seen them interact as a pair. However, the female of a male who had been trapped might be taken. All such behaviour is rare and in one of Kummer's studies, during 1000 hours of observation, no adult male hamadryas baboon was ever observed to mate with a female outside his harem. In some primate groups, some sharing of mates occurs; for example, male anubis baboons could appropriate a female for a few hours or days, and in chimpanzee groups, several males might mate openly with a receptive female. The woolly spider monkeys or muriqui, studied by Strier (1992) for 1200 hours, were only observed to chase aggressively on nine occasions and even males near a sexually receptive female did not fight. They did sometimes remove sperm plugs which would make their own fertilisation more likely to be successful.

2.4   THE EVOLUTION OF ALTRUISM

Why should not every individual act in ways which result in their own gain, in the short-term and perhaps also in the long-term? Put in terms of human qualities, why not be selfish, or indeed vindictive, all the time? As described in Section 2.3, competition occurs at the gene and cell level as well as at the individual and group level. Trivers (1985, p. 137) points out that: genes may bias meiosis in their favour or suppress the action of genes from the other parent; mitochondria from the mother sea urchin *Paracentrotus* sp. may destroy those from the father; the B chromosome in the grasshopper *Melanoplus* sp. appears to be solely parasitic; and in some circumstances cells from one organ seem to benefit at the expense of other cells and the organism as a whole. These examples are perceived as surprising by most biologists but examples of competition between individuals, especially those who are not closely related to one another, are perceived as normal. The logic behind this paradox is based on some knowledge of the degree of relatedness of the protagonists.

Within the body of a multicellular animal, the genetic complement varies a little but there are very many cells with the same genes. Hence mechanisms for minimising inter-cell competition, such as apoptosis as a defence against cancer development, have evolved and are generally effective. As Ridley (1996, p. 33) emphasises, genes which result in the suppression of parasitic parts of the body are likely to spread in the population. This is true despite the extensive specialisation of organs within the body and the consequent diversity of cell types and hence of active sections of the genome. Specialisation which is comparable in several ways with that within the body also occurs in groups of individuals, and mechanisms for minimising undesirable conflict or promoting cooperation exist within individuals which live in groups. The reason why these mechanisms exist is that there are many ways in which the actions that result in short-term gain for certain individuals within a group result in long-term disadvantages for those individuals. The disadvantages may be of various kinds, including consequences of cumulative destabilising effects within the group, or specific retribution by other group members. This retribution is itself part of a general mechanism for minimising destabilising or generally harmful actions. Given the great complexity of the societies of various species of animals, natural selection must have resulted in the spread of genes whose effects are to reduce the most adverse effects of competitive acts and to promote various forms of cooperation, occurring either simultaneously or with a time lag.

When would a gene which promoted altruism spread in a population? If one cell incurs some cost when acting in a way which benefits another cell, this is not altruism if the two cells are genetically identical. However, as soon as there is a genetic difference between them, it can be called altruism. This is true even if most of the genes present in each individual are the same. This is the case, albeit to decreasing extents, in this series: if the individuals are close relations, or members of the same species or members of different species in a class of animals. Worker ants can be altruistic to their sister worker ants, brother mammals can be altruistic to one another and parents can be altruistic to their offspring. The importance of being a relative is very strongly emphasised by those who are surprised by the existence of altruistic behaviour. Alexander (1987, p. 3) wrote:

> We are evidently evolved not only to aid the genetic materials in our own bodies, by creating and assisting descendants, but also to assist by nepotism, copies of our genes that reside in collateral, non-descendant, relatives.

The emphasis by Alexander and others, of the importance of helping relatives rather than individuals in general, was based on the observation that altruism is commonest between close relatives and the erroneous assumption that the degree of relatedness reflects arithmetically the extent of shared genes. Close relatives share more genes than those of the same species which are not close relatives. However, as explained in Section 2.1, many genes are common to all members of a species, even if some of these genes are non-functional. It may well be that genes which promote altruism are widespread. If an altruistic act is to be carried out, it might be addressed only to close relatives, or to those who could be close relatives, but it might also be addressed to any who bear the same gene or to those who might reciprocate, encourage reciprocation, or carry out similar group-stabilising actions. As mentioned earlier, reciprocity may be direct and specific with the return benefit very similar to the initial altruistic act such as shared food for shared food. It may also be different but of similar value such as mating opportunity for food, or indirect with the altruist receiving later benefit from an individual who is not the same as the original beneficiary. In all cases, if the altruist benefits overall, the gene for altruism is likely to spread.

Alexander (1987, p. 86) suggests that altruism spreads because of rewards whilst rules spread because of punishment. In fact, a gene which promotes altruism should spread if its net effect is beneficial to the fitness of its bearers and if it cannot be supplanted by another which confers greater benefit. A gene promoting altruism would be more likely to spread in the population if there was some means of assessing the likely benefit to the recipient, the cost to the altruist and preferably also any possible longer term benefit to the altruist which might result from the action. Some of the immediate risks to the altruist and benefits to the recipient should be quite easy to assess, as should be the ratio of one to the other in more extreme cases such as very low cost and very high benefit.

Discussions of how altruistic behaviour might have evolved have often included reference to natural selection based on the differential fitness of groups. One champion of this group selection view was Wynne-Edwards (1962) who argued that many social behaviours are adaptations for regulating population size. However, few would now accept that evolution of characters for the good of the species can occur. Detailed arguments for the role of group selection in the evolution of altruism are presented by Sober and Wilson (1998). For example, on p. 26–29 they present explanations of why altruists may increase in overall frequency if groups with more altruists produce more offspring. Part of their basis for the assertion that group selection plays a significant role in the evolution of altruistic behaviour is the Price equation which was discussed by Hamilton (1975) and is presented here in words.

$$\text{global frequency of altruistic gene P} = \text{average gene frequency} + \frac{\text{covariance of average group size and average gene frequency (before selection)}}{\text{average group size}}$$

The first component on the right-hand side of this equation is the consequence of selection acting at the gene level whilst the second is the group selection component.

The extensive arguments of Sober and Wilson (1998) are intended to explain the group selection aspects of a situation such as the following. They argue that if animals live in groups whose members could act altruistically and collaborate, or could just compete, it might be that in some conditions only the collaborator groups would survive because of the stabilising and other beneficial effects of collaboration. However, the key question is whether it is correct to speak of group selection components as being involved in the selection process. If those individuals who have genes which promote their altruistic behaviour in a group have more descendants than those who do not have such genes, the genes for altruism will obviously spread in the population. This will occur if bearers of the gene become more numerous in sets of groups which make up a population, for example because non-collaborator groups tend to die out. The gene will spread whether or not its effect is to make an individual more successful within a small group. However, selection is acting at the level of individuals bearing certain genes. The individuals with the altruism gene produce more offspring because they are in groups in which the gene has a beneficial effect. It is not necessary to postulate some kind of group selection.

Once altruism occurs and is reciprocated, the possibility of cheating becomes important. A variety of characteristics of individuals, any of which would tend to promote altruistic and moral behaviour, are listed below:

(1) Affection for certain types of individuals – perhaps those which are close relatives or group members, or are likely to be – which reduces the chances that harm will be done to them.

(2) Affection for those same individuals which increases the likelihood of carrying out behaviour which is beneficial to them.

(3) Ability to recognise individuals which might be beneficiaries or benefactors.

(4) Ability to remember the actions of others which resulted in benefit to oneself or to others in the group.

(5) Ability to remember one's own actions which resulted in a benefit to another individual.

(6) Ability to assess the risk or benefit of one's own and other's actions and either to compare these or to avoid high risk and try to attain high benefit.

(7) Ability to detect and evaluate cheating.

(8) Ability to punish or facilitate the punishment of those who cheat.

(9) Ability to support a social structure which encourages cooperation and discourages cheating.

(10) Having a desire to conform.

This last quality may promote the occurrence of altruistic acts by means of positive feedback but may also promote immoral acts. Suppose that an altruism-promoting gene appears in animal A. It will not survive in the population if its effects prevent A from reproducing but may spread to some extent amongst the offspring of A if it has no substantial adverse effect on reproductive success. If it has the effect of benefiting the relatives who also bear it, it will spread more readily. Once it is present in many individuals in the population, there is a greater potential for its action to result in further spreading since more bearers might be benefited. It is not necessary for there to be reciprocation of the altruism for the gene spread to occur, but the net cost to the altruist in terms of offspring production would have to be outweighed by the overall benefit, in terms of the spreading of the gene in the population. Most of such examples would be low cost activities. It would also be necessary that no gene whose effects were to reduce or prevent effective altruism could spread and negate the advantage of possessing the altruism-promoting genes. Explanations of how selection for cooperative behaviour may occur are presented by Bell (1997, p. 506, p. 525).

Another kind of altruism-promoting gene might be linked with genes which encourage reciprocation of such altruism and assessment of any cheating. A more complex set of gene effects is involved here but the arguments concerning their spread are similar. The beneficial effect of the initial altruistic action, however, may also accrue to the altruist when some reciprocation occurs. Hence a greater initial cost, or potential cost, of the altruism may be tolerated. In this case, if the genes spread widely in the population, the altruistic act could be directed towards any individual and not just a close relative if the likelihood of reciprocation was above a threshold level related to the initial cost. The likelihood of spread of genes promoting such altruism which could be reciprocated directly or indirectly would depend upon whether genes promoting other strategies were more successful. These other strategies might involve a variety of forms of cheating.

When two or more possible strategies exist, each of which could be promoted by a gene, useful information about the likely result of the competition between these genes can be obtained by the use of game theory. An application of game theory which is relevant to consideration of when to be altruistic and when to act so that you gain, whatever the effect on others, is the 'prisoner's dilemma', in which two individuals may either cooperate, or defect and betray one another, for specified pay-offs. The commonly investigated scenario is that in which cooperation reciprocated gets three points, cooperation unreciprocated gets zero points, and defection gets one point if the other does likewise and five points if the other cooperates. When computer-simulated games were played in which a long series of encounters was modelled, the strategy which was most successful was 'tit-for-tat' in which each player began by cooperating and then did what their opponent had done at their last play. However, where both players used this strategy but one player defected at any point, cooperation ceased completely. Since escalating violence is not the norm it seems unlikely that this exact strategy is used in real life. A strategy called 'generous tit-for-tat' which randomly forgave 30% of transgressions would lose to 'always cooperate' which in turn would lose to 'always defect'. The strategy 'simpleton', which involves staying with an action which wins but switching to the other if it loses, could replace 'tit-for-tat' but lose to 'always defect' (Ridley 1996, p. 76).

The problem with using such game theory results is that they are too simple when the sophisticated intellects of any social vertebrate are considered. Modifications have included the insertion of a delay between plays and the insertion of random 'noise' which changes the actions on some occasions without the player knowing (Axelrod 1984, 1997). Even with such changes, the models are too simple. As Kitcher

(1993) points out, in real life individuals select their opponents, respond to what they do and break off interactions altogether at times. A further difference from reality is that games are not just played by two individuals but often by several group members and many of the interactions which occur in groups are closely monitored by those in the vicinity. Most members of social species show some degree of specialisation so the possibilities for reciprocation are complex. The 'tit-for-tat' strategy is certainly absent in some situations, for example Heinsohn and Packer (1995) found that some lionesses defended the pride on each occasion that it was necessary whilst others lagged behind when such an attack was occurring. The roles and relationships within the group of lionesses seemed constant and not at all like those considered in the models.

A further challenge to simplistic models of reciprocal altruism arose because although the modelling of the prisoner's dilemma showed 'tit-for-tat' as a successful strategy in small groups, it did not do so when group size was more than a few dozen. It is my view that it was naive to expect that any simple model could explain all, or indeed much, of altruistic behaviour and that several different mechanisms promote it. Boyd and Richerson (1990) argued that most altruistic behaviour could be accounted for as conformism. *Individuals in a group show conformism when they tend to behave in the same way as other members in their group and copy widely used strategies and activities.* There is much evidence that this does occur, that there are benefits from copying strategies and that such conformist behaviour tends to act as a positive feedback system which accentuates group characteristics. However, if there are no other constraints, injurious behaviour is just as likely to be copied as altruistic behaviour and conformism cannot account for the origins of altruism, only for some of its increase once it has been successful for individuals and has developed in a group.

Improved understanding of how altruistic behaviour might have evolved is likely to come from combining sophisticated modelling methods with information obtained from studies of real life situations.

In this way, rather than over-simple general strategies, combinations of strategies which utilise the real abilities of the animals concerned can be considered. It is now clear from the modelling studies of Riolo *et al.* (2001) that tolerance and cooperation in a group-living species could arise if a strategy existed of benevolence to individuals bearing the same recognisable characteristic as the actor. This could occur even if there was no direct reciprocation. Such a mechanism could be the only altruistic behaviour in a species, or could coexist in a species with more complex altruism which is reciprocated by a known individual or by another group member who recognises the actor.

3 Biological capabilities needed for altruism and morality

3.1 CAPABILITIES

Any consideration of altruism, especially reciprocal altruism, or of moral codes depends upon a certain level of sophistication of brain functioning. If this level was not needed during evolution until the human species arose, then it is of little use to consider other species when trying to understand the basis for human morality. In this chapter, the abilities of humans and other kinds of animals for information processing, recognition of others, awareness, feelings and cognition are discussed. Different degrees of ability and the extent to which these qualities of individuals have evolved are considered.

3.2 WHICH BRAINS WOULD ALLOW RECIPROCAL ALTRUISM?

In order to reciprocate an altruistic act, it is necessary to remember and evaluate who conferred the benefit, what degree of benefit it was and what would constitute a similar benefit. These capabilities would also be used in order to identify any individual who cheated and failed to reciprocate. It is also necessary to have an adequate system for control of actions. An adequately functional brain would have to have evolved in order that the capabilities would exist. As Wilson (1978, p. 2) says:

> The brain exists because it promotes the survival and
> multiplication of the genes that direct its assembly. The human
> mind is a device for survival and reproduction, and reason is just
> one of its various activities.

Whatever the level of analysis and decision making, it is the brain which does it. When considering the more complex of normal decisions, there is nowhere outside the brain which can be used, except of course to consult another individual and hence their brain. Referring to such issues, Wilson (p. 6) says:

> The oracle which these philosophers consult resides in the deep emotional centres of the brain, most probably within the limbic system.

We have biases about ability in man and other species. Everything which we have read is written by humans and there is a widespread assumption that humans have superior abilities when any level of brain function or its consequence is under consideration. Most people are persuaded by evidence of various kinds that humans have evolved from non-human primates and, even if they ask questions about the likelihood that such a change would have occurred, they expect non-human primates to be different in very significant ways from other kinds of mammals because they are like humans. In the same way, there is a desire to discover that mammals are significantly different from other vertebrates and are very different from other phyla of animals. Often the term used when making such comparisons is more or less advanced. This concept is a result of the biased assumption that the significant evolutionary path was that which led to man. This biologically naive view is widespread, even amongst biologists. There are many examples of animal features where the most efficient, or safest, or most successful outcome is not that which obtains in man. However, the view of the golden route of advancement to man persists and is particularly prevalent when brain function is under consideration. Early studies of brain anatomy revealed a proportionally large neocortex in humans and quite a large neocortex in other primates. The conclusion was drawn that all high-level processing occurred in the neocortex and that animals with no large neocortex were not capable of high level thought. Those coming to such conclusions were somewhat disturbed by the fact that ungulates such as cattle and sheep also had a large neocortex but they looked for evidence for automatic behaviour requiring no high level thought in animals with a small neocortex. It was rather difficult to find such evidence because birds, fish, octopus and even insects displayed complex learning ability. Despite this, many scientists persuaded themselves that there was some qualitative difference from mammals or from man in the learning or other behaviour and that their prejudice for a sharp distinction between humans and every other species and between primates and non-primates was justified.

The true situation is that there are many brain functions which are not necessarily limited to a particular anatomical region of the brain. In birds, much of the high-level processing occurs in the striatum rather than the neocortex. Fish have different parts of the brain developed according to the most important sensory function in that group of fish but the processing in the expanded optic or olfactory regions of the brain is not limited to analysis of optic or olfactory input.

Conclusions about brain processing capabilities cannot be drawn on the basis of anatomy alone but must be based on what the animal can do (Heyes and Huber 2000). Measurement of learning or other ability must be objective and not biased by the kind of testing which is most convenient for the experimenter. For example, monkeys and rats can press levers but cows cannot easily do so and different operants must be devised. As explained in Chapter 1, Section 2, brain size is not necessarily a good indicator of intellectual ability. Barton and Dunbar (1997) conclude that 'brain size is very crude as a neurobiological variable' and explain that some animals may have a smaller brain to body size ratio because they have evolved larger body size. The considerable learning abilities of ants are difficult to understand, given the small size of their brains, if brain size is of any significance. The complexity of the brain appears to be greater in socially living animals than in non-social animals (see Chapter 1, Section 2). It has also been suggested that in order to exploit some kinds of food, a more elaborate brain is needed. For example, where fruit or other food occurs in widely scattered patches so that optimal routes between patches must be found, this would require better spatial cognition, probably involving the hippocampus. Hence if animals do have more elaborate brains, it may be in order that they will have good social cognition for 'the processing of any information which culminates in the accurate perception of the dispositions and intentions of other individuals' (Brothers 1990) but it may be for other reasons. However, the idea of a linear scale of intelligence increasing from fish via reptiles to mammals and primates in particular is not at all well supported by evidence from behavioural studies (Macphail 1982). The studies of food-caching in scrub jays (Clayton and Dickinson 1999, Emery and Clayton 2001) have shown that not only can the birds find food which they have hidden but they can recover perishable food such as moth larvae earlier than less-perishable food such as peanuts. Also, those scrub jays which observe others hiding food modify their own caching behaviour in a way which reduces the likelihood of it being found.

It would appear that some representatives of each of the groups of vertebrates have the ability to form and retain associations to the degree required for some reciprocal altruism to be possible. The complexity of appreciation which a human or a chimpanzee has of itself and of its relationships with other individuals appears to be greater in certain respects than that which can be demonstrated for animals other than anthropoid apes and man. However, there are also many examples of the sort of similarities in appreciation between humans and other animals which suggest that complex long-term relationships are not impossible in many social species.

3.3 THE CAPACITY FOR RECOGNISING OTHERS

Most people can recognise many hundreds of people and use names for a proportion of these. The recognition is by sight of the face or body shape, sound of the voice, odour, or, especially in blind people, the feel of the face. Parent-offspring recognition is usually particularly efficient but even brief meetings may be sufficient to allow recognition on all future encounters. Dunbar (1996) suggests that the optimum group size for humans is about 150 because this allows very efficient recognition and knowledge of one another. This is stated to be the number of people in a typical hunter-gatherer band, a typical religious commune, an average address book, an army company or an easily run factory. These are the people who are more likely to be helped and more likely to be regarded as friends. With recognition and knowledge, of good qualities, comes desire to help and to extend relationships. If hostile acts or cheating are remembered, appropriate retribution might be exacted.

In any careful study of socially living animals, it becomes apparent that individuals react in different ways to at least some of the members of their group. This could be because those individuals always behave in the same way, for example they might always be aggressive. However, with sufficient, carefully observed interactions, it is possible to deduce that some of the group members recognise one another. Evidence from observations of repeated interactions can be confirmed by experimental studies. Darwin (1859) observed that ten to fifteen thousand cattle on a ranch in South America subdivided themselves into groups of forty to one hundred which kept together and Albright (1978) recommended that herds of one hundred or more cattle should be split into smaller groups on the basis that it is difficult for the cattle to recognise more than seventy to one hundred individuals. Studies of social behaviour in heifers and cows by Broom and Leaver (1978) and by Benham (1984) indicated that individuals behaved in a consistently different way towards the various members of their social group. Observations of this kind led Moss and Poole (1983) to conclude that African elephants could recognise and remember six hundred other individuals. Hagen and Broom (2003) conducted an experiment which required cows to approach and walk past one cow rather than another in order to get food, a task which they learned readily. This showed that they could discriminate between the two cows and use the information.

In studies of vervet monkeys by Cheney and Seyfarth (1990, p. 4) calls by different group members elicited different responses and tape-recorded calls of infant monkeys played to an adult elicited the response that the adult looked towards the mother of the infant. On another occasion, when a female monkey was attacked by the mother of a juvenile, the sister of the attacked monkey, who observed the attack, threatened the juvenile. This juvenile had not been with the mother so the sister must have recognised it (Cheney and Seyfarth 1986). In an experimental study by Dasser (1988) macaques were rewarded if they selected the correct picture of other social group members after being shown a picture of the mother, offspring or sibling of the animal in the picture. Vervets also behaved in a way which indicated recognition of members of other social groups (Cheney and Seyfarth 1990, p. 48). It is known that monkeys have a preference for the odour of close relatives, even if they have not met them, but the behaviour described above indicates discrimination of individuals and a concept of the relationships of the individual.

The recognition of individuals of other species, especially humans, is reported for many companion animals, laboratory animals and zoo animals. In some cases, the discrimination of a human is based on the clothing worn but there are many examples of people being responded to in a way which implies recognition whatever they wear. Humans can also recognise individuals of many other species. When de Waal (1996, p. 175) met a bonobo which he had not seen for six years following transfer from one zoo to another, both recognised one another. The encounters in the first zoo, when the bonobo was adolescent, had included a regular greeting before periods of behaviour observation by de Waal and 'a few close and friendly encounters in his night quarters'. After the six-year separation, the behaviour of the male bonobo was very friendly and identified by those people present as indicating a friendly relationship. A reunion between stump-tailed macaques after a two-year separation (loc. cit., p. 176) indicated that they remembered one another.

There are many studies of pigs, sheep, dogs, pigeons, parrots and other social species which indicate that they can discriminate between individuals of their own species and other species and can use the information in a way which suggests that they have concepts of individuals and of some of their qualities. Humans categorise people, simply stated, as friends, enemies or strangers and are generally much more willing to help friends. It would appear that animals of many other species have the capability to do the same and sometimes do so.

3.4   AWARENESS AND CONSCIOUSNESS

Most moral actions necessitate the use of complex concepts and hence of high-level processing in the brain so where the extent to which morality exists in different species and individuals is under consideration, the degree to which they are aware or conscious is relevant. A distinction which is made by some people in discussions about all of these topics is that between mind and brain. The brain is supposed to be the functioning organ of the body whilst the mind is a more nebulous parallel construct which is used in explaining many of the complicated aspects of human life. As mentioned in Chapter 1, Section 2, it is my view that there is no useful distinction between mind and brain and only the word brain is needed. The mind–brain separation stems from a failure to understand general biological functioning and the all–pervasiveness of evolution. The basis of mind or brain must have evolved, just as foot-shape evolved, but even some biologists have found it difficult to accept this. The thinking process is a part of the system which has evolved and even the most complex brain processes can have a function. In all arguments in which the word mind is used, it is the brain which is meant. Within the brain there is a range of levels of functioning but there is no justification for referring to one kind of functioning as mind and implying that it is not brain functioning. Dennett (1991, pp. 33–39) also criticises the making of a distinction between mind and brain.

The term 'aware' is used to describe an individual who is perceiving sensory stimuli and processing them so that their qualities are evaluated. However, an individual can also be aware of an idea or a mental image triggered by memory rather than current sensory input. Griffin (1991, p. 12) considers that:

> awareness involves the experiencing of interrelated mental images.

and this may often be true. However, we cannot know for certain whether individuals share such mental images so a more useful definition is that:

> awareness is a state in which complex brain analysis is used to process sensory stimuli or constructs based on memory.
>
> *(Broom 1998)*

Studies of a variety of non-human species and of normal and brain-damaged humans make it clear that there is a range of degrees of awareness. The gradation of awareness has been described under five headings by Sommerville and Broom (1998) and these are summarised here.

(1) Unaware but responsive

Following some sensory input in an intact animal, either no brain processing takes place, as in a spinal reflex response, or no higher level processing occurs, as when a primer pheromone elicits no immediate response but modifies subsequent physiological functioning.

(2) Perceptual awareness

A perceived stimulus results in an automatic response which may be modifiable, e.g. scratching to relieve irritation, or not modifiable, e.g. blinking when an object passes close to the eye. Some pain falls into this category although in most cases the response is much more flexible.

(3) Cognitive awareness

The sensory input or remembering of an event results in a flexible response which is appropriate but largely automatic. For example, recognising and responding simply to offspring, competitor, ally, dwelling place, food type or many cues whilst driving. Simpler forms of frustration would involve cognitive awareness.

(4) Assessment awareness

The assessment of a situation by an individual and deduction of its significance in relation to itself so that complex responses can be made. Examples include complicated feeding procedures such as blue tits opening milk bottles, vertebrate prey responding to predators and many human social responses. Self-awareness is a kind of assessment awareness as it requires an appreciation of the qualities of and integrity of the self as an entity in the environment. Much of fear and anxiety must involve assessment awareness.

(5) Executive awareness

Assessment of a situation, deduction and planning in relation to long-term intention. This may involve deductions about the feelings of others, imagination and the mental construction of elaborate sequences of events. Examples include complex communication with conspecifics in humans and possibly other social animals, and the making and use of tools in an original way. Anticipation of future events and appropriate planning would appear to occur in a variety of species, especially social species.

Human patients with various kinds of brain damage have degrees of functioning of which they say that they are unaware, a condition which Weiskrantz (1997) calls blindsight. Amnesia subjects state, and clearly believe, that they have forgotten about events but can be demonstrated to have some memory of them. When there is damage to an area of the striate cortex in the brain (ibid, p. 17) human patients say that they are blind in a part of the visual field connected to that area. However, presumably because of alternative neural pathways, monkeys and people with damage which completely prevents output from that brain area can respond to visual stimuli in the corresponding area of the visual field. A person with such damage could show good visual discrimination but be unable to report anything about the experience. Weiskrantz (p. 24) also reports that a human patient with no sensation of touch in the right side of the body, caused by lesions in the left parietal lobe of the brain, when blindfolded and touched on the right side could point to the locus of stimulation. In each of these cases, there is a loss of aspects of awareness but it is clear that sensory functioning is still occurring and Weiskrantz

suggests that such results are of fundamental importance to our understanding of awareness and consciousness. Some authors have suggested that there is a general awareness module in the brain but as
Weiskrantz (p. 44) points out, there is no evidence from patients with
brain damage for the existence of such a module. Indeed, the general
significance of information about blindsight seems to be rather limited because absence of awareness of some type of sensory input does
not mean that there is any deficiency in other aspects of awareness.
Also, it seems possible that, where there is damage to an area of the
striate cortex, the high-level brain processing associated with awareness of sensory events in the relevant visual area is still occurring in
some part of the brain but is blocked by an output associated with the
damage.

There is a wide range of usage of the term 'conscious' which
makes definition difficult and has resulted in preferred usage of 'aware'
by scientists. The widespread medical and veterinary use refers to an
individual whose responses indicate that sensory systems, including
at least their simpler brain connections, are functioning. Blood and
Studdert (1988) define conscious as:

> capable of responding to sensory stimuli; awake; aware.

At the other extreme, Gallup (1983) refers to consciousness as the
demonstrable capacity to reflect about the self, specifically the ability to recognise oneself in mirrors. Most people, however, would not
think about whether individuals can recognise themselves in a mirror when deciding whether or not they are conscious. As Weiskrantz
(1997, p. 77) puts it:

> no one would have a problem in declaring that a comatose animal
> is unconscious.

Some of those who write about consciousness seem to wish to create a
definition which excludes all but well-functioning humans and many
use definitions which make identification of consciousness very difficult where the subject cannot speak. Rosenthal (1990, p. 16) says:

conscious states must be accompanied by higher order thoughts (a thought about a thought) and non-conscious states cannot be so accompanied.

Humphrey (1986, pp. 93–94) states that there is no consciousness in a human body until it recognises itself in a mirror or makes guesses about other peoples' feelings. In Humphrey (1992):

to be conscious is essentially to have sensations: that is to have affect-laden mental representations of something happening here and now to me.

Weiskrantz (1997, p. 52), commenting on this, says that 'to me' is not necessary in the definition and 'I am not concerned with whether awareness is "self-awareness"; indeed I think that particular concern has been over-stressed in discussions of consciousness'.

Whether different degrees of higher level brain functioning are referred to as awareness, as in this chapter, or as consciousness, there remain the questions as to whether non-human animals are aware or conscious and how such functioning has evolved. Bradshaw (1999), invoking the precautionary principle of Cameron and Abouchar (1991, 1996), argues that continuity of morphology, physiology and biochemistry of the brain, as well as observations of behaviour, are so clear between humans and other vertebrate animals that we should assume that they have consciousness in case they do. Bradshaw, in common with the author and many others, dismisses the argument that an individual which cannot talk or demonstrably recognise itself in a mirror cannot be aware or conscious in the Humphrey (1992) sense. Continuity in some aspects of awareness and consciousness seems more likely than a sudden discontinuity between anthropoid apes and humans. Thorpe (1974, p. 363) said 'I consider animals to be capable of reflection and to that extent of self-consciousness' and Griffin (1976, p. 99) argues for continuity across animal species including man in various functions including having mental experiences.

The evolution of awareness is perceived by Crook (1980, e.g. p. 36) as being a consequence of the increasing complexity of organisation of functional systems in life such as feeding, predator avoidance and reproduction. When discussing the evolution of consciousness, Alexander (1987, p. 10) concentrates on assessing costs and benefits and reciprocity, especially in relation to cooperation in aggression and group-hunting. The role of social behaviour in the evolution of brains and especially of higher order processing in brains is discussed in Chapter 1, Section 2.

Awareness of the physical environment may be at the perceptual awareness level. One example is an ant which ejects from the nest anything which smells of oleic acid, even a fellow worker. Another is a person standing on a road who moves out of the path of an approaching car. Cognitive awareness is indicated by the bees studied by Gould and Gould (1988). Foragers were given nectar in a boat on the edge of a lake and then the boat was gradually moved further from the shore. The bees continued to dance when they returned indicating the direction of the nectar source. Those bees which responded to the dance visited the nectar if the boat was close to the shore, stopped if it was not and ignored the dance thereafter. However, there is evidence that many animals have assessment or executive awareness of aspects of their environment. For example Geist (1971, p. 43) described an occasion when he approached a flock of wild big-horn sheep which he had not visited for several months but to which he usually brought salt. The sheep could observe the direction in which he was walking and when he moved out of sight behind vegetation and hid, the sheep which were attempting to get the salt did not search the area where he had disappeared but attempted to intercept him at the place where he would have been if he had continued in a straight line. Two examples of awareness of the physical environment quoted by de Waal (1996, pp. 82–83) concern zoo observations. Bonobos at San Diego Zoo had a two-metre-deep dry moat around their living area. They could enter the moat by climbing down a chain. On several occasions, when the dominant male in the group climbed down into the moat, a younger male pulled up the chain making an open-mouthed play face at him and an adult female rushed to the scene, put the chain down into the moat and guarded it until her mate climbed out. On one occasion in the Arnhem Zoo chimpanzee colony, the seventh in a row of car tyres on a horizontal log had been filled with water by a keeper hosing the enclosure. An older female attempted unsuccessfully to remove this tyre for about ten minutes. She had been observed by a young male whom she had sometimes taken care of and when she moved away, he approached the log, removed the tyres one by one until he could remove the one with water in it and then carried it, still full of water, to the female. She accepted it and scooped out the water with her hand. These last two examples illustrate assessment awareness of the physical environment and probably executive awareness of the needs of other individuals in order that the helping action could be carried out. However, in considering all of such evidence, negative evidence should also be taken into account. Cheney and Seyfarth (1990, pp. 284–286) reported that vervet monkeys showed no response to a fresh python track, or a stuffed Thompson's gazelle put in a tree to simulate a leopard kill, or a cloud of dust produced by Masai people and their cattle, despite the fact that all of these could indicate potential danger to the monkeys.

Awareness in social situations often has to be of a high degree but the immediate response of a primate mother to the distress cry of her baby requires only perceptual awareness. Responses of vervet monkeys to tape-recorded calls of members of a neighbouring social group (Cheney and Seyfarth 1990, p. 65) illustrate circumstances where the minimum requirement to explain the actions was either cognitive or assessment awareness. If the neighbour's call came from the expected direction, the response was a brief look. However, if exactly the same call came from an unexpected direction, the look was of longer duration and the response was sometimes to run into the trees in that direction and give leaping displays. Another example of calling and of response to it is that of Marler et al. (1986) who observed that bantam chickens gave a rapid call if they found food which was attractive and which they were willing to share but gave a quieter, slower call if the food was of less good quality and they were not willing to share. The other birds responded by approaching when the first was heard and not approaching when the second was heard. A very different response was that of a matriarch elephant when a young female was anaesthetised with a dart (Eltringham 1982, p. 52). The matriarch stood over her trumpeting and attempting to lift her to her feet, indicating awareness that the young female had a problem and needed help. Awareness of responses to a need for help was indicated by the observation by Hediger (1955) of a female gorilla who pretended to have her arm trapped in the bars of her cage and then caught the keeper when he went to free her.

The studies in which apes were taught signs also provide much evidence of awareness, for example when Savage-Rumbaugh and Lewin (1994) taught the bonobo Kanzi a sign for herself and a sign for bad and then put the two signs together, the bonobo was visibly distressed. Since neither sign alone had such an effect, self-awareness is indicated. Disturbed or excited responses to mirrors have long been described for members of human races unfamiliar with them. Anthropoid apes have similar responses and apparent identification of self as the image has been reported for orang-utans in 1922, chimpanzees in 1925, and bonobos and gorillas more recently. The observations included chimpanzees and orangs looking backwards and forwards from the mirror image to the real object and a gorilla picking her teeth with the aid of a mirror. The experiment used by Gallup (1982) involved putting a spot of paint on the face and later observing that the spot was touched by the finger when the mirror image was seen. However, this test is inappropriate for many species and much other evidence of self-awareness is available. As de Waal (1996, p. 71) points out in his useful review of the subject:

> apes do not need reflective surfaces to gain self-awareness. They are used to watching themselves in the social mirror: the spectators' eyes.

This comment would also apply to other social animals. A final area of study which might be mentioned in relation to awareness is deception. When a dog on a lead wishes to stop during a walk but has previously been prevented from doing so except when it needs to urinate, it may show signs of wishing to urinate and succeed in stopping. The stops may be more frequent because the human holding the lead is deceived. There are many examples of deception in monkeys (Byrne 1995, p. 203) and in humans (Trivers 1985, pp. 415–419) with various objectives. In many of these examples, prediction of the likely future actions of others and an understanding of how the deceiver is viewed by the deceived are needed, so executive awareness is involved.

3.5   FEELINGS AND EMOTIONS IN RELATION TO MORALITY

As described by Broom (1998), one way in which feelings can arise in an individual is as a consequence of sensation or perception, for example feelings of pain or sexual pleasure. Another is as a result of emotions, an emotion being a physiologically describable electrical and neurochemical state of particular regions of the brain, which may result in other changes in the brain, hormone release or other peripheral changes but which need not involve awareness. Examples of such feelings are anxiety or lust. A third way is as a consequence of complex or simple brain processes, for example achievement pleasure, guilt or boredom.

> A feeling is a brain construct involving awareness which is associated with a life regulating system, is recognisable by the individual when it recurs and may change behaviour or act as a reinforcer in learning.
>
> *(Broom 1998, 2001b)*

Feelings can be positive or negative in that they promote approach or avoidance. Other examples of feelings include malaise, tiredness, hunger, thirst, thermal discomfort, fear, grief, frustration, guilt, depression, loneliness, general suffering, jealousy, anger, eating pleasure, exhilaration, other sensory pleasure and general happiness. Each feeling can vary in strength and will involve some complex brain processing. The distinction is made here, and by Broom (1998), between emotions which are physiologically describable and may or may not involve awareness, and feelings which are brain states that necessarily involve higher level functioning and are recognisable by the subject. Hence the terms are inter-related but not interchangeable.

There are many circumstances where the existence of a feeling is evident from the behaviour of the individual but actions and the use of words can be faked and many actions are not unique to particular feelings. Hence, neither observation of behaviour nor human reports are entirely reliable evidence for feelings. Despite this, it is often possible to deduce, with a high probability of being correct, that an individual is feeling, for example, pain, guilt, anger, exhilaration or eating pleasure. For some feelings it is helpful to use physiological evidence, for example adrenal hormones in body fluids or brain scans, to identify and assess them. However, it is seldom easy to be able to conclude that a feeling is not present in an individual. Feelings of all kinds can exist without any behavioural or physiological indication of their presence. Chronic pain, grief, depression and jealousy can often exist without obvious signs and even acute pain can be suppressed, for example by endogenous opioids acting in the brain. Hinton (1999) describes a great variety of verbal and other behavioural responses to guilt, shame, etc. in various human societies and Feldman (1997, pp. 82–105) describes a variety of pleasures which he divides into sensory and propositional according to their origin. Both Feldman, considering pleasures and hedonism, and Blum (1980, p. 1), referring principally to sympathy, compassion and human concern, state that modern philosophers have paid insufficient attention to the importance of feelings and emotions in the formulation of their ideas.

In the past, many philosophers, scientists and medical practitioners have not considered feelings to be of much value or importance. Blum (1980, p. 2) argues that this situation is greatly affected by the views of Kant that:

emotions and feelings are transitory, changeable and capricious.
They are weak, subject to variations in our mood and
inclinations . . . likely to be unreliable, inconsistent, unprincipled,
or even irrational . . . Feelings and emotions are entirely distinct
from reason and rationality.

Blum argues against this position. Skinner (1973, p. 25) stated that
'feelings are at best by products' and (1974, p. 17):

what is felt or introspectively observed is not some non-physical
world of consciousness, mind or mental life but the observer's
own body. This does not mean . . . that what are felt or
introspectively observed are the causes of behavior.

Further, he said (1978, p. 124):

One feels various states and processes within one's body, but these
are collateral products of one's genetic and personal history. No
creative or initiating function is to be assigned to them.

This view of feelings as solely an accident of individual development
with no function or relevance to any other individuals would not be
held by most behavioural scientists now. As Marian Dawkins (1993,
p. 5) points out, the actions of people are much affected by a belief
that these might cause pain, happiness or sorrow in others. People are
not only concerned about their own feelings but about those of others.
However, the idea that feelings are things which have to be overcome
in order that the real problems of life can be solved is still widespread.

Feelings serve some useful functions and involve awareness
(Broom 1998). Since both the functional systems in animals and the
ability to be aware have evolved, it is logical to consider how feelings
might have evolved. Marian Dawkins (1977) stated that:

It is reasonable to assume that subjective feelings (like other
characteristics) evolved because those which possessed them were
fitter than those which did not.

and

> feelings must be a product of natural selection. They are a part of biology.

In a much more extensive exposition of such views, Cabanac (1979) said:

> We experience feelings of hunger because that is part of our mechanism for rectifying a food deficit and getting something to eat. We experience fear and pain because they are part of our body's way of removing us from situations which are life threatening. Conscious experiences are there as survival aids.

Similar arguments were presented by Wiepkema (1985) and by Broom and Johnson (1993). Wiepkema asserted that feelings are involved in monitoring the effectiveness of regulatory actions, being positive when regulation is successful and negative when it is not. Broom and Johnson (1993, pp. 33–34) said:

> A final but crucial point about the evolution of adaptation to the vicissitudes of the physical and social environment is that a very important part of that evolution has been the development of the complex appreciation of the interactions of an individual with the world in which it lives, which we call feelings. Complex brains, like those of vertebrates, have complex systems for regulating these interactions which are not just the product of automatic responses to stimuli. If an individual has a system of feelings which involves changes in its mental, and perhaps in its hormonal, functioning because a certain kind of body regulation is difficult or because an anticipated event has not occurred, such an individual will have increased fitness in comparison with a genetically different individual which has no such system.

The arguments about how much of the occurrence of each of the different feelings is adaptive and hence about the extent to which that feeling might have evolved is presented by Broom (1998), see also

Broom (2001b) for further detail about the evolution of pain. The general argument is that, whether feelings were originally epiphenomena of other brain processes, or functional brain processes which ceased to have a central function, or an original part of life-regulating systems, if they had a positive effect on the fitness of individuals bearing the genes which were necessary for their occurrence, these genes would have survived and spread in the population. If, on the other hand, the feeling had harmful effects, or no positive or negative effects, the genes which promoted those feelings would have disappeared rapidly or slowly from the population. These arguments apply to non-humans as well as to humans.

Some feelings will be associated particularly with the likelihood of occurrence of moral actions. One individual might attempt to avoid causing harms to another because such harms could result in retribution, or social instability, or because the individual harmed is closely or distantly related, or because a social debt might thereby be incurred. In order to avoid causing harms, an estimation of the effects of actions on the feelings of the other individual would have to be made. Pain, fear, discomfort, etc. in the other individual would have to be recognised. Anxiety may be associated with moral actions in that the individual has concern about whether deductions based on the observation of the behaviour of another are correct and whether judgements about the consequences of one's own actions and the relative value of the consequences of different altruistic acts are correct. To some extent, frustration and depression might also be consequences of moral decision-making processes. The feeling which plays the most obvious role in encouraging moral actions is guilt, which occurs when the individual has behaved in a way that they or their social group members would normally condemn or punish. This feeling could be advantageous to the individual in that it forces the allocation of attention channels and processing capacity to a situation of importance in relation to future decision-making. Guilt occurs much more in social situations than in individuals who are by themselves and there may be outward manifestations of the feeling of guilt which convey useful information to others in the social group. Blushing, like other indications of guilt, will often be an honest signal, even though it can sometimes be contrived. Grief will also promote moral actions in that it amplifies the significance of important life events and draws the attention of others, who observe its manifestations, to the strength of relationships and the importance ascribed to life and to an individual. Anger can also have a role in moral behaviour (see below). Some feelings of pleasure occur when close relatives are able to succeed in some way, or when friendships are cemented, or when favours are done, or when collaboration is effective.

The views expressed above are supported by authors from various backgrounds. Blum (1980, p. 25) refers to altruistic feelings and argues that these can be strong and are more than just related to personal knowledge and state. Gert (1988, p. 47) says:

Pain is an evil. No rational person has any doubts on this matter.

He explains this view, making it clear that the causing of pain is morally wrong. The statement is not intended to be an argument against the biological idea that pain is adaptive and has evolved. Planalp (1999, p. 160) says:

messages loaded with emotion have two essential meanings: a judgement of good or bad and an imperative to keep things as they are or to change them. This is the core of emotional theory.

She goes on to say:

Anger stems from the judgement that something is wrong (often unjust) and that action should be taken to fix it. Love stems from the judgement that something is right and that action should be taken to sustain it.

The comments are perhaps too general because anger can occur in an individual who is thwarted or bested in some entirely fair way and love is often to do with what is perceived as good rather than necessarily right. However, the general principles expressed are that these emotions and feelings play an important part in furthering moral actions. Rottschaefer (1998, p. 84) says:

> there seems to be growing evidence for an evolutionary basis for basic emotions.

Brandt (1996, p. 32) also argues in favour of functional feelings which have evolved:

> many of our desires and aversions . . . arise mostly from a history of pleasant experiences of certain types of object, activity or situation. These pleasures themselves can be explained either as a result of conditioning or . . . perhaps because of evolutionary survival value.

In a discussion of the mechanisms underlying moral capacity and the evolution of such mechanisms, Rothschaefer (1998, pp. 84–86 and 94–97) emphasises the importance of feelings such as guilt and anger. He considers empathy to be a particularly important part of these mechanisms and refers especially to its emotional components. The ability to appreciate the state of other individuals is considered to rely greatly on deductions about the feelings of others and on one's own feelings. Many of these components of moral decision-making and behaviour are considered to occur in a range of animal species, not just in man. The idea that emotions are sometimes the enforcer of moral acts and tend to stabilise behaviour and relationships by reducing the extent of erratic behaviour is also presented by Brody (1998). Clark (2000, p. 140) emphasises the important role of feelings like that of shame in reducing the likelihood that acts which are morally wrong will be carried out. The role of a variety of feelings in moral behaviour is described in detail by Planalp (1999, pp. 162–186). For example (p. 162):

> Emotions . . . draw attention to, assert and calibrate whatever
> moral standards we hold. The consequences of feeling disgust,
> guilt, shame, anger at injustice, remorse, gratitude, hate, jealousy
> and envy are discussed in relation to morality. Again sympathy
> and empathy are considered to be important.

All of these arguments are different from those of Kant. Blum (1980, p. 135) criticises Kant for emphasising duty rather than sympathy in moral actions. The Kantian view that feelings are unimportant fails to take account of the substantial role of feelings in the regulation of behaviour and of their existence as evolved mechanisms rather than just epiphenomena. However, the idea that short-term feelings should not be allowed to overcome carefully thought out deductions about what to do is an important one. This argument is fallacious in that careful thought about an issue will often lead to a feeling, rather than just countering feelings. Once it is accepted that many feelings are a consequence of very high level processing in the brain, the distinction is seen to be between hasty, ill-thought-out conclusions, which may or may not be right, and more carefully evaluated conclusions, whether or not these are associated with a feeling.

3.6 COGNITIVE RESPONSES TO MORAL ISSUES

Cognitive brain processes or behaviour are all deduced to involve some degree of processing complexity but cover a wide range of complexity. The evidence concerns the nature of the associations which are formed amongst the various incoming stimuli and existing brain constructs. In many definitions the word intelligent is used. Although it is the outcome of brain changes which is the evidence for the extent and kind of cognitive function, neuropsychologists are able to monitor brain changes that are associated with some aspects of the cognition. The increasing complexity of concepts which appear to be within the capabilities of human children during development were described by Piaget (e.g. 1932). Many authors have referred to levels of cognitive ability in a range of animal species but whilst such reviews have sometimes been descriptive, many have been idealogical in that their aim was to delineate a supposed sequence which led to the human as a perfect culmination. Much evidence of cognitive ability has already been presented in Chapter 1 Section 2, Chapter 2 Section 2, Chapter 3 Section 2 and 4 of this book. The idea that social living led to some of the major developments in cognitive ability has been described. Whilst there is much evidence that there must be such abilities in order to explain many examples of social interactions in various species, it should not be assumed that only social events require high levels of cognitive ability or that all social behaviour requires it. The concept of Machiavellian intelligence, presented by Byrne and Whiten (1988), referred to intellectual ability to deal with social situations and to change tactics creatively as the game evolves. However, efforts to emphasise its unique links to social life are criticised by Strum *et al.* (1997), who give examples of simple cognitive tasks in social situations and complex tasks, for example navigation in humans and other species, in other situations. It is clear that some impressive cognitive ability can occur in non-social situations, e.g. the chimpanzee insight learning reported by Köhler (1928) or the navigation by birds reported by Emlen (1970), whilst other abilities may be encouraged in their development by social factors, e.g. the learning of hundreds of words by a parrot (Pepperberg 1990) or learning to wash sand from sweet potatoes by Japanese macaques (Kawai 1965). A large number of examples of such ability are entirely confined to social situations.

There are some actions which are moral, in that they have the actual or potential effect of conferring benefit on others at some cost to the altruist, but do not necessarily require a high level of cognitive ability. In many cases it is not possible to know much about the level and nature of brain processing which is involved when a moral action occurs. However, very many moral actions must require a high degree of awareness and cognitive ability. On many occasions when an individual, whether human or other species, prior to an action has to evaluate the consequences of that action for the welfare of another individual, some sophisticated brain processing is likely to be involved. Staying the hand which might otherwise strike a blow, or refraining from a bite which could kill need not be associated with subtle assessment. However, avoidance of taking food so that another can have it, or helping another to achieve an objective, or teaching another something useful, or preventing another from encountering danger will usually require an appreciation of the needs, state and probability of success of the other. When a sick or distressed member of a social group is helped, as in the whales, children, rhesus monkeys, Japanese macaques or elephants mentioned in Chapter 2 Section 2, especially Section 2.2.8, the helper appears to respond to the signs of disability in the other individual and to want to assist the other to be able to carry out normal functions. An appreciation of normal functioning from the point of view of the other and some distress at the inability of the other would appear to be necessary for such helping actions to occur. Animals of species who have little or no ability to help in such circumstances do not show the same interest or responses in such circumstances. The responses of animals to the dead of their own species is probably also related to their ability to help a weak individual prior to death. There are reports of anthropoid apes, whales and elephants spending time and energy trying to help a dead conspecific. Some anecdotal reports suggest that horses and cattle are disturbed by dead herd members. However, studies of deer, sheep and pigs indicate that observers of herd members being shot in a field or stunned and killed by bleeding out in a slaughterhouse are not disturbed unless there is evident distress in the animals before death (Anil *et al.* 1996, 1997). It is the distress of one individual, rather than the perception of the dead individual, which affects group members. Many animals either do not have experience of seeing dead conspecifics, or have no possibility of making any adaptive response to them. The variability in the extent of showing, helping or grief responses is probably dependent on the probability that adaptive responses can be shown.

The report (Goodall 1990, pp. 64–66) of an aberrant female chimpanzee who killed and partially ate a baby chimpanzee from her group is of interest because of her behaviour and because of that of the others in the group. Other group members investigated the dead body of the baby but did not eat it and did not treat the female who had killed it in a different way afterwards. It is clear that the baby's body was not treated as food but that the killing of that young animal was not perceived by an observer chimpanzee as a harm to itself. These same individuals might punish a fellow group member for failing to back them up in a dispute with other individuals. We do not know how they perceived the dead infant but it is clear that the vast majority of the members of a chimpanzee group make strenuous efforts not to harm young individuals in their group or even those which they encounter from other groups. As mentioned in earlier chapters, refraining from harming other individuals is a widespread behaviour, especially in social animals, and since refraining has some cost in most cases and there is an undoubted benefit to others, it is moral behaviour. Even amongst rival animals, sympathy may be evident. de Waal (1996, p. 44) describes a male chimpanzee who feigned a limp when in view of a rival but not when out of view. This behaviour inhibited attack by the rival. The feigning of the limp, whether or not it stemmed from any experience with a real limp, indicates awareness of the sympathetic response of the rival otherwise its occurrence need not have been limited to the times when the rival was able to observe.

Behaviour which deceives others may sometimes involve self deception also. Trivers (1985, pp. 418–419) lists a variety of circumstances in which people indicate by their behaviour, including their statements, that they are aware of what would be moral behaviour but delude themselves as to their own actual role. He points out that people might: deny responsibility for harmful outcomes of their actions, exaggerate beneficial outcomes, use present knowledge to rewrite recollections of past events, perceive themselves to be altruists and their partner to be selfish, or fail to perceive things with negative connotations. We know that many species are capable of deception of others, and probably of themselves, but in most of these cases the ability to appreciate what constitutes a moral act is also very likely to be present.

3.7   WHAT IS NEEDED BIOLOGICALLY FOR MORALITY?

Morality concerns actions which could affect other living individuals. It is possible to go through life behaving in a moral way irrespective of who is encountered or how often. This is a strategy which has clear advantages if the individuals concerned are able to recognise one another, if there are likely to be repeated encounters and if the occurrence and consequences of an action are likely to be appreciated and remembered. There are also some advantages, in terms of avoiding dangerous instability in a group, even if the only condition which is met is continued membership of the same group. As pointed out in Chapter 2, Section 1, long lifespan and low dispersal rate will tend to increase the likelihood that altruistic behaviour will occur. The advantage to be gained from altruistic behaviour in long-lasting associations among individuals will depend upon the key resources, or other factors, which affect survival, and hence on the nature of any likely competition or need for collaboration. For example, altruistic behaviour which minimises group instability will be valuable if collaboration in finding or obtaining food is very advantageous, or if the primary food source is widely available without too much competition and predator avoidance requires maintenance of a social association. The members of a flock of starlings trying to find food in harsh winter conditions, or of a herd of wildebeeste grazing on the African savannah and attempting to avoid lion attacks seldom show group disruptive behaviour even if refraining from doing this means that there is some cost to individuals in lost food or extra need for energy utilisation. Very short-lived animals, or those which very seldom encounter others, or those which must compete vigorously for resources are the least likely to show altruistic avoidance of group disruption, or any form of mutually useful collaboration.

Individuals which do not live socially but which associate with a mate or with offspring will behave altruistically towards the mate or offspring, at least for some of the time. Again, the minimal form of altruism is avoidance of competition but this will often involve considerable costs, for example in lost food. Much greater sacrifices are made in food provision, defence, help in thermoregulation, teaching, etc. The abilities required for altruism to be shown towards offspring need not be great. A means of discrimination between own and other offspring is needed but this may be done by knowing the location of the offspring or it may be that the offspring respond to their parents, for example to the calls in colonially nesting birds. The period when offspring may attempt to prolong the period or extent of parental care can involve complex evaluation of need and subtle deception, and in order to do this substantial cognitive ability would be required. Collaboration between mates in various aspects of parental care is demanding of cognitive ability in respect of recognition of the other and, especially, evaluation of the relative contributions of own efforts and of the efforts of the partner. Reciprocity of altruistic acts and direct collaboration must occur and be assessed. Where prolonged group-living occurs, there are far more demands on cognitive ability and a greater likelihood of, and frequency of, moral behaviour. Self-sacrificing collaboration between parents in order to rear young would be regarded by most people as moral behaviour, as would much of parental behaviour without parental collaboration. However, a robot might be programmed and successfully feed young animals and we should not think of using the word moral to describe its behaviour, so another quality would normally be taken into account before morality is recognised.

In emphasising the biological basis of morality, arguments have been presented in this book for moral behaviour in those non-human species which have sufficient cognitive ability and awareness. However, others do not think in this way, for example Rolston (1999, p. 233) refers to reciprocal altruism but says:

> Since the baboon, though on sentry duty, is not a moral agent, he has no moral duty.

Views on the subject of what is needed for morality are contrasted by Wolff (1978) who says that biologists consider that:

Natural selection operates on social behaviours that promote reproductive advantage, whereas the individuals whose moral behavior has evolved are not, or need not be, aware of the reasons for the selective fitness of their behavioral phenotype. By contrast, moral philosophers, and at least some psychological theorists of morality, consider as moral only those forms of human behavior for which intention, deliberate choice among equally determined actions, and awareness of the social consequences of alternative actions can be assumed.

Dennett (1987) describes three orders of intentionality: first-order intentionality is intent to change the behaviour of others; second-order intentionality is intent to change the mind of others by passing ideas; and third-order intentionality involves knowledge that another, who might be a teacher, is intending to change one's mind. The first two seem to overlap greatly because behaviour must often be changed by conveying an idea; for example, one small bird can change the behaviour of another by giving the specific alarm call on the approach of an avian rather than a ground predator. This transmits that idea, the evidence being that the typical and appropriate response to the first call is remaining immobile or diving into cover whilst that to the second is flying up into the air. Even the dog barking to deter the approach of a potential rival is conveying an idea. If the rival dog appreciates that the first dog is trying to deter approach, it has Dennett's third-order intentionality.

A more useful categorisation when considering whether an individual is acting in a novel way would seem to be one which, like the different orders of awareness described in Chapter 3, Section 4, is based on the complexity of concepts. In addition, associated with the awareness, there must be some control of own actions as mentioned by Dennett (1994) and in rather unspecific terms by Fischer and Ravizza (1998, pp. 27, 89). To those accustomed to investigating the motivational state of animals, the idea of animals as automata is confined to very simple animals such as *Amoeba* or *Paramecium*, or to some circumstances which require very rapid responses, and the kind of frequent but coordinated response such as those involved in locomotion. Otherwise, there is a considerable degree of flexibility in the control of behaviour. Does morality require the understanding of all of the issues involved in the situation, or rather how much understanding is necessary? Suppose that a person is told, or otherwise discovers from the example or instruction of others, that a certain action is moral or immoral but that person does not understand why this is so. Are they acting in a moral way when they perform, or avoid performing, the action? A young child might do this but so may adults who have not thought through all of the consequences of actions for themselves and for their community. If understanding is considered essential before an action can be classified as moral, many human actions which are regarded as good could not be accepted as moral. Actions of other species which would be categorised as good in the same way as the human actions above would not be categorised as moral by those who see no evidence of understanding. However, they would be considered as moral by those who judge on the basis of the effects of the action and the general capabilities for awareness of the animal irrespective of any demonstrable capacity for understanding at that time.

In the earlier sections of this book it is argued that perceptual functioning, motivational systems, cognitive ability, awareness and various feelings have evolved. If all of these components of moral behaviour have evolved then morality itself has evolved. However, is any of morality culturally based and does this mean that it has not evolved? There are certainly cultural traditions which refer to what behaviour is right or wrong. However, abilities upon which these depend must have evolved and it is my view that the capacity to be moral has evolved. Wilson (1978, p. 167) asks:

'Can the cultural evolution of higher ethical values gain a direction and momentum of its own and completely replace genetic evolution?' and answers this 'I think not . . . Human behaviour – like the deepest capacities for emotional response which drive and guide it – is the circuitous technique by which human genetic material has been and will be kept intact. Morality has no other demonstrable ultimate function'.

Hence Wilson considers that morality is vital for survival and has arisen in the same way as any other capability of living organisms. A list of characteristics of human morality is presented by de Waal (1996, pp. 210–211) who says:

If we break the relevant human abilities into their component parts, some are recognizable in other species.

He then goes on to consider briefly culture, language and politics and says:

It is hard to imagine human morality without the following tendencies and capacities found also in other species.

1. Sympathy-related traits
   (a) Attachment, succorance and emotional contagion.
   (b) Learned adjustment to and special treatment of the disabled and injured.
   (c) Ability to trade places mentally with others: cognitive empathy.
2. Norm-related characteristics
   (a) Prescriptive social rules.
   (b) Internalisation of rules and anticipation of punishment.
3. Reciprocity
   (a) A concept of giving, trading and revenge.
   (b) Moralistic aggression against violators of reciprocity rules.
4. Getting along
   (a) Peacemaking and avoidance of conflict.
   (b) Community concern and maintenance of good relationships.
   (c) Accommodation of conflicting interests through negotiation.

de Waal emphasises that in 1(c), 2(b) and 4(b), 'humans seem to have gone considerably further than other animals'. This view is clearly at odds with that of Kummer (1978, pp. 44–45):

> The biological function of morality would be twofold; first to increase the help and reduce the damage done to social companions; and second to increase predictability both in the helper and in the competitor. . . . With this possible exception, it seems at present that morality has no specific functional equivalents among our animal relatives. Their societies benefit their members even though their individuals are essentially guided by selfish opportunism. Human morality is intimately related to the evolution of cognitive qualities, which made it both necessary and possible.

Whilst there have been considerable developments in our knowledge of the social behaviour of animals since Kummer wrote these words, it would seem that many people had and still have an inability to admit similarities between humans and other species. Kummer suggests (1978, p. 42) that his conclusion that there is no morality in other species could be because the methods of description of behaviour were too crude and that the tendency to always use the simplest explanation may be wrong. He also appears to be missing the point that a mixture of behaviour which aids the actor and behaviour which aids others is still partly altruistic and that an action which aids another now and influences the other to be more likely to return the favour later should be considered as evidence for a moral code.

4 **Ideas about morality**

WHAT IS RIGHT AND WHAT IS WRONG?

Most people would say that an understanding of what is right or good and what is wrong or evil is fundamental to the way in which they decide what to do in life. It is, therefore, the key issue in philosophy. Brandt (1996, p. 1) presents three goals of ethical theorising:

> [first] to ascertain which states of affairs are desirable in themselves (and how desirable they are); second, to determine which sorts of actions are morally right or wrong, praiseworthy or blameworthy; and third, to ascertain whether a commitment to always doing the morally right thing is desirable from the point of view of the agent's own well-being.

In many writings from the past on this subject and in some today, no clear distinction is made between social, political, legal and religious meanings of right and wrong. This is not just because of poor quality thinking, the borderlines between these meanings are vague and some attempts to make sharp distinctions have slowed the development of understanding.

4.1.1 *Concepts of right, good, wrong and evil*

Right in the sense of good should not be confused with right in the sense of correct. It is correct to say that sugar will dissolve in water but the statement is not good or morally right. However, even after this distinction is made, within the moral sense the terms right and good are complex. When we use the word good, is it the good of an individual or some universal good to which we allude? Blum (1980, p. 96) refers to a good as universal if it is:

something which everyone ought to perform, or which it would be wrong not to perform.

The good of an individual may coincide with this but need not do so. Some definitions of good concentrate on the individual performing an action without necessarily considering overall good effects or even intentions but when evaluating a quality of a person, or an action, most people would consider the universal aspects. It is clear that there are many different kinds of good, even if there are underlying principles which encourage many of them. As Anscombe (1958) said, rephrasing the words of earlier writers, '*Bonum est multiplex*'. Although there is much discussion about the different types of good, more is written about the different types of evil and lists of what should not be done are often longer than lists of what should be done. Gert (1988, p.47) argues:

> Evil plays a much more important role in morality than good does.

This may be true in the sense that it is generally easier to specify and hence to understand what is evil than what is good but an appreciation of both good and evil is necessary in order to decide how to behave in a moral way in a variety of circumstances. Aristotle thought of something as good if it optimised human welfare. That which is morally right, according to Bentham (1789), 'will contribute maximally to the happiness of sentient creatures'. One aspect of this view is that happiness or pleasure is the only good and pain, in the very general sense, is the only evil. A second aspect is the utilitarian argument that the greatest overall good should be sought. This view was explained further by J.S. Mill (1863) who referred to aiming for the *summum bonum*, greatest good, whilst implying that the *summum malum*, greatest evil, should be avoided. A third aspect of Bentham's view is that the term 'sentient creatures' does not refer exclusively to humans. In Bentham's statement, whether an action is good or evil is determined by its actual effect. The argument could justify the use of intolerable means to justify a good end.

Another widespread view of what is good or bad places particular emphasis on what is desired by the individual concerned, so it takes account of the motivation of that individual. Hobbes (1651, Part I, Chapter 6) says:

> Whatsoever is the object of any man's appetite or desire; that is it which he for his part calleth good.

Three much more recent statements by Gert (1988, pp. 48, 50, 183) are:

> 'a definition of evil as the object of an irrational desire', to 'define a good as that which no rational person will avoid without a reason', and 'To have a moral vice is to have a disposition to unjustifiably violate a moral rule.'

In each of these statements there is reference to rationality or use of it but the key aspect is the desire to do something or to avoid doing something. A detailed exposition of the argument that good things are those which are desired is presented by Brandt (1996, pp. 37–49) and then (pp. 49–60) some limitations to the argument are mentioned. In its simplest form, it is clear that fulfilling desires can lead to something which is not good for any individual and Ridley (1996, p. 253) suggests that:

> The Hobbesian search for a perfect society ended, therefore, in the gas chambers of Auschwitz.

The importance of rationality as a foundation for morality was emphasised by Kant (1781, 1788). There is reference to judgement in definitions of right and wrong which depend on rationality. Kant considered an action to be right if it would be judged that every person should act in that way in such a circumstance. This is made explicit in the definition by Firth (1952) of an action as 'morally wrong' if it:

> would be disapproved of by any person who was factually omniscient, impartial and devoid of emotions towards particular persons but otherwise normal.

Similarly, Westermarck (1906, pp. 1 and 17–18) said that:

> 'It is wrong to do A' means the same as 'I have an impartial
> disposition to disapprove of acts like A.'

However, there are often practical difficulties in determining ration-
ally whether each person should act in a particular way. Indeed, it is
possible for there to be a good action of which most rational people
would disapprove. A flaw in the argument that rationality can be the
whole basis of morality is pointed out by Midgley (1994, p. 149):

> Kant, when he made morality essentially a matter of reason, took
> for granted an emotional background which he did not notice.

The underlying biology, not just that concerned with emotion, plays
a part in determining what individuals judge should or should not be
done. Plato (370 BC) considered that ideal moral laws just exist. Likewise, some of those who have discussed the concepts of good and bad
have rejected complex rational arguments or consideration of all of
the effects of actions and have simply asserted that what is good or
bad is self-evident or intuitively true. However, it is clear that different people from different backgrounds come to different conclusions
as to what is self-evident and 'intuition' must depend upon ability to
make deductions based on individual experience. Brandt (1979) considers that acts are intrinsically good or bad and that evaluation is
necessary to know this. Evaluation depends upon information and
ability to process it. If, as a result of lack of information, an act occurs
which harms others, is it a bad act? On the basis of its effect it is
bad but on the basis of motivation it is not. Similarly, if an individual has information but poor ability to judge what should or should
not be done, a harmful act may be carried out, but is it a bad act? It
can be argued that potentially harmful acts should not be carried out
unless there have been adequate attempts to obtain information and
to consider consequences. There is clearly a difference between what
is culpable and what is not but significant harms cannot be excused

because of failure to obtain available information or to consider the evidence using one's capabilities.

When considering the effects of actions, some acts will result in net benefit to the actor and to others whilst other acts are altruistic in that there is a net cost to the actor. The followers of Schopenhauer (1818) might say that no action can be good if the perpetrator benefits as a result. Many people, e.g. Blum (1980, p. 85), reject such a view and it seems entirely unsound to me. The idea that all life must involve suffering and that anything which leads to a benefit, particularly a benefit which is associated with pleasure, is wrong involves a failure to understand biological functioning and how it has evolved.

4.1.2 Where do right and wrong come from?

Conflicting ideas about how concepts of right and wrong arise in individuals have had various far-reaching consequences in human society. Plato considered that humans are born virtuous but become corrupted by exposure to society, and that there are ideal moral laws which determine what is moral behaviour. This view of morality was followed by Rousseau (1755) who spoke of 'the noble savage' and believed that being nearer to natural origins meant having less sin. Kropotkin (1902), a champion of the importance of cooperative behaviour, was clearly influenced by this idea. Anthropologists such as Margaret Mead have sought to gain evidence for this view and have sometimes been duped by their subjects into finding the evidence (Mead 1928, Freeman 1983). Recent anthropologists such as Leakey, studying the humanoids which preceded *Homo sapiens*, have also emphasised the likely peacefulness of the hunter-gatherers whom they described, despite finding spears and crushed skulls. Aristotle's position was somewhat different from that of Plato in that he argued that people should observe, choose what to do, evaluate the consequences, and strive for what they think is right. A more extreme version of this position, held by many people but typified by Huxley (1893), was that people have animal aspects against which they must continually fight. The idea of slaying the dragon of an animal past or that (p. 82):

> Laws and moral precepts are directed to the end of curbing the cosmic process

assumed that knowledge of right and wrong was absent in, or minimal in, other species and in our ancestors but could be acquired and used. This position seems to me to be just as naïve as that of Rousseau. As recently as 1994, Wright argued that humans are potentially but not naturally moral. One of the central arguments in this book is that there is a genetic basis for moral behaviour in humans and other species but since all genes interact with environmental variables in complex ways, the extent of moral behaviour will vary. Wright thinks that 'natural' means inevitably present but, since everything can be affected by environmental variables, nothing is inevitably present. His other arguments are that in stable, well-organised societies, moral behaviour will be more successful and widespread than in transient societies with less repeat contact between individuals, but in every social group moral strategies are effective. An action is right or wrong according to whether it has beneficial or harmful effects on other individuals and whether or not the perpetrator could know of those effects. Most individuals of a variety of species can perceive that their own actions cause some benefits and harms to others and can act morally.

The idea that humans are ethical by their biological nature is held by many, for example Ayala (1987). However, Ayala considered that moral norms are part of cultural evolution, and that the capacity for moral behaviour is not present in other animals. This position seems illogical to me. If the potential to act in a moral way is present in individuals, it must include all of the sensory, motor and analytical components. In particular, each individual must be able to evaluate the effects on others of its actions. At least some moral norms would be appreciated without the need for instruction. Control of actions so as to behave in a moral way will be much more efficiently learned if information is received from others but the potential to take advantage of such information is in itself complex. A range of gene effects must be involved, including some which will be effective in all socially living individuals, not just humans in a limited range of modern societies.

A further view that the biological basis of morals should be considered is that presented by Richards (1993) and supported by Petrinovich (1998). Richards was unwilling to accept any moral principle unless it could be 'justified by facts'. This position, if carried to its logical conclusion, would seem to require a degree of scientific knowledge much greater than we have now, otherwise moral principles which are vital for the effective functioning of human society could not be accepted. A demand for too high a degree of rigorous proof is undesirable in a situation where other sources of information are available and where the demand might conflict with conclusions drawn following the use of the precautionary principle.

The proposal that morality in general, and ideas of what is right and what is wrong in particular, has a biological basis does not mean that all kinds of biological order are desirable or relevant. Leopold (1949, p. 224) proposed that:

> A thing is right when it tends to preserve the integrity, stability and beauty of the biotic community. It is wrong when it tends otherwise.

This view, which is expanded and discussed by Johnson (1991), is difficult to defend as a definition of right and wrong, firstly because extreme harms to individuals can occur in the course of achieving these objectives. If the biotic community of a small island was being damaged by the people in a small village and a group of seals, the community might be preserved by killing the humans and seals with strychnine but the action would not be right. Secondly, if any change in community integrity is seen as wrong, there would be no possibility for any substantial evolutionary change within that community to be right. For example, a change in a grazing mammal species which means more efficient harvesting of grasslands could significantly alter the plant population structure, with consequent effects on insect and nematode worm populations, but I should not consider this as morally wrong. In the same way, humans evolve and develop new abilities but this does not mean that every effect which humans have on ecosystems is morally wrong. On the other hand, some effects caused to ecosystems by humans who are, or could be, aware of what they are doing are so undesirable at the individual or population level that most people would consider the human actions morally wrong. Whilst some small changes in ecosystems are inevitable and some species of animals and plants would become extinct in any area, the human engineered destruction of types of marshland, coral reef or rain forest, often with associated extinction of species, is a moral issue. In the same way, an action which caused severe harm to one or a few individuals, or slight harm to a large number of individuals would be wrong and would be worse than causing slight harm to one individual.

The argument that moral acts and codes exist because of the action of natural selection does not mean that evolutionary arguments are themselves codes for living. It is proposed that where a moral act increases the chances of biological success, the genes which promote its occurrence are likely to spread in the population. Hence, competition amongst genes can result in the promotion of altruistic acts as well as acts that only promote individual survival and reproduction at the expense of others. As mentioned earlier, some morally right actions will be successful only if society structure is appropriate. A particular strategy in a social situation may be successful on average but lose out when certain anti-social strategies are being used. However, group disruption is costly to the individual using the anti-social strategy, as well as to others, so the moral strategy still does well overall.

4.1.3   Goodness and intention

As mentioned above (Section 4.1.1) some qualities are thought of as virtues which benefit only the actor. Hobbes (1658) refers to personal virtues such as prudence, temperance and courage and distinguishes these from moral virtues. An action, attitude or strategy which never confers benefit on any other individual should not be called morally right. Whilst each of the personal virtues mentioned could result in benefit to others, it is the benefit itself that is critical in deciding whether or not to call the virtue moral. Hence, it is clear that many of the qualities which are considered to be virtuous are not necessarily evidence of morality. Similarly, actions or attitudes which some might refer to as sinful but which never harm another individual are not morally wrong. However, in the development of individuals and in the organisation of the lives of individuals, the kind of control of behaviour which is associated with personal virtue can increase the likelihood that moral behaviour occurs.

If an act which benefits others is carried out with the intention of there being some beneficial consequence for the actor, is it right and good to do it? Aristotle (340 BC Section 9.8) questions whether a person who dies to save a friend is acting altruistically. He points out that the glory resulting from the action is a great reward and suggests that the person 'prefers a short period of intense pleasure to a long one of mild enjoyment'. St Augustine of Hippo (AD 354–430) was one of many who have considered whether it is right to give to the poor because of the pleasure and glory which may result. Frances Hutcheson considered that any giving which is motivated by vanity or self-interest is not benevolence but his pupil Adam Smith considered that a deed is still good whatever the motivation. Sen (1977) points out that sympathy at the torture or pleasure of others is egoistic and may help one's own utility but is nonetheless an important agent for good. Ridley (1996, p. 21) argues that:

> what matters to society is whether people are likely to be nice to each other, not their motives.

I agree with this view and consider that if we have capacities and mechanisms which promote altruistic behaviour, that does not reduce the good effect or negate the altruism. If it is a good act, in that it confers a real benefit, then it remains a good act however much benefit accrues to the perpetrator. When an individual's actions are evaluated, a good act with a substantial bonus effect for the actor would not be regarded as highly as a good act with little or no bonus. However, it is in the interest of all members of society to promote the likelihood of good acts.

4.1.4   Rules, principles and ideals

Lists of virtues and sins, of things which are right or wrong, have been produced by many people. In some cases, these are presented as rules of conduct or codes for living (see Chapter 1, Section 1). However, the term 'rule' has different connotations for different people and seems inadequate as a descriptor to some. Midgley (1994, p. 120) says:

> morality . . . has been, among other things, a panorama of ideals, a way of developing the feelings in a particular direction, a set of arts for visualising better kinds of life, for working together on the understanding of human destiny. . . . Morality is not, just rules.

She goes on to argue (p. 121):

> Our question constantly takes the Hobbesian form, how did an original society of egoists ever come to find itself lumbered with rules that imposed consideration for others?

This question suggests that people sat down and thought up the rules but there must have been some widespread willingness to acknowledge such rules which was based on a propensity to behave altruistically and detect cheats.

Brandt (1996, pp. 78–79) states that the earliest report of Greek morality was that by Homer in the tenth century BC. The moral code for a warrior required:

(1) courage, acting so as to have a good reputation (fame);
(2) protection of guests and suppliants;
(3) loyalty to one's friends and relatives (philoi);
(4) not displaying arrogance or demands beyond one's due (hubris);

(5) telling the truth and respecting agreements, including the marriage vow;

(6) returning favours;

(7) self-control in the sense of acting wisely in view of the possible consequences for oneself.

Other parts of Homer's writings, and those of Hesiod in the eighth century BC referring also to non-military Greeks, add condemnation of contempt for the dead, violence, crooked dealing and being unkind to the weak. Brandt sums up these requirements as:

(1) to do no violence (except in war) and to be kind to the poor, children, the hungry, suppliants and guests;

(2) to be honest in property dealings and not to steal, break contracts or cheat by using false measures;

(3) to speak the truth, especially when much turns on it;

(4) to show respect and kindness to aged parents;

(5) not to commit adultery;

(6) to be courageous and secure a good reputation;

(7) to return favours;

(8) to show self-control.

Other codes for living are discussed in Chapter 5 but some more recent attempts are worth listing. Ross (1930) argues that the fundamental, self-evident moral principles are:

(1) to keep promises;

(2) to make reparation for injuries wrongfully caused to others;

(3) to reciprocate services rendered us by others;

(4) to assist in bringing about a distribution of happiness in accordance with merit;

(5) to make others better off in respect of virtue, knowledge and pleasure;

(6) to improve ourselves in respect of knowledge and virtue;

(7) not to injure others.

The approach of Griffin (1986) was to attempt to list things which are intrinsically good for everyone:

(1) personal accomplishment;
(2) freedom to decide what to do, by one's own lights, without constraint;
(3) having the basic capacities to move one's own limbs, have the minimum material conditions required for life and have freedom from pain and anxiety;
(4) understanding of oneself and the world;
(5) enjoyment;
(6) having deep personal relations.

Coming from the other direction, Gert (1988, pp. 98, 126, 136, 154) says that nobody should:

(1) kill;
(2) cause pain;
(3) disable;
(4) deprive of freedom or opportunity;
(5) deprive of pleasure;
(6) deceive;
(7) fail to keep a promise;
(8) cheat;
(9) fail to obey the law;
(10) fail to do duty.

Prohibitions to commit adultery and to steal are not added because they are covered by other edicts.

Some of these rules or codes principally impact on the subject's individual or personal virtue whilst others concern moral virtue because they affect others. Those which relate to impact on others would be relevant in all human societies and some non-human societies. It is of interest that Piaget (1932, p. 402) thought of some as coming from outside the individual and some as coming from inside:

> the morality prescribed for the individual by society is not homogenous because society itself is not just one thing. Society is the sum of social relations, and among these relations we can distinguish two extreme types: relations of constraint, whose characteristic is to impose upon the individual from outself a system of rules with obligatory content, and relations of cooperation whose characteristic is to create within people's minds the consciousness of ideal norms at the back of all rules.

Whilst it is clear that individuals will learn about rules from other members of their society, this sharp distinction between external constraints and internal ideas about cooperation is misleading. Each individual would have the structure which would help in the setting up of the moral system using information gained from the social environment. Each aspect of the moral code that an individual has would be a result of interaction between the predisposition to obtain information and the actual information obtained. Wherever people live in a complex stable society, there will be far more similarities in the functioning of that society than differences between societies so the resultant moral codes will vary little from one society to another.

4.2   OBLIGATIONS, RIGHTS AND EVALUATION

4.2.1   *Which individuals should be considered?*

When considering how an individual should behave in respect of possible effects on other individuals, the conclusion may well be different according to which other individual might be affected: human adult; human child; human foetuses of various ages; non-human animal of various kinds; communities of organisms of various kinds; and future generations of any of these. This point is made by Gert (1988, p. 13) who states that an action is morally relevant if it is done to:

(1) presently existing moral agents, e.g. adult human beings;
(2) actual moral agents, present or future, including future generations;

(3) actual or potential moral agents, present or future, including neonates and foetuses;

(4) existing sentient beings, including many animals but excluding foetuses;

(5) actual or potential sentient beings, present or future, including future generations of animals and animal foetuses.

Gert limits the term 'moral agent' to adult human beings which I would not do. See Chapter 7, Section 3 for further development of this point.

4.2.2 Deontology: Kant and rights

The deontological approach to the organisation of human conduct, in which the structure is a set of duties pertinent to all individuals, has been followed by adherents to various religions and by many who have not thought of themselves as religious. One of those who argued for a deontological approach to morality is Kant whose categorical imperative states that an act is wrong if the agent could not consistently will that the principle underlying such an act should be a universal law. Hence the individual, aware of the underlying law, should assess what action duty dictates using rational thought and carry out that action. A moral act could not be grounded on a feeling of pleasure according to Kant's view. This interpretation of Kant's position is supported by Guyer (2000, p. 133) but Guyer also points out (p. 130) that in an essay written in 1762 and published in 1764, Kant argued:

> that the faculty for representing the true is cognition, but that for serving the good is feeling, and that these must not be confused with each other' and 'the judgement: this is good, is fully indemonstrable, and is an immediate effect of the consciousness of the feeling of pleasure.

From his later writings, it is clear that Kant's view changed because in 1785 he declared that freedom is the source of all value. Guyer (p. 131) explains Kant's (1788) mature moral theory as being the freedom of will to use the categorical imperative in deciding what should be done. O'Neill's (2000) explanations of Kant's thinking about what is just make it clear that he was far from an impractical idealist and some of his followers have misrepresented him in various ways. However, the common expositions of his views largely ignore the biological functioning of individuals. As Blum (1980, p. 82) puts it:

> The full moral dimensions of friendship are difficult, if not impossible, to focus on within a Kantian framework, with its emphasis on obligatory conduct, on impersonal considerations, on universal attitudes.

Those following the Kantian school of thought about moral actions were concerned to advocate rational thought and to suppress what they feared as natural but dangerous aspects of their own functioning. In doing this they failed to appreciate the very substantial role of awareness and of feelings in general; as explained in Chapter 3, Sections 4 and 5 these are very important parts of the mechanisms which we and other species of animals use in coping with events in life. Moral acts involve some degree of awareness, although this may be only a feeling of obligation 'I should help X', rather than an extensive understanding of all aspects of the situation. Also, an individual could, in a moral way, set up a system in the form of a habit or response which later operated automatically so the moral component occurred before the act itself.

Although Kant had a substantial impact on the deontological approach to morality, many based their views of right conduct on a range of obligations or duties without using his rather limited framework. The source of an obligation or duty to others might be stated as God, or a holy book, or parental instruction but in most cases the individual would have observed, or calculated based on related observations, the consequences of following or not following the obligation. Such observations may well have reinforced or modified the ideas about what should be done. The idea that people might act on a duty-based moral structure without any regard for consequences is naive. Indeed, many of the rules which are used involve predicting consequences in simple or subtle ways in order to avoid actions with unacceptable outcomes.

Another rule is that just to seek pleasure without concern for all consequences is wrong and the basis of many duty-based structures is that if a bad thing is done, the consequence is a punishment, usually executed by society and by your own conscience.

Arguments about the importance of freedom to control one's life led to the idea that such freedom is a right which all should have. A moral structure based on a set of obligations could be re-stated as a set of rights. Nozick (1974) presents the view that:

> Individuals have rights, and there are things no person or group may do to them without violating their rights. So strong and far-reaching are these rights, they raise the question of what, if anything, the state and its officials may do.

Nozick regards rights as so clear cut that only a minimal state is needed to protect citizens. Such strong proponents of a rights structure for determining what are proper actions regard the stated rights as absolute, so they cannot be mitigated by other circumstances. Francione (1995, Chapter 4, p. 5) describes a right as:

> a type of protection that does not evaporate in the face of consequential considerations.

A key issue here is the establishment of what is a right. There are few so-called rights which would be accepted as valid in all circumstances. The oft-proclaimed right to free speech can cause great harm to certain individuals and hence can be morally wrong in my view, as can the 'right' to drive a car as fast as you wish, or to carry a gun. Midgley (1994, p. 112) quotes a letter in *The Guardian* of 3 January 1993 by T. Radford:

> Can we deny a mother's rights to shop in the genetic supermarket for healthier babies?

It is my view that the concept of rights causes too many problems. All behaviour and laws should be based on the obligations of each person to act in an acceptable way towards each other person rather than to assert the rights of anyone. Hence it would be better if any public statement which refers to rights, such as national constitutions and laws, were rewritten to avoid the use of the term rights. Such statements should provide guidelines for the behaviour of each person rather than asserting what the individual who is the object of an action can demand.

4.2.3   Utilitarianism

The narrow meaning of consequentialism in ethics is that the extent to which an act is morally right is determined solely by the goodness of the act's consequences. This approach was extended into utilitarianism by J. S. Mill (1843) who argued that the right act or policy is that which will result in the maximum utility, or expected balance of satisfaction minus dissatisfaction, in all the sentient beings affected. Feldman (1997, p. 3) explains the position futher.

> In its typical formulation, act utilitarianism presupposes that on each occasion of moral choice, the agent confronts a set of possible acts. For each possible act there is a consequence. The consequence contains all the subsequent events that would occur as a consequence of the act if it were performed. Each consequence has a value determined by the amount of good and evil it contains. Act utilitarianism is standardly taken to be the view that the agent's moral obligation is to perform the act that has the best consequence.
>
> *(p. 6)*

> 'general' utilitarianism requires a person to perform an act if the consequence of universal performance (to the greatest extent possible) of similar events would be better than the consequence of universal performance (to the greatest extent possible) of acts similar to the alternatives.

Feldman also states (p. 11):

> If a good is deserved, its value is enhanced and if they do not deserve a good which they receive, its value is mitigated.

He has gone so far as to say (1975):

> Historically, utilitarianism has been associated with the idea that
> the only intrinsic good is pleasure and the only intrinsic evil is
> pain.

Since pleasure and pain are feelings which may be transitory, this
statement could be interpreted as an argument for sometimes acting
for short-term effect, whatever the longer term consequences. Those
who present the utilitarian arguments might say that they use the
words 'pleasure' and 'pain' in a very wide sense but the common
usages of the words, and the scientific meanings, are narrower and
if these more normal meanings are used, utilitarianism according to
Feldman's meaning would be a code for living which is at odds with
biological mechanisms and with most people's ideas about what is
right and wrong.

Although many aspects of utilitarianism are helpful when deciding what is morally right (e.g. Feldman 1980), as a general approach
it is flawed. Acting in such a way that general happiness or general
good is promoted will be entirely desirable in some circumstances,
but following such a philosophy does not take account of the fact that
humans and other animals interact with and have concerns for individuals. Hence the mechanisms underlying moral codes are based on
effects on individuals as well as on collections of individuals. General repugnance at causing harm and delight at causing good effect
start with consideration of certain individuals and then go on to consideration of collections of individuals, or of individuals in a certain
category, or of sentient beings in general. It is very difficult to start at
the general and consider individuals only inasmuch as they are part
of the generality. In fact it is too difficult to do so. An example of the
flaw in the extreme utilitarianism approach is that, following this
approach, an individual could be caused extreme pain or other poor
welfare, or could be killed if the overall effect were good. This individual might be a dangerous criminal or an entirely innocent person
but should they be tortured, caused prolonged misery, or killed? Most

people would not wish an innocent person to be killed, however great the resulting good, and those who hesitated on the issue might be swayed to that view if the person were their neighbour, their mother, or themselves. In part this is because the killing of any person can have harmful consequences for the person who kills, for the people who condone the action, for those who observe the action or for those who hear about it. The careful reasoning of the utilitarian who decides that the killing should occur is not always known, or even comprehensible, to all of those who are aware of the killing. Hence it may be that, following a consequentialist argument, any killing may have much greater bad consequences than the effect on the individual who dies. These consequences are difficult to assess and a moral code which is based on rules, duties or obligations and which has developed over many generations is likely to work better in any society.

4.2.4 Moral values and decisions

Individuals usually act in a way which indicates that they place value on certain relationships, certain actions of others, certain qualities of others, including life itself and perhaps also aspects of the wider biological environment. The existence of these values affects decisions about what to do or not to do. The actions carried out by the individual and the consequences of those actions also have an effect on the happiness of the individual. The basis for arguments about how moral decisions are taken is clearly an important matter for debate. Criticisms of the utilitarian position have been made by many, including Williams (1972) and Midgley (1978, p. 299). Those who would consider themselves deontological ethicists would maintain that certain rights, rules or principles take precedence over utility. However, as mentioned above (Section 4.2.2) both Kant's approach and that of advocates of the rights approach also have flaws. It is proposed in this book that the bases for the values which individuals have, and the ability to assess the best course of action, generally that which promotes cooperation and group stability, have evolved because those individuals which had such qualities were more likely to be successful. The moral structure is a set of values, feelings of obligation, desires to please and the utilisation of a capacity to analyse many of the consequences of actions for a range of individuals. Neither a rights-based approach nor a wholly utilitarian approach is adequate to further moral ends but elements of both deontological and utilitarian approaches are necessary.

4.3   KNOWLEDGE AND CONSCIENCE

Views about the roles of knowledge, reasoning and understanding in moral behaviour have ranged from the one extreme that only knowledge and reasoning are required for morality, to the other that most knowledge is dangerous and some knowledge is antithetic to moral action. Kant's view of morality as depending on reasoning has been mentioned already. He considered morality to be of a unitary nature, based on a single foundation, which seems to have implied that, prior to knowledge acquisition, there is no guiding mechanism and no feelings are involved in reasoning. Some hold this view now but most would consider understanding to be putting knowledge into an existing framework and tempering it with the consequences of other kinds of responses, including those of a more emotional kind, before decisions can be taken on moral issues. The Buddhist idea of self-knowledge would also seem to be of this latter kind and Tu (1978) said 'morality or spirituality is not internalised by but expressed through learning' (see also Chapter 5, Section 1). The idea that knowledge is dangerous or harmful has for some been an absolute idea, referring to the knowledge of all people, and for others has assumed that whilst most people could not cope with knowledge, a few morally competent individuals could cope with it. Whilst there are occasions when knowledge of a particular fact may result in harm to the person who knows it or to another, it is quite illogical to generalise from this that knowledge promotes immoral behaviour. As explained in Chapter 5, some factual knowledge may undermine the structure of a religion, with its associated moral code, but the important moral elements of the religion will survive this. It is my view that the expansion of an individual's knowledge, like improved cognitive ability, is much more likely to increase the likelihood of moral action than to reduce it.

A more widespread conclusion as to the role of knowledge in moral behaviour is not that it is dangerous but that it is not particularly important. Hume (1739) argues that 'the passions' constitute an integral and legitimate part of human nature which have recognisable causes and uses. He stated, in the light of this position, that:

> Reason is, and ought only to be, the slave of the passions.

Among the more recent proponents of this position was Freud (e.g. 1930) who considered that many of the most important forces driving human behaviour are 'unconscious' and not readily available to self-reflection. Few people would now be as extreme in their views as Freud since the evidence for experience and conscious thinking altering judgements about important issues in life is so compelling. However, there is evidence for elements of structure guiding the acquisition of information (Hinde and Stevenson-Hinde 1973) and for the significant role of feelings in helping to control behaviour (Broom 1998), so Hume and Freud had some useful contributions to make to the arguments. Supporters of the view that knowledge and judgements based on it are far from being the major components of moral decisions and development include Murdoch (1970) and Blum (1987). Wilson (1993, pp. 7–8) went so far as to say:

> When people act fairly or sympathetically it is rarely because they have engaged in much systematic reasoning . . . The feelings on which people act are often superior to the arguments that they employ.

Darley (1993) also expresses doubt about whether there are principles of moral judgement based on cognitive processing. Hart and Killen (1995) point out that there are:

at least three interrelated, but different issues involved in Darley's claim:

(1) the rejection of general, global structures that reflect moral principles, such as the ones proposed by Kohlberg;
(2) the question of how principles, of any sort, are applied to actual contexts; and
(3) the relationship between moral judgement and moral action.

They conclude that moral principles which guide action do exist, that most philosophers, including Kant, have considered content important when moral judgements are made, and that both analysed inputs about the social situation and preconceived judgements are used to determine action. An important problem which results from the Freudian view is that people who believe that knowledge can have little effect on what they do because they are automata driven by internal forces, other people, fate or genes may use this as an excuse for anti-social behaviour (Midgley 1994, p. 84).

There is a widespread view in many human societies that we are all endowed with a conscience. The conscience, which is thought to lead to feelings such as remorse, guilt and shame, should block some anti-social behaviour and promote good actions. For Blum (1980, pp. 3–4), 'Morality has primarily to do with obligation' and the term 'altruistic emotion' seems to parallel 'conscience'. For Blum, and for many others, actions based on conscience are not rapid responses to perhaps trivial stimuli. He says:

> 'Altruistic emotions are not like changeable moods' and 'Acting from altruistic emotion is not characteristically acting on impulse.'

The world of stimulation may be suspect and should not be given too much weight when important decisions are being taken. However, the key questions concern where the conscience comes from and how it acts. Since conscience must be a construct in the brain of the individual, and all structures in all individuals arise as a result of interaction between genetic information and the environment in which the individuals develop and function (see Chapter 2, Section 1 and Chapter 4, Section 5), conscience must arise as a result of such interaction. As Elzanowski (1993, pp. 272–273) says:

> value experience has first to be accepted as a natural phenomenon, as an objective source of subjectivity.

The taking of decisions about moral issues depends on motivation systems. An array of sources of information results in the existence of causal factors, an assessment of all of whose relative levels determines what action is taken (Hinde 1970, Broom 1981, McFarland 1985). Conscience is the name given to a collection of inputs to the centre for making decisions about which behaviour will occur. These inputs will be of various kinds based on feelings, previous experience and current stimuli but are grouped together under this heading of conscience because they relate to moral issues. This view has similarities to that of Nagel (1970, p. 3) who argues:

> I conceive ethics as a branch of psychology. My claims concern its foundation, or ultimate motivational basis . . . The view presented here is opposed not only to ethical relativism but to any demand that the demands of ethics appeal to our interests.

However, Nagel does not use the term motivation in the same way as do those involved in ethological and psychological research, e.g. see the references cited above. I would say that all of the causal factors form part of motivational state and some physiological changes and all behaviour are the result of motivation. Hence motivation does not just refer to actions of which the individual is aware and which involve calculated intent. Nagel's preoccupation with motivation, which involves intent in his arguments about moral behaviour, causes problems for an overall understanding of morality. A moral action could occur without full realisation of the consequences. Indeed, very few people analyse the consequences of all of their actions, or are aware of their intentions at the time of carrying out some moral acts. Hence using Nagel's narrow view of motivation, very few actions are moral. I see no reason why an action should be considered not to be moral because it 'appeals to our interests'. Some moral actions are motivated in part by feelings and desires, whilst other moral actions have a short-term cost to the actor but confer a long-term benefit because of increased stability in the social group or because of increased esteem for the actor from others in the group. Actions are not disqualified from being moral in either of these circumstances. Nagel says that his view is opposed to ethical relativism, i.e. to the idea that there is no universally valid moral principle. I support this view of his since I argue that there are some moral principles which are common to all humans and to some other species of animal as well. Given the distinction between moral codes and customs which concern sexual behaviour, I would argue that most moral codes are the same for all humans. Hence my stance is ethical objectivism, but although some of those codes may exist in other species, others probably do not. Methods of achieving objectives often vary among individuals so although the conscience may be similar, the strategies used to achieve the result vary. Some individuals show what would be widely described as more emotional responses whilst others seem more calculated. Males and females may differ in the strategies used. There may also be differences between males and females in the degree to which effort or sacrifices are made to achieve moral objectives. The extent of investment in the young varies between males and females, not just in humans, and the certainty about parenthood varies. Hence one sex, usually the female, may sacrifice more for their offspring, or for others inside or outside the social group. Fathers may themselves possess, and may pass on to their offspring, genes which tend to extract more investment from the mother and mothers may have, or pass on, genes which promote her interest in future breeding by reducing her investment in the current young. For genetic and environmental reasons, conscience may vary somewhat amongst individuals.

Much has been written about how the conscience should be used. The following points are based on ideas presented by Anthony

Freeman (pers. commun.). It is not always easy to distinguish between conscience and self-interest and conscience may not allow a full understanding of why an action is right; for example, the distinction between justice and mercy may not be clear. Advice for those who may be too lax in using their conscience includes:

(1) suspect your conscience if you feel unwilling to enquire too deeply into an issue;
(2) weigh factors opposed to your interest as carefully as factors supporting your interest; and
(3) seek guidance from wiser people rather than from peers or less wise people.

On the other hand, advice for those who may be too scrupulous includes:

(1) do not doubt the honesty of your judgement on the basis of factors which become apparent only after the decision has been made;
(2) a small element of self-interest does not make a whole action selfish; and
(3) a good action is not rendered evil just because it happens to give pleasure to the actor.

A person who acts in a moral way, presumably according to their conscience, has often been considered to be of 'good character'. Hence there have been various views as to the origin of good character. One hundred years ago in Britain and in several other countries, moral qualities were thought to be very much determined by character, a nebulous concept which depended largely on the familial line of the person. The persons in society who were poorer or categorised as being of lower class were thought of as having less character and a less developed moral code because of their family origins. Those who wrote down these views were almost always from the higher class, probably wealthier, part of society and it was in the interests of that group to perpetuate differences between social strata. Little effort was made to find out whether the moral differences actually existed and there was no clear awareness of the differences between moral actions and customs. Hence, many of the supposed moral inadequacies of the lower classes might now be regarded as just differences in sexual customs or manners. Many persons in society looked up to those whom they believed to be their betters and expected that such people would set an example with regard to issues of real moral importance. The origin of such attitudes may lie in the general success in becoming leaders of persons who were able and valuable to other group members. However, the trust would be misplaced if the leader had assumed power with largely selfish intent, or had inherited power without themselves having the qualities which would be of value to the group. Issues relating to development of character are discussed further in Chapter 4, Section 5.

4.4   MORALITY IN RELATION TO CODES
OF SEXUAL BEHAVIOUR

4.4.1   *Morality and the biological basis for sexual codes*

I have argued that moral acts are those which confer a benefit on other individuals which may or may not be closely related to the actor. This includes acts which support the structure of the society within which the actor lives and acts which, in addition to benefiting others, confer a short- or long-term benefit on the actor. Hence acts which are immoral are those which cause harm to other individuals, including those immediately affected and those which will be affected although they are distant or as yet unborn. Harms involve poor welfare, either that involving difficulty in coping or that involving reduced fitness (Broom and Johnson 1993, pp. 74–86). In many societies, various aspects of sexual behaviour are included in moral codes. Indeed, for many people the ideas elicited when reference is made to moral or immoral behaviour largely concern sexual behaviour. The argument presented here is that most sexual behaviour is not a moral issue at all and that, although some sexually motivated actions are immoral, in general the importance of sexual behaviour in morality has been greatly over-stated. There are reasons why people may include in codes for living some condemnation of some sexual behaviours which are not related, or are only indirectly related, to morality. Much of the sexual behaviour which is regarded as transgression of a code is in the code because it is of importance to guarding of the mate by males. This and other biologically based origins for sexual codes are briefly explained here and an attempt is made to distinguish the morally important from the morally trivial. There are differences among societies in attitudes to sexual customs which are greater than differences in real moral issues.

Some codes of sexual behaviour have an obvious biological basis. In some cases this is clear because of the knowledge which we now have and about which former generations would have known less. If individuals never mate or form sexual liaisons only with a member or members of their own sex, they will have no offspring. Parents who wish their own genetic line to continue would be likely, in general, to discourage such behaviour. There could be compensations for parents in some circumstances, for example, in some societies, social benefit for those whose offspring became priests, monks, nuns or castrati with great singing ability.

Mating with siblings, offspring or parents involves a great degree of inbreeding which may reduce the quality or survivability of the offspring. Hence, codes of living which proscribe such liaisons or long-term sexual partnerships are founded on mate-selection mechanisms which have arisen as a result of natural selection.

The minimisation of disease risk is a major factor affecting codes of sexual behaviour and of other social behaviour. For example, the likelihood of contracting infectious disease can be reduced by not welcoming sick strangers, staying in your own community rather than travelling, living in a monastery or being a hermit. Avoidance of sexually transmitted disease can be made more likely by codes of sexual behaviour. Lethal diseases, such as syphilis and diseases which are debilitating or harmful to future reproduction such as gonorrhoea, have been a risk to all humans until very recently and so have affected codes of living. A code of behaviour which condemns promiscuous mating would reduce the risk of contracting such diseases for those who abided by it. It would also reduce the general risk of the spread of the diseases in society if many people abided by it. This general effect would not be of great importance to those who did not carry out promiscuous mating but it could be relevant to them because of the risk for their offspring. The reduced risk posed by venereal disease, particularly syphilis, which resulted from improved medical treatment in the twentieth century must have resulted in less fear of the possibly lethal consequences of sexual intercourse with a new partner. The advent of acquired immunodeficiency syndrome (AIDS), a new, potentially lethal, sexually transmitted disease, in this social climate did not result in a rapid enough change in sexual practices to prevent its spread in many countries. The origin of the disease in Africa and the relative difficulty for foreign travellers to go to some countries, e.g. countries with communist governments in the 1970s and 1980s, had an effect on the distribution of AIDS across countries. However, data from the United Nations AIDS Programme (e.g. published in Die Presse (Vienna), 11 July 2000, p. 3) gives indirect information about sexual codes in different countries. All countries in which more than 5% of adults were human immunodeficiency virus (HIV) positive at the end of 1999 were in the southern half of Africa. Other countries with more than 1% were in the Caribbean and Central American region, or in South East Asia. Some countries with higher incidences of AIDS than others in their region were holiday destinations for people from the United States or Europe. The countries with less than 0.1% were Islamic countries in North Africa and South East Asia, former communist countries in Eastern Europe, Scandinavia, Cuba, China, Mongolia, Korea, Japan, Bangladesh, Philippines, Indonesia and New Zealand. Within many countries in which the incidence of AIDS is substantial, sub-groups in which promiscuous mating is frowned upon remain largely free of the disease.

A quite different area where natural selection acts is on factors which directly affect reproductive success. Females restrict their sexual behaviour in a way which maximises their chances of producing viable, good quality offspring. In many species the female is capable of mating during a limited period only. Human females who are in an early stage of pregnancy, where foetal loss is most likely, may feel nausea which results in reduced desire for vigorous activity including copulation. As mentioned in Chapter 1, Section 4, efforts to protect offspring may lead to increased sexual activity. van Schaik *et al.* (1999) showed that the risk of infanticide by male monkeys increased the likelihood that the mother monkeys would allow and encourage mating. Sometimes in human society, a mother must encourage sexual intercourse rather than risk an attack on her child. Infanticide does occur in modern human society, by mothers as well as by fathers, but especially by stepfathers (Daly and Wilson 1988).

Although the effects on female sexual behaviour mentioned above are significant in humans, and very substantial in species where there is no mating possible on most days of adult life, the most substantial effects on codes of sexual behaviour are those resulting from male uncertainty about paternity. In species in which the offspring develop within the mother, until they are capable of locomotion and interaction with her, while she is certain that she is the parent of a particular individual offspring, the male with whom she consorts has much less certainty. It is often difficult to recognise alien offspring and the recent results of DNA testing, which show that as many as fifteen percent of the children of married couples are not the offspring of the father, demonstrate the magnitude of uncertainty about paternity in our society now. Indeed it may transpire that this discovery has substantial effects on attitudes in human society in the near future. The consequence of the problem in a wide variety of species is the development of adaptations for mate-guarding or sperm competition. It is proposed here that important aspects of sexual customs or codes are aspects of mate-guarding by males so, before considering those customs or codes, the topic requires some brief discussion.

One guarding method used by human males is to stay with the mate, especially at times when mating is likely such as at night or when few other people are around. Another aspect of mate-guarding is to insist that the female should wear clothes and act in a way that minimises the likelihood of other males being attracted to her. Prohibitions of being seen by men, for example by wearing a yashmak, or of speaking to men, or of visiting certain places have this effect. Much more extreme measures include requiring the wearing of a chastity belt which allows urination and defaecation, but prevents copulation, or the very widespread practice of clitorectomy which prevents much of the sexual pleasure during copulation. The male may himself enforce sexual loyalty by punishing actual or potential transgressions, or visiting at unexpected times to make female deception more difficult, but he will also set up a structure in his society so that others in the group look for and report transgressions. There is often a reciprocal aspect to this monitoring and reporting, in that the male or female reporter may be rewarded by the male concerned but cheating in such circumstances is probably much commoner than with real moral issues. The costs to the male of being deceived, and having to invest in children who are not his own offspring, are considerable but the deception per se has hardly any cost to the mother or to group stability. It is only the consequences of the male's actions if the female is found out and the subsequent actions of the other male which might have such costs. Mate-guarding in itself is not morally wrong but some of the methods used can be questioned on moral grounds. The whole life of many women is greatly affected by some of these mate-guarding methods. It is my view that the severe restrictions placed on women by, for example, sections of medieval Christian society and of modern Islamic society are morally wrong. Clitorectomy in any society is wrong. Murder in any circumstance is wrong, yet 'le crime passionel' involving the killing of an unfaithful wife caught 'in flagrante delicto' is regarded as different from other cases of murder in many countries. The codes of conduct in various societies make male unfaithfulness much less reprehensible than female unfaithfulness. Whilst this difference may have some biological basis, largely that males are stronger than females, I think that it is morally wrong. Hence, whilst mate-guarding by either males or females is morally acceptable, some methods, including harmful sexual customs inspired by male mate-guarding, are not morally acceptable. It is necessary to look again at all sexual customs and to consider the true magnitude of any harms caused by transgression. Harms caused to individual males have been over-emphasised in the development of some sexual customs and harms caused to individual females or to females in general have been under-emphasised. As a consequence, some supposedly immoral acts related to mate-guarding are morally innocuous or trivial. Others are more important but, overall, the imbalance in most societies between male interests and female interests in the formulation of codes relating to sexual behaviour is morally wrong. Some actions which are described as immoral are not immoral at all. Others are treated as being of major importance when they are of minor importance. In every case we should concentrate on true morality and not over-emphasise benefits to certain males.

4.4.2 Transgressions of sexual codes in relation to morality

Sexually related actions which are condemned in the codes of some or most societies:

(1) may cause real harm to the individuals concerned;
(2) may be a problem to males attempting to guard their mates;
(3) may have associations with reciprocal altruism; or
(4) may have consequences for social stability.

Each of these aspects will be considered for a range of actions.

Rape can result in death, or injury, and, even if physical injury is avoided by a woman who acquiesces but does not consent to the act, leads to adverse psychological effects and these alone are sufficient reasons for it to be considered morally wrong. In addition, rape of a woman by a man may result in pregnancy, or future reproductive problems, or psychological effects associated with these. A particular anomaly concerning rape is that the view of others in society about the magnitude of the harm to the woman is affected by her position in society. The rape of a woman who is poor has often been viewed as much less serious than the rape of a women from a rich and influential background. To some extent this is a consequence of the protective ability of the male relatives.

The influence of male mate-guarding on the attitude of society to rape is stronger condemnation of the act than might otherwise occur because each male considers that a woman such as the one raped could be his partner or future partner. It may be that the mate-guarding male may suspect that female infidelity is involved. This possibility has sometimes been rated, by males and hence by society, as more important than the act of rape itself. It puts pressure on women to resist rape vigorously, even if this resistance puts them at risk of being killed or severely injured. If a woman has not resisted she may be suspected of having encouraged the rapist. The difficulties of understanding a given situation are worsened because there is the possibility, probably rare, of a woman encouraging sexual advances and then accusing the man of rape after reflecting on the consequences of the situation. However, the commonest miscarriage of justice would seem to be that which occurs when women fail to report rape because of fear of being suspected of having encouraged the rapist, or of not being believed. Reciprocal altruism amongst males tends to minimise the occurrence of rape in stable social groups. A male refrains from raping the wife or daughter of another because of favours owed to that male and the risk that he will rape in return. Rape has a substantial destabilising effect on societies because cooperative social relationships are difficult to maintain if an individual in the group is known to have raped. Any violent assault has this effect but rape is often regarded as much more significant. Rapists are likely to become outcasts and outcasts are more likely to be rapists. Males away from places where they are known and males in tribal conflict situations such as wars are more likely to rape. In some cases it is an act of aggression against the other tribe or society and not just an action which is desired but socially prevented in the normal environment.

Adultery normally causes no physical harm to the participants although there can be significant psychological problems over a long period. However, for the mate-guarding male, adultery by his spouse is often more of a problem than rape because the infidelity of the spouse is clear and may mean the ultimate loss of the spouse. Hence reactions to it are sometimes strong. The points about reciprocal altruism made above in relation to rape also apply to adultery. The effects of adultery on social stability are less than those of rape, because they usually affect fewer group members, but can still be considerable. In general in human society, monogamy results in a more stable society than any form of polygamy. Serial polygamy, like that where divorce and remarriage is commonplace, results on average in there being more disturbed children who disrupt society than in a more monogamous society. However, serious failure in a marital relationship can also lead to major disturbance in the children of the marriage and both single parents and subsequent marriages can provide a stable environment for children so the above statement refers to the average, and not to each, case.

Pre-marital sex could cause harm if an unwanted baby is produced or if a venereal disease is contracted so it is not surprising that there are codes in many societies saying that it is wrong. In many cases, however, the social sanctions are for females rather than for males. This is logical in that the female is left with the baby but it is not morally right and in many societies there are social systems for ensuring that the father shares responsibility. The mate-guarding aspect is rather in the form of daughter-guarding and the destabilisation of society is greatest if a baby is born and the mother is too young to rear the baby adequately. If the pre-marital sex is between individuals who are committed to a permanent partnership, none of these problems exist but the contract of marriage is often thought of as the best guarantee of that commitment. Parental and societal disapproval of a partnership is generally greatest if it seems unlikely that the partner will be permanent and a contributor to care.

Display of the body and flirtatious behaviour would not cause harm to others but might be a challenge to the mate-guarding male or to a paired female. If it is the male or female's partner who is behaving thus, the risk of attracting other males is clear. Display by others does not cause a problem. Hence the male's attitude when the subject is his wife may be quite different from his attitude when it is someone else. There is no doubt that the sight of body or behaviour can elicit sexual excitement in males or females. There may be consequences for social group stability if the behaviour leads to rape or socially harmful sexual liaisons. However, there is evidence that the likelihood of such anti-social sexual behaviour can be reduced if males have access to female display acts, such as strip shows, or sexually explicit pictures which encourage sublimation of sexual urges or masturbation rather than the anti-social behaviour. Whereas some codes for living condemn flirtatious behaviour unreservedly, e.g. the Bible, it would seem better for the promotion of moral behaviour if individuals are advised not to show such behaviour in an uncontrolled way or in inappropriate circumstances, rather than not to show it at all. Controlled display, in the form of publications, videos and shows, to each of which access is restricted, should be encouraged because of its beneficial effects.

Copulation in public is generally regarded as far less acceptable than displays or interactions which fall short of this. It would not cause direct harm so it must be impact on others which is perceived as the source of potential problems. The mate-guarding male might see in it a potential to arouse which increases the chance that his partner will mate with someone else. A mated female might have the same concerns. If there is such an effect, there could be a destabilising effect on society. It may be that the potential for other males to intervene and mate with the female is the greatest risk so neither partner would wish to take that risk.

Prostitution is condemned in much the same way that strip shows and sexually explicit books or videos are condemned. On the other hand, many men are willing to use prostitutes. If disease and pregnancy are prevented, the physical harm to the prostitutes may be small. Some individual women may be able to deal with the mental effects by the use of particular mental, behavioural and social strategies. However, until the relatively recent advent of effective condoms, none of these harms could be prevented. Many women are harmed by prostitution but have little or no alternative because of financial or other circumstances. Men may be concerned that their wives or daughters could become prostitutes, but generally the mate-guarding male would see little problem in prostitution. The net effect on social stability is probably positive because the likelihood of rape or mate-stealing is reduced. This would appear to be a situation where in former times the harm to the prostitutes resulting from disease and pregnancy was too high for the practice to be condoned and the risk to men of venereal disease was very great. With both of these risks gone or substantially reduced, the arguments against prostitution appear to be much reduced. However, the argument that prostitution can be acceptable refers only to the situation where the prostitute receives no net harm.

Homosexual acts within stable partnerships between healthy adult individuals would appear to involve no harm to the participants except that, as far as biological fitness is concerned, they will not produce offspring. There is no challenge to the mate-guarding male, and such relationships are obviously reciprocal between the partners. There is no challenge to social stability unless there is vigorous social disapproval and it would be the actions of the disapprovers which caused problems. Bentham (1748–1832, published 1984) was of the opinion, on the basis of consequentialist arguments, that such sexual non-conformity caused no harm and was not a sin. Banner (1999, p. 273) points out the problems associated with such arguments and explains the positions of those who consider actions as well as consequences when deciding how homosexuality should be viewed. I consider that it is acceptable for individuals to live as a stable homosexual couple. If the individuals involved in the homosexual act are not a stable couple, there is less reciprocity and a little more risk of societal destabilisation, especially in an intolerant society, but still the act is innocuous. Promiscuous behaviour is somewhat more likely amongst homosexuals, because there is no risk of unwanted baby production, but as a consequence there is somewhat more risk of venereal disease. This became apparent during the early spread of AIDS although the major spread of AIDS has been through heterosexual contact.

Any sexual act directed towards an immature male or female has a considerable potential for harm to that individual, including long-term psychological effects, which are made worse according to the amount of force involved or injury resulting. Such acts by sexually mature individuals should be strongly discouraged but they should be distinguished from exploratory behaviour by one immature individual towards another which is not harmful. With effective education about sexual development, the transition from exploration and interest to knowledge and caution about the consequences of normal sexual activity can be effected.

Pleasure in sexual activity has been misguidedly condemned in some societies (see Chapter 3, Section 5). The distinction between sexual behaviour which harms others and that which does not should be known by all and the harm caused by a small proportion of sexual activity should not be generalised to all. Sexual pleasure helps to reinforce pair bonds and supportive relationships in mated couples and to reduce social disruption and is a wholly good thing (Broom 1998). Sexual pleasure resulting from masturbation is also harmless or beneficial. It is most unlikely ever to prevent normal copulation and hence to reduce biological fitness and may significantly reduce the likelihood of anti-social sexual behaviour.

Words which mean copulation or which refer to sexual organs are taboo in many societies, and often used as swear words: a bizarre situation. It seems unlikely to me that the normal use of such words would influence the hearers and cause them to initiate anti-social acts. Their use as expletives must be a consequence of the prohibition on their use and could increase the aggressive feelings when the actions are contemplated. It would seem that any kind of prohibition on the use of the words is undesirable.

4.4.3   Sexual codes and sin

It is against this complex background that the relationship between immorality and sexual behaviour has to be considered. Kant (1780 approx.) says:

> Sexuality exposes man to the danger of equality with beasts, but how can there be such a danger?

Midgley (1978, p. 45) argues that a parallel with beasts implies no danger at all. More recent authors have been concerned that sexual desires and behaviour are part of the bad side of human nature. Williams (1989) argues that:

> just about every . . . kind of sexual behaviour that has been regarded as sinful or unethical can be found abundantly in nature.

However, in commenting on his view, de Waal (1996, p. 16) questions the logic of assuming that animals are sinful because they show such behaviour. I do not consider that much of sexual behaviour is sinful at all (as mentioned above in Chapter 4 Section 4.1).

There is much written about differences in sexual codes in different human societies. For example, Barash (1979, p. 143) describes how one wife can be shared by brothers in the Toda of Southern India, the Tupi Kahawit of Brazil and the Tre-ba of Tibet. Amongst the Pahavi-speaking people of Northern India, brothers will together buy one wife and will then buy others if they can afford to do so.

The term 'sin' should be restricted to actions which are morally wrong in that they cause, or might cause, significant harm to any other individual, to society, or to the environment. Behaviour which is not ideally efficient in increasing the functional development of the individual showing it, or which is concerned with sexual activity which harms no other individual, should not be called sin. Sexual codes and customs should be re-assessed to check the extent of truly harmful effects and particular attention should be paid to actions or rules whose real raison d'être is to help in male mate-guarding without conferring real benefits or preventing real harms.

4.5 DEVELOPMENT OF MORALITY IN THE YOUNG

For many years now, those who study the development of behaviour, and of biological characteristics in general, have considered that the qualities of every characteristic are a consequence of interactions between a genetic programme and information derived from environmental variables. These variables are wider in their variety than just those which contribute to learning, or those whose effect is mediated via sense organs. The functioning of some of the genetic programmes depends to a large extent on environmental factors which vary little from one individual to another so the characteristic is similar across individuals, whilst others depend on factors which may be very different in different individuals and different circumstances, so the resultant characteristics of individuals are diverse. Hence, whilst it is of interest to consider the relative roles of genetic and environmental factors, it is erroneous to refer to any characteristic as genetically controlled, or instinctive, or innate and there is nothing which does not depend in part on genetics. This understanding was absent in the past and this is reflected in some statements and ideas about the development of origins of moral behaviour. For example, Durkheim (1894) and his followers considered that society was the only source of morality. Much more recently, Dawkins (1976) argued that individuals start their life bad and have to be taught to be good. He also considered that as natural selection acts on the adult phenotype in relation to moral behaviour, the study of the development of moral acts was not very important.

Following Dawkins' view, Ruse (1982, p. 324) said that children have to be taught not to lie, bully and cheat. The critical point here is whether or not there are genetic programmes which make the learning of some moral rules likely and easy. Since most functioning systems in man and other animals develop in this way, it would be surprising if the very important moral regulatory mechanisms did not. One way in which instructive programmes could work is for feelings to promote preferences for good consequences of action and mitigate against bad actions. Some moral behaviour is very simple and can easily develop in most humans and many other species. Other moral behaviour is sophisticated and likely to be rarer.

The data collected by Piaget (1932) included details of the rules of childrens' games. Piaget pointed out that children seem to look for systems with rules and that they adhere closely to these rules once they are learned. He also examined many stories and situations involving children and tried to establish what children of different ages regarded as good or bad conduct. He considered that children paid attention to the consequences of actions and to the intentions of others and formed their own opinions which would not necessarily coincide with those of their parents. The idea that children were just instructed in moral matters by their parents was dismissed. However, although there is a valuable step towards understanding how morality develops here, Piaget tended to over-emphasise the idea of autonomy and independence from external pressures, a position previously presented by Kant. Williams (1981, p. 5) points out the deficiencies of this position in that it should:

> allow more room than Kantianism can allow for the importance of individual character and personal relations in moral experience.

Killen and Nucci (1995) further explain:

> Likewise, Piaget did not theorise about the importance of the individual or personal relations in personal development . . . children develop a sense of fairness and justice through a reciprocal recognition that the desires of others are similar to the desires of the self.

Another important methodological approach was that of Kohlberg (1969) whose initial study was of seventy-five boys aged ten to sixteen who were asked a set of questions at three-year intervals for twelve years. As a result of this, Kohlberg listed the following six stages of morality and proposed in his earlier writings that it was necessary to go through one stage in order to be able to attain the rest.

(1) Being guided by expectations of unpleasant consequences such as punishment.
(2) Acting so as to gratify own needs and sometimes those of others by conforming to group behaviour.
(3) Doing what is approved of by others and avoiding dislike and rejection, including showing concern for others and loyalty.
(4) Considering obligations and duties, being motivated to follow the law, defer to authority, and support societal institutions by not doing what it would be bad for everyone to do and which would induce guilt.
(5) Considering contractual commitment to laws and institutions according to their general utility and rights to life and liberty which deserve adherence in every society.
(6) Considering individual conscience as based on universal principles such as equality of human rights and dignity of individuals.

The list is carefully considered and constructive for further discussion, but these stages would seem to reflect increases in knowledge, changes in ability to express concepts and changes in expectations of what answers the questioner wanted. Also, there must be questions as to how similar a list would be produced by females or people not immersed in the general philosophical position prevalent in the United States at that time. As Brandt (1996, p. 89) points out:

> There is, however, only modest empirical support for the allegedly necessary sequence of Kohlberg's stages.

Kohlberg eventually abandoned the idea of the necessary sequence. However, Kohlberg (1969) did suggest that the six stages might reflect cultural evolution, a point picked up by Crook (1980, p. 396) and it is worth considering in relation to the possible evolution of the various stages. Stages 1 and 2 could operate via sets of strategies, like

tit-for-tat and others described in Chapter 2, Section 4, and could occur in a wide range of social animals. Stage 3 is also readily explained
by various kinds of reciprocal altruism and some elements could be
widespread amongst species. Stage 4 requires a more elaborate form of
reciprocal altruism and a well-structured society but its functioning
depends in part on feelings such as guilt and anxiety as well as on the
cognitive ability required to initiate them and to act appropriately.
Stages 5 and 6 are difficult to identify without verbal evidence but
they are still based on principles present in Stages 1–4.

Although Piaget (1932) does describe the behaviour of some
young children, most of his ideas, and those of Kohlberg (1969), about
the development of morality are based on data collected from, or
about, children of seven or older, or from young adults. Using the general hypothesis presented in this book that many aspects of morality have evolved in various social species of animals, and knowing
from recent research that the cognitive capabilities of young children
develop to a very high level before seven years of age, the assumption that morality does not emerge until after six years of age seems
strange. Studies of the behaviour of fifteen to eighteen-month-old children (e.g. Rheingold and Hay 1978) resulted in descriptions of sharing
of favoured toys and food, caregiving to dolls, etc. and taking turns
in acts. Similarly, Dunn and Kendrick (1979) describe the early appearance of comforting responses and Zahn-Waxler and Radke-Yarrow
(1982) found evidence of concern for individuals in distress by sixteen
months of age. Hoffman (1982, 1984, 1988) followed Hume (1777) in
focusing on the importance of empathy during moral development. He
referred to generalised or global empathy as occurring before one year
of age, empathy which indicates recognition of the other individual
as different from the self in one- and two-year-olds, empathy which
involves the offering of help appropriate to the immediate needs of the
other by three years of age and empathy extending beyond the immediate situation and individuals in later years. Hoffman considered empathy to be a native disposition, probably the result of evolution. The
evidence for a significant role for empathy during the development

of social interactions is good but the fact that behaviour is based on empathy does not mean that the whole of it is explicable as empathy. The detail of each action must depend on the specific experiences of the individual interacting with the feeling of empathy.

The role of parents, and other significant individuals in the environment of the developing child in shaping moral behaviour is clearly important. Parents and others provide examples and often offer direct instruction about what is right and wrong. The child is likely to observe that a parent is careful throughout life not to act in certain ways which are harmful to others but, as Alexander (1979, p. 274) points out, they may also teach their children how to cheat without getting caught (see Chapter 2, Section 2.9). Three significant disciplinary methods used by parents (Rottschaefer 1998, p. 244) are power techniques, such as use of force, threat or deprivation of privilege, love withdrawal including expressions of anger and disapproval, and instructive techniques involving pointing out the effects of the child's behaviour on others. In the course of development, the young child is not viewed as passive but as actively constructing social and moral categories based on experience from parents, peers and own observations (Damon 1983, Hart and Killen 1995). This allows the young individual to develop:

(1) sensitivity to the emotions and needs of others;
(2) cooperative versus competitive orientations toward the use of common resources;
(3) provision of care to infants, the elderly, the ill and others in need;
(4) social problem-solving skills that permit the successful resolution of conflict with others;
(5) the development of standards for truth-telling and trustworthiness;
(6) awareness of and adherence to social conventions and moral norms.

(Hay et al. 1994)

4.6 MORALITY AND LAW

What is the basis for laws? Are legal codes the same as moral codes? In his book about the life of Thomas More, Ackroyd (1998) explains that in sixteenth century England the distinction between law and religion was not at all clear. A statement by the religious leaders of the time was regarded, in public and to a large extent in private, as legally and morally right. The role of the religious leaders included pronouncements on law. However, from More's own writings (1516) it is clear that he was aware of the role of those motivated to protect their possessions in the formulation of legal and social codes, for on his imaginary island 'Utopia' there was no money, private property or social distinction and virtue was taught and rewarded with happiness. More's cynicism about the organisation of society was not made entirely explicit but the linkage between law and morality was criticised by Luther (1525) who spoke of:

> judgement according to love . . . without any law books.

The codes of conduct produced in religions are the earliest forms of what we might now call laws. As stated already in Chapter 1, Section 8 and explained further in Chapter 5, moral codes are the central part of religions and the laws which are produced in the name of religion include a substantial moral component. However, laws did not always remain under the control of religious leaders and religious leaders have sometimes been so affected by their power that they did not conform to or advocate some of the moral codes which were the foundation of their religion. Hence, whilst some laws are readily recognisable as promoting particular moral actions, or leading to sanctions following immoral actions, other laws have the effect of promoting inequalities in society or reinforcing prejudices which are not morally right. Whilst protection of valuable individuals in society is useful to all members of a social group, there are limits to the privileges which should be permitted to a wise person, or to a military leader or useful figurehead. Laws in many societies have protected the person of the leader, the property of the leader, or the persons and property of an elite group within the society. The aims of many laws were not just that monarchs and their property were defended but also that those with property were protected against those without. Only two hundred years ago it was possible for a person in England who stole a sheep to be hanged or to be deported to Australia and made to work for the government or a land owner. Some laws penalised persons outside the society very heavily because of tribal conflicts, for example on my first visit to Carlisle in the north west of England, I learned that there was a law that any Scotsman found on the streets after dark was subject to the death penalty. This law, probably unenforced for three hundred years, has now been repealed!

In addition to protecting persons and property, some laws are important for the support of trade. Indeed, Ridley (1996, p. 202) went so far as to say:

> Government, law, justice and politics are not only far more
> recently developed than trade, but they follow where trade leads.

Various rather immediate forms of cheating during trade are penalised by laws but there are questions as to whether these laws always lead to a just result in that some forms of very severe exploitation of others are not penalised. Other kinds of laws seem to protect individuals and have some moral aspect to them but are designed to minimise actions which members of society see as a general threat, for example laws against drunkenness, drug-taking or homosexuality. Laws designed to prevent fast driving, or to stop roads being blocked by parked cars, or to raise taxes in order to build roads have a moral component in some cases but not in others. The whole question of the extent to which law and morality have features in common and differences is discussed by Brandt (1996, pp. 237–281). One of the ironies of such a comparison is the difference between moral standards for individuals and moral standards for governments. As Gert (1988, p. 242) points out, governments can violate moral rules which apply to individuals, for moral purposes. It is acceptable for governments, but not for individuals, to tax or imprison people.

Some of the laws which were obviously unfair to certain members of society, especially those which penalised the poor but not the rich for similar misdemeanours, are not now in force. In deciding what should be the law and what should not, the views of the articulate voting members of society have been more and more taken into account. Democratic systems of government have the particular advantage that the views of the majority of members of society can gradually prevail. Devlin (1965, p. 13) argued that a system of criminal law should conform to the actual moral standards of the community. He famously proposed that an action is contrary to the morality of a community if a reasonable person, the man on the Clapham omnibus, would find it reprehensible or disgusting beyond the limits of toleration. Devlin refers to changes in the view of the average reasonable person over time and it is clear that attitudes to, for example, suicide, assisted suicide, abortion and re-marriage have changed over a period of fifty years. This method of changing laws does not lead to rapid change on some moral issues, however. Rawls (1971) states:

> In a just society the liberties of equal citizenship are taken as settled, the rights secured by justice are not subject to political bargaining or to the calculus of social interests.

He then goes on to explain that, in the twentieth century American citizens were very far from equal and some justice was subject to political bargaining. He argued for social control and hence laws which would secure as close an approach as possible to the equal distribution of society's rewards. Others do not have this view and consider that it is reasonable for laws to allow some members of society to have almost unlimited advantages over others in terms of possessions because of aristocratic parents, wealthy parents, intellectual ability, ruthlessness or chance. Many people, but not Rawls, argue in favour of a meritocracy, in which greater rewards go to those with most ability or other merit. If this occurs without carefully considering what constitutes merit, each person might attempt to skew the general view of merit so that their own qualities are considered meritorious, or so that abilities such as being able to compete and make money, which happen to be popular in a particular culture or section of the community, are so considered. Both evaluations could be wrong. Another problem is that the consequences of unevenness of distribution may be that those with least merit starve, or that the least rewarded people act against society by becoming criminals.

Laws are based in part on the consequences of actions and in part on the intentions of the individual carrying out the action. A person who causes death by a completely unavoidable action is not regarded as culpable. However, some blame attaches to anyone carrying out a dangerous action, for example driving a motor car, if any death results. The law is only broken if the person is regarded as careless or irresponsible. An intentional action, such as causing death, is legally worse than an unintentional action and a planned, intentional action is worse still. All of these features of law would be taken into account in any moral judgement.

The extent of punishment is an important feature of law. Whether crimes are regarded as serious or minor and whether punishment is by fine, community service or imprisonment are related to the society's idea of the severity of the punishments. This principle is also common to other moral judgements. However, there is a basic question about whether punishments for wrong-doing should be in proportion to what has been done, or related to what is likely to occur in the future (Plato about 380 BC). The future conduct of the individual and the effects on others when they know about the punishment and the crime, i.e. the deterrent effect, is proposed by Plato as being more important than consideration of the magnitude of the crime itself. Both the magnitude of the crime and deterrent effects play a part in decisions about punishment in modern law. The deterrent effects are clearly dependent on the extent to which the information is disseminated to others. Another factor which is taken into account in determining punishments for some, but by no means all, crimes is the financial consequence for individuals or organisations harmed by the crime. This leads to some great anomalies in punishment when the situation is viewed from a wholly moral perspective.

The general conclusion must be that whilst some laws and their enforcement seem to be of great moral value, others are not just. Morality and law can sometimes be at odds with one another.

4.7   CONCLUSIONS ABOUT THE EVOLUTION OF MORALITY

The idea that the various aspects of morality have evolved implies that human morality has or had parallels or antecedents in our immediate ancestors, other primates, other mammals and other vertebrate animals. In Chapter 2 the very great overlap in gene complement between humans and some other animals and the widespread occurrence of cooperative and altruistic behaviour in animals, especially social animals, are explained. Then in Chapter 2, Section 4 the possible ways in which altruism might have evolved are considered. All of this is unconvincing unless the abilities needed to behave morally are present in the individuals, so the evidence for awareness, feelings and cognitive ability in a range of species is presented in Chapter 3. Human ideas about morality are presented in this chapter and the important distinction is made between customs and moral behaviour. In particular, in Chapter 1, Section 4 and Chapter 4, Section 4 the extent to which codes of sexual behaviour should be regarded as part of morality is discussed and it is concluded that the true morality component of any code should be assessed and that the moral component of functions such as male mate-guarding should not be over-emphasised. In the same way, not all laws should be treated as if they indicated what is morally right, for example those laws which perpetuate tribal differences, or social prejudices, or protection of the persons and property of the powerful.

Based on all of this evidence it is argued that morality has a biological basis and has evolved. Reciprocal altruism has been important in the evolution of morality but it is not all of the biological basis, as other mechanisms, such as feelings of empathy, compassion, love and guilt, are also involved. The way in which this fits with current philosophical arguments concerning morality has been questioned, for example Rolston (1999, p. 215) says:

> In view of the debates about altruism and its relation to genetics, we would take caution to recall that neither in deontological ethics nor in utilitarianism, the two main Western traditions, is altruism the pivotal principle.

This implies that, because altruism is not of central importance using either kind of argument in its pure form, it is not important. However, as argued in Chapter 4, Sections 2 and 3, neither deontological nor utilitarian arguments in their pure form are tenable, even though aspects of each seem to be essential in explaining and understanding morality.

The emphasis placed on the evolution of morality in this book does not in any way imply that moral actions are automatic or independent of environmental effects. Each behaviour of each individual is a consequence of interaction between genome and environment. When formulating decisions about what is, or is not, a moral course of action the individual will be taking account of many sources of information. It is the capability to come to appropriate moral conclusions which has evolved. Some universal actions have effects which are very disturbing and aversive to the perpetrator, for example, causing injury to another individual and, hence, producing abnormal body form, or much blood, or exposing normally invisible tissues, or causing the production of severe distress sounds. These effects can be perceived and can reduce the likelihood of repetition of the action without high level cognitive functioning and it is easy to see how the aversive perception itself might have evolved. Other immoral actions may have effects which are much more difficult to process and appreciate and it will be less easy to understand how mechanisms promoting morality would have evolved. However, in all cases moral actions can be promoted by natural selection, even if they are never wholly determined by genetic influences.

A similar position to that adopted here is presented by Chisholm (1999, p. 26):

> our moral sentiments are (1) contingent, facultative for achieving a future (even if we cannot live to see it) that is valuable for our ultimate reproductive success (or would have been in our evolutionary past), and (2) that these moral sentiments represent the relationship between current and recent indicators (sociological or cultural) of the evolutionary value of our futures and the state of our nervous system, which we tend to experience as a variety of love – the personal moral command to promote human flourishing.

Chisholm goes on to emphasise, as does Dennett (1995), that it is misleading to think that reproductive success is promoted by every step of causal pathways. Dennett considers some pre-conditions which are necessary for morality but he does not present a firm opinion as to whether or how morality has evolved.

If the system underlying moral action has evolved, there are implications for the concept of free will because the individual does not have control of all aspects of the system. However, each individual still has to take decisions and how these are taken is far from predetermined. A rigid, automatic system would not work because of the multiplicity of stochastic processes which affect each individual. Hence, free will is vital for the effective functioning of a system which involves many, partly predictable variables.

5 The origins and value of religion

5.1 THE MORAL CORE OF RELIGION

Religion of some kind is ubiquitous in human society. This is not surprising if man is an essentially religious animal as stated by Thorpe (1974), see Chapter 1, Section 8 and Chapter 5, Section 4. The definition presented in Chapter 1, Section 1 is: *a religion is a system of beliefs and rules which individuals revere and respond to in their lives and which is seen as emanating directly or indirectly from some intangible power.* The religion forms the basis for individuals' practices and attempts to know and conform with what is right. A great diversity of religions is included by this definition.

The proportion of people in the world who are actively involved in religious practices is difficult to assess but Bruce (1995) estimated that in 1990 it was 14% in the UK. A much larger proportion of people is substantially affected by fundamental aspects of one or more of the religions prevalent in their own society. Indeed, many who never attend religious services would acknowledge themselves to be part of a religion, and many who would not say this organise their lives according to a code of living which stems from a religion.

A central theme of this chapter is that religions have a common moral code which is central to their functioning. They also differ in more peripheral aspects which may be conspicuous and regarded by some as of central importance (Chapter 5, Section 2). Parts of the moral core of any religion are widely known, but the extent of the moral component is often not fully appreciated. People who live in a society with one dominant religion are often ill-informed about other religions and especially about their moral aspects. The reason for this may be allegiance of a tribal nature to the religion in their own society, even if they are not actively involved in it. Indeed tribal rivalries are often linked with religions in a way which is nothing to do with the religions themselves. One of the consequences of these situations is that people tend to substantially over-emphasise the importance of the conspicuous aspects of religions and hence the differences among religions. Even those who write comparing religions (Smart 1998), or trying to explain religions (Hinde 1999, p. 239) dwell much more on differences than on similarities. When the impacts of religions on people over their lifetimes are thoroughly considered, the moral impact is so great in comparison with that of the more trivial, peripheral aspects of the religions that the similarities among religions are seen to be much greater than their differences. Some examples of key statements in various religions are given here to demonstrate this point. In appreciating these statements it is necessary to see through the jargon, which is familiar only to the initiated, to the actual message in the teaching which is intended for these people.

Buddhism originated in the teachings of Siddhatta Gotama (480–400 BC). The first commandment of Buddhism is non-injury to others 'ahimsa' and compassion on all beings e.g. 'I have made the vow to save all beings. All beings I must set free' (Vajradhvaja Sutra 280). In achieving the 'Noble Path' an individual should carry out good actions in terms of their effects on others and refrain from bad actions but the intention and quality of action are regarded as important, not just the result. There are prohibitions on the killing of humans and other creatures and a ban on drugs which modify the brain because mindfulness is part of the training for the path. As Harvey (2000, p. 52) puts it:

> 'The degree of wholesomeness of an action is seen to vary according to the degree and nature of the volition/intention behind the action, and the degree of knowledge (of various kinds) relating to it. A bad action becomes more unwholesome as the force of the volition behind it increases, for this leaves a greater Karmic "trace" on the mind.' Also (p. 21) 'A gift is said to be "purified" by the donor, the recipient, both or neither, according to whether they are virtuous and of good character or not.'

The route to enlightenment, 'nirvana', clearly involves altruism, as is clear from Suttoripata, I, 8:

> Contented, easily supported, with few duties, of simple livelihood, controlled in senses, discreet, not impudent, he (the individual aiming at a good life) should not be greedily attached to families . . . Just as a mother would protect her only child even at the risk of her own life, even so let one cultivate a boundless heart towards all beings. Let one's thoughts of boundless love pervade the whole world – above, below and across – without any obstruction, without any hatred, without any enmity.

As pointed out by Rolston (1999, p. 315) with reference to such Buddhist teaching, 'Many religions urge altruism'. The Hindu Law Books of Manu lay down duties, the stories of the God Visnu and the Goddess Kali are a source of moral inspiration and the God Siva is vengeful to those who transgress.

Mencius (or Meng-tzu) lived around 400 BC and was perhaps the major interpreter of Confucianism. Tu (1978) explains his fundamental teaching as follows.

> Each human being, Mencius seems to assert, is endowed with a 'moral sense', also known as the sensibility of the hsin. Inherent in the hsin are the four generations of the four basic human feelings: commiseration, shame and dislike, deference and compliance, and right and wrong.

The later teacher of Confucianism, Wang Yang-ming (1472–1529) argued that people should attempt to eliminate selfish human desires (ssu-yü).

The Ten Commandments of Judaism and of Christianity are clearly stated details of a moral code which requires the adherent to think of others. This code and a range of good qualities are described as 'God given', a term which can be equated with 'moral' in both religions. Augustine of Hippo (354–430) is one of many Christian teachers who spell out a number of moral actions as 'God given' or 'God's will' and then argue that all should try to ascend to God. Perhaps the clearest instruction in Christian teaching is to:

> love your neighbour as yourself
>
> *(Leviticus, 19: 17)*

The idea of loving God and loving your neighbour are regarded as inseparable. In modern Christian teaching 'your neighbour' is interpreted very widely. The mechanism for acting in a 'Christian' way is often stated as being to obey your conscience (see Chapter 4, Section 3). The great importance of altruism in following a Christian way of life is emphasised by Grant (2001).

Whatever an individual does will be known to God (or Allah) according to Judaism, Christianity and Islam. The idea of an all knowing deity is a very strong means of encouraging good behaviour and discouraging acts which harm others. If an individual believes that any action will be known, the likelihood of harm being done to others is very considerably reduced. The extent of this knowing is exemplified by Gert (1988, p. 266) as follows:

> 'Why should I be mad?' can be answered by: 'Because God commands' or 'Because God will be pleased if you are' and 'God knows when one only seems to be mad'.

The Qu'ran (Koran) makes it clear that Allah will reward and punish according to the morality of the individual's actions.

> 'He causes whom He will to enter into his mercy. But for the evil doer He hath made ready an afflictive chastisement' (Sura LXXVI, 31) and 'Verily the day of severing (the good from the bad) shall be the appointed time of all'.
>
> *(Sura XLIV, 40)*

The idea that all bad things which are done will be known is also stated in other religions but as Tu (1978) puts it 'the primary focus is self knowledge . . . as the ultimate source of morality . . . makes no appeal to the "wholly other"' in Mencian Confucianism, Chuang

Tzu Taoism and Ch'an (Zen) Buddhism. I interpret this statement as meaning that there is no deity who is wholly divorced from man. The inevitability of retribution if morally wrong actions are taken is still important although it is hoped that individuals will seek to achieve nirvana and hence avoid the need for any punishment.

The view that the key moral codes are the central part of all religions seems well supported by the holy writings of each religion. All include parables with a moral message, actual statements of moral codes and an idea of goodness personified in God or a god-like concept, or condition such as that in Buddhism. They also explain a mechanism by which those who cheat in reciprocal altruism situations or who carry out wrong or anti-social acts will be found out and punished sooner or later.

5.2 OTHER ASPECTS OF RELIGIOUS PRACTICE

Both simple and elaborate moral messages require a structure if they are to be purveyed within a community. This structure will be more effective if it is attractive to, or operational for, all humans so it is likely to take advantage of widespread human qualities and preferences. However, it will also be substantially affected by cultural variations in the particular human society. Hence religions would be expected to have three major kinds of components. In addition to the especially important moral components which have some genetic basis, there would be other components which have arisen as a consequence of natural selection and culturally determined components.

Most religions encourage the people in a society to meet one another at a certain time and place. Such meetings provide an opportunity for socially supportive behaviour to be encouraged and anti-social behaviour to be revealed and condemned. All individuals in the community are usually encouraged to attend such meetings but there is useful effect even if only one or two are gathered together. The group of people who meet together is called a church by Christians. The location of the meeting, which Christians also refer to as a church, becomes a focus of the religion and people change their behaviour when they are in the mosque, temple or church. In order to promote this, activities which might be morally questionable are discouraged or forbidden in the religious building or centre.

The argument for moral behaviour, as presented in this book, is relatively complex and more easily comprehended principles are needed for any religion. One help in providing these is the concept of a deity. The idea of someone whose behaviour is perfect, or of the person whom you can aspire to be or of someone who is aware of your transgressions, so you cannot do wrong without consequences, is a helpful part of religious structure for most people. Deities are often conceived of as somewhat similar to you, perhaps as an ideal mother or father figure. The statements of such a deity will carry weight and can be as simple as 'love your neighbour as you love yourself', or 'thou shalt not kill'. If the other members of the religious community support such a statement then it is easier to accept. Such a situation leads to the development of a belief structure.

The propensity for humans to accept belief structures is discussed by Hinde (1999, e.g. p. 53). The structure starts with the moral code and with the description of the deity or deities and it requires the participating persons to make statements of belief. People feel strong when they and many others are saying the same thing. This is especially true when each appears to have carefully considered the statement. However, there is also great appeal in ritualised statements whether spoken or sung. The repeated affirmation of faith is comforting and to be present in a group who are all chanting or singing the same thing can be comforting. The language and the particular nature of the chanting or singing will be different in different cultures. There will also be some cultural variation in the exact nature of the belief statements. Some of the statements are of faith in a deity and of willingness to behave according to the moral code. Others are more detailed and concern events chronicled in a holy book. These events may be miraculous, so to affirm them implies considerable acceptance of the details of the religious structure. All of these belief statements together constitute the doctrine or dogma of the religion.

Variations among the sects of a religion are usually associated with some variation in the composition of this dogma. Religions vary in the extent to which people are expected to accept the doctrine. For Hindus, there is much emphasis on conduct and the doctrine is a general guide. Jews are expected to accept a series of statements about belief and acceptance of even more doctrine is required from Muslims and Christians. Some sects of each religion are less rigid than others in the extent to which belief statements are required to be made and in the extent to which they must be made in the presence of others.

Holy books, like the Hindu Bhagavadgita, the Christian Bible or the Muslim Qu'ran, are a source of moral teaching and of the structure which helps the religion to function. They are revered because of their content: even narratives that have been written in the past by persons now unknown to us are sometimes treated as absolutely correct in every detail. During periods of history the Bible, the Book of Common Prayer and the Qu'ran have been taken literally in every detail. There are those who accept all aspects, for example of the description of the origin of the world, others who question this but do not question key statements of faith, such as the Christian Creed, and others who accept general principles but do not necessarily accept any wording of these books. The holy book may be seen as a prescription, a guidebook, or a source of inspiration but it has a significant effect on morality in the community.

Part of the structure which convinces people of the importance of following the moral code is to emphasise the importance of the deity or deities by attributing great powers to him, her or them. A deity who is all-knowing and able to exact retribution is likely to be thought of as being able to do other impressive things such as originating the physical universe, creating man and other species, causing the Sun to rise, making volcanoes erupt, causing great floods, transforming one substance into another, bringing the dead to life and curing all ills. Attributes associated with the proper regulation of human life are often mixed up with those associated more generally with living organisms and those concerning the physical world. Those who adhere to a religion may be asked to believe in individuals who can place stars in the sky, fly, or walk on water. These abilities seemed much more feasible at the time that the ideas developed than they do now that we have much more knowledge of the functioning of the physical world. However, there are some which seemed improbable seventy years ago when we had some knowledge, which seem credible with present knowledge, for example curing of sick people who had faith in the healer. Some of the actions and abilities of God, Allah and other deities described in holy books are part of the structure supporting the essential core of the religion but are not necessarily believed by persons who adhere to the religion. Individuals vary in which parts of the holy writings they accept and religious sects vary in how much acceptance they demand.

Some religions have several or many deities whilst others have one deity but many saints. Whilst there has been a trend, historically, towards monotheism, there are difficulties for many people to understand the concept of one god who is beneficent but also vengeful. Minor gods or saints vary in the area of life with which they are or were most concerned and hence are useful as role models and contributors to different parts of teaching. These also make easier the idea of communication with the deity. If God/Allah is so all-knowing and powerful, it could be difficult to talk to Him. There has, however, been some decline in the extent to which there is prayer via saints, for example in the Christian Catholic church and in Islam where the saint cults of 'Low Islam' are looked down on by many in 'High Islam'. Talking via, or with reference to, a saint may help. Of course priests and other holy persons also help in respect of communication with deities.

Prayer is a significant part of most religions. It may be communal and hence part of a familiar and comforting ritual, which consolidates social bonds within the group, or it may be individual. The prayer whose words are set out for all to use include exhortations to moral behaviour but also requests for aid which may sometimes include aid for acts which reinforce tribal decisions or which are aggressive towards other communities. Individual prayer, whether in a social situation or outside it, will often include both pleas for help which confers direct benefit on the person praying and requests for assistance in efforts to behave morally. Prayer can also take the form of a discussion about how to deal with short-term and long-term problems in life. There can be discussion with others directly, discussion as with others but in their absence, discussion with a deity, and requests for help or apologies to a deity. Each of these might be considered as prayer, although some would limit the use of the term to the last or to the last two situations. A private prayer may increase the chances that an individual will act in a moral rather than an immoral way, sometimes because a statement in a prayer cannot be ignored as easily as when the idea in the statement is never properly enunciated. Where the prayer is shared with others, the likelihood of cheating in social situations will generally be reduced even more. These good effects can occur whether or not the prayer is knowingly addressed to God.

Prayer in its widest sense is carried out by every person. However, many would not appreciate that and would laugh at the more ritualised forms of prayer such as prostrating yourself flat on the ground with your head towards Mecca, or kneeling on the ground and placing the hands together. There are many traditions and rituals in human societies and, whether they are within or outside religions, they may give pleasure and reassurance to those who are involved. They may also increase loyalty to the group and hence encourage the furtherance of its aims.

To outsiders, the most obvious characteristics of a religion are its symbols, images, public celebrations and buildings. When the largest and most elaborate building in an area is a temple, church or mosque, it is difficult to ignore it. If many houses in an area have a candle in the window or a symbol on the door because it is Eid, Divali or Christmas and if there are processions of people walking through the streets with or without accompanying music, the attention of all is drawn to the religion. Within religious buildings and elsewhere there may be symbols such as the cross and images of saints and of deities which are the focus of group or individual activities. Religions are supported by the various aspects of structure mentioned above. They often come to be seen as being of great importance in themselves. If they support the moral core of the religion and do no net harm then they are desirable.

5.3   GOODNESS, GLORY AND PARADISE

The concept of goodness or rightness, which is discussed at length in Chapter 4, Section 1 and other parts of Chapter 4, is a central issue for all religions. The difference between the philosophical discussion in Chapter 4, Section 1 and the teaching about goodness presented within religions is that the latter incorporates some of the structures and means of achieving goodness as well as the concept itself. Hence if belief in an all-knowing deity, or acknowledgement of adherence to the religion, or attendance at meetings associated with the religion, or reverence for religious symbols, books and buildings are necessary components of the structure which underlies the moral code, then these may be part of the teaching about goodness. It may therefore be said that to love God or Allah, to pray, to make a pilgrimage, or to attend or build a temple are good. The person who is not an adherent to the religion might need more information about intentions and consequences in order to decide whether or not the action is good. Some actions which most people would categorise as bad have been pronounced good and carried out in the name of a religion, mostly for tribal rather than truly religious reasons (see Chapter 5, Section 6). However, most of the religious structure aspects of what is regarded as good are either innocuous or weakly good when assessed by people outside the religion, as they would not have survived for long within the religion were this not so. For example, an important Christian command is 'Thou shalt love the lord thy God and love thy neighbour as thyself'. When analysed by an outsider, the first part is either good or innocuous and the second part is either good or very good depending on the interpretations of 'God' and 'neighbour'. Buddhist teaching focuses on the intentions of individuals and the effects of their actions on other people and other sentient beings. The importance of intentions is emphasised by the view stated by Harvey (2000, p. 53):

> An action performed without intending to do that particular action, for example accidentally treading on an insect, without any thought of harming . . . is not blameworthy and generates no bad karmic results.

Harvey also explains that (p. 49) Buddhism is different from 'act utilitarianism' because the end cannot justify the means:

> only wholesome means have the ability to conduce to wholesome ends

The Buddhist view of goodness involves elements of deontological, utilitarian and motivational approaches. In this and other religions there are different levels of goodness as well as different levels of evil.

Buddha is a reflection of the ideal state of an individual, and God and Allah are generally conceived of as perfect individuals. However, it is assumed that people who are themselves good and who have a high level of ability and of consciousness will have a more accurate concept of the deity. When Christian people have what they believe to be a religious experience of God, the image described is somewhat like themselves or like familiar depictions and is not like the deities of other religions. Those who report such visions or experiences have often gained considerable status, and sometimes influence and wealth, as a result of doing so. Nevertheless, the reports are almost always of kind, good deities. Presumably those who have visions of devils are less likely to report them but the vision of God as other than good is almost unknown. The idea of perfection is discussed in much detail by Buddhists as their philosophy is that it is achievable, even if only in the course of several lifetimes. The Noble Path requires eight factors to become fully satisfactory and according to Harvey (2000, p. 37) these are:

(1) right view or understanding, (2) right resolve, (3) right speech, (4) right action, (5) right livelihood, (6) right effort, (7) right mindfulness and (8) right concentration or unification.

In following the path or stream, a range of spiritual fetters have to be destroyed, including ill-will and sensual desire. There are some parallels in what is being aimed at here with the Christian idea of future resurrection. This seems a peculiar concept to many commentators on Christianity but Midgley (1994, p. 8) explains:

> What is envisaged at the resurrection is not, then, that corpses revive but that the soul develops other faculties to replace the body.

The rather woolly term 'soul' seems here to mean a spirit of an individual which continues after death.

Belief in some kind of after-life or reincarnation is a very important part of the Buddhist, Jain, and Hindu religions and is also important in Christianity and Islam. The fact that individuals have effects on others after they are dead is obvious. Influences and memories do not disappear when the individual dies. Hence, in that sense there is after-life, but the belief of many is in a much more tangible existence than that. The after-life for the Buddhist occurs on Earth but for Christians and Muslims it occurs in Paradise or Heaven, or in Hell. Pictures from Bibles and other Christian books often portray Paradise as a situation where the needs of all are provided for and all people are good. They may also show a child, a chick, a lamb and a lion resting together. This indicates a condemnation of normal inter-specific biological relationships and perhaps a fear of man's biology. Other representations of Heaven or Paradise refer in words or pictorially to glory and God's presence. In many cases the portrayal of Heaven or Paradise is of a place which contains persons with whom the artist might identify, whereas Hell also includes other humans and non-human beings of various kinds. Hell and fear of it has been a major weapon urging people to follow religious paths. The ultimate good state for Buddhists is 'Nirvana' where there is an end of every-thing which is unsatisfactory ('dukkha'), including suffering, and a destruction of attachment, hatred and delusion. It must be attained by a good and wholesome path.

5.4 THE EVOLUTIONARY BASIS OF RELIGION

5.4.1 From morality to religion

If morality has evolved and morality is the core of religions then the basis for religions has evolved. All human societies have a propen-sity for religion because religion provides a valuable structure for the moral code which is valuable in all of those societies. The religious framework makes it easier for the average person, or perhaps more im-portantly the likely transgressors of moral codes, to understand what should and should not be done. Those societies which formed such a framework were more likely to remain stable because anti-social, dis-ruptive actions would have been less likely to occur. They were also less likely to have uncooperative, unproductive individuals among their members.

In the course of the evolution of religion in humans, much of the moral code would have been established early on but the extent of observance of this code would have varied among individuals. The reli-gion would have developed in order to provide a structure which en-couraged the widespread observance of the moral code. Genes whose effects promoted the religious structure underlying morality would have spread in the population because of the beneficial effect on the bearer of the gene of the effective presence of the moral code in the so-ciety. The monitoring of moral behaviour and the principle support for the religious framework of the moral code may well have come more from females than from males because the resultant paternal care, male contribution to group activities and overall group stability had a greater benefit for females. However, once the religious framework for morals started to become established, males would have wanted to be involved in managing it and would have contributed to its devel-opment, perhaps as much eventually as females. The less desirable, tribalistic aspects of religion might have been more male than female influenced.

A number of predispositions of humans to respond to moral and other aspects of religion have been mentioned already. Wilson (1975, p. 562) said:

> human beings are absurdly easy to indoctrinate; they seek it . . . men would rather believe than know.

As quoted in Chapter 1, Section 8, in 1978 Wilson reiterated his view that humans have a predisposition to religious belief. In an argument close to that presented in this book, Crook (1980, p. 185) said:

> It seems likely that in history the legitimation of the complex reciprocities of political structures took the form of ethics rooted in religious propositions enunciated and maintained by a priestly gerontocratic structure. The origin of the major world religions with an emphasis on reciprocal altruism occurred in states where economics were moving towards the K end of an r-K continuum (India, China, Rome) and whose interior politics were increasingly dominated by legalism. The ethics of ego-transcendence by way of reciprocal altruism may thus have historical origins that are not divorced from socio-ecological and biological considerations.

Crook repeated this view (p. 287):

> under K conditions ethics emphasising altruism are more likely to have evolved. Indeed this latter principle is likely to underline [sic] the history of the religious systems that legitimated the major civilisations of the medieval period.

Crook refers only to the religions of the most elaborate civilisations and hence ignores the early development of each of these religions and religions in other human societies. The records and artefacts of early human civilisations do not reveal much about the ethical aspects of their religions. However, just as we now believe that high levels of human intellectual ability were present in human society many thousands of years earlier than was believed until quite recently, it may well be that elaborate religious structures supporting moral codes were present in very early human societies. The work of anthropologists investigating religions in modern and recent human societies, which had little contact with other religions, shows that moral codes concerning the true moral issues rather than just sexual and other customs were always present. In some cases, anthropologists sought to emphasise that these societies were different from Western European or North American society, or sought to make the societies appear ideal, so it is difficult to evaluate the work. It is clearly of great interest for early historians and anthropologists to look again at data with a view to checking whether or not evidence exists concerning the evolution of religion in general and of moral aspects in particular.

The high degree to which humans have evolved a propensity to respond to details of information from the culture in which they develop, in such a way that they readily respond to new crazes and behaviour fashions, is emphasised by Dawkins (1982, 1993, 1995). Much more wide-ranging than the examples quoted by Dawkins are the 'pan-cultural' 'relatively stable characteristics' of man discussed by Hinde (1991, 1999, p. 17). These include aspects of perception, responsiveness, motivation, emotion, and cognitive processes as well as various strategies for attaining goals. Much evidence pertaining to capabilities needed for reciprocal altruism and morality are detailed in Chapter 3 and some of these characteristics, and those referred to by Hinde, are qualities which the majority of people have and which predispose them to religious involvement. The commitment of people to relationships with other individuals (Hinde 1999, p. 98) also facilitates the more personal aspects of religion, both with other individuals in the same group and with the deity. It is easier to talk about personal problems with someone whom you know well or feel that you know well. The attraction of certain kinds of rituals to people has been discussed in Chapter 5, Section 2 and the likelihood of conformism within human groups in Section 3. People are also likely to respond to prophets with interest and enthusiasm and prophets have played a major role in Christianity, Islam, Buddhism, Judaism, Taoism and Hinduism (Hinde 1999, p. 49). Not all of these characteristics of humans are relevant specifically to the moral aspect of religions, and some are especially related to other aspects as explained in Chapter 5, Section 2, but the biological basis for moral behaviour, and for religious structures supporting it, is quite clear.

5.4.2 The concept of God in relation to the evolution of religion

We know from scientific information, such as that in Chapters 2 and 3, and from personal knowledge that any society is more than the sum of its parts. Societies themselves have qualities which influence what happens within them and modify the behaviour of individuals, most frequently in a beneficial way. Hence it might be said that there is a spirit within the society. Relationships amongst individuals who emanate from different societies and relationships between societies can also be influenced by such qualities of each society. There is considerable empathy between individuals who come from different social groups, even when these groups are very distant from one another. The more communication there is, the more empathy there is. When disaster strikes in any place known to us, we feel sympathy for those involved. Evidence of oppression or hardship elicits responses from the vast majority of individuals who receive the evidence. There is empathy for all and it crosses species barriers. All of these empathic feelings mean that throughout the world there is a common spirit. Human actions do not occur in isolation and the spirit is bigger than any individual and involved in all actions. This spirit is of great importance to humans and other sentient beings and is the essential part of the concept of God.

A point which has been made by many writers, for example Midgley (1992), is that arguing from supposedly objective science is not sufficient to deal with all issues and (p. 73) that to get rid of reverence for something greater than ourselves is harmful. The scientific method is of great value in many situations but it has not yet been possible to investigate some areas of potential knowledge. We should consider all available information and use appropriate strategies to improve understanding rather than depending solely on the results of scientific investigation. The idea that each individual is monitored by something which is not a particular human is useful for the individual in organising how to behave.

The concept of God as a spirit linking all sentient individuals is reconcilable with the biological background and usable by all. The spirit is dominated by the good qualities of the individuals. The monitoring of the actions of individuals, which involves deliberately or accidentally checking on whether beneficial acts are reciprocated and whether anti-social acts occur, is carried out by various other individuals. Most important sins will be discovered and many good deeds will be noticed but it is logical to say that God is involved in the monitoring. Similarly, wrong actions are likely to have consequences sooner or later and, whoever is the actual agent, they can be attributed to divine action.

Prayers are often communicated to other individuals and the conscience, which is affected by other individuals, may guide the person who has spelt out the problem. Hence it may be said that God is hearing prayers and helping via the individual concerned and via others. When people get together to take part in a religious service, provided that on some such occasions they think seriously about moral issues, they should be more likely to do the right thing and it is reasonable to say that they are in the presence of God. Acts aimed at glorifying God will do so provided that the intent and consequence are good rather than harmful on a worldwide scale. However, actions carried out in the name of religion which cause net harm will be against the interests of God. Individual people will have a different image of God and this does not matter. It is their consequent action which is important.

The meaning of God presented here is linked to existing and formerly existing sentient beings. God has power over physical events only in as much as the collective of sentient beings, individually or jointly, has such power. Hence God cannot significantly alter the passage of the Sun, or the timing of the dawn, or the explosion of a volcano. God did not create the universe but started to have an impact after sentient beings had evolved and interacted significantly with one another. Hence it could be said that God was involved with the creation of the moral and social world. There could be links with sentient beings outside Earth but at present, as far as we know, there are no links so God is the spirit of sentient beings on Earth. God will exist as long as there are such beings to have some influence. It is not illogical to think of a set of gods or a Trinity which together make up God, neither is it illogical to consider only one indivisible God with different qualities. The arguments about the number of natures and substantive existences of Jesus, which were sufficient to split the Orthodox and western Christian churches (Binns 2002, pp. 63–70), do not alter this concept of God. God is the same for all religions, and indeed for all sentient beings who have contact one with another, but God's actions will vary somewhat according to local circumstances. As communication amongst individuals improves, the influence of God should become stronger. It will be more difficult to avoid being found out if more individuals are monitoring and prepared to try to encourage good actions rather than bad.

There is no need to postulate a devil or anti-god. Hell is universal disapprobation and whilst there might be physical punishments for wrong-doing, punishment can be effective without this and there is certainly no need for any concept of a fire and brimstone hell. Nirvana and Heaven are useful concepts to describe what each individual, and sentient beings collectively, should aim at. In them, perfect individuals would have perfect relationships and each would be close to God.

5.5 THE EFFECTS OF NEW KNOWLEDGE ON RELIGION

Philosophical positions take a long time to develop and a long time to change. The same is true for the more influential religions. Even though new ideas can arise and spread rapidly through populations,

those concerning moral issues are generally either of minor importance in life or are returns to a previously existing position.

Both the religious framework for moral codes and the other,
more peripheral, aspects of religions are likely to have developed over
a long period and to be resistant to change. In the past, religions must
have been the subject of various attempts to undermine them, indeed
genes which promoted such undermining would certainly appear in
the population. Hence each religion would be expected to have change-
resisting qualities. These qualities are valuable when the net effect of
the religion on individuals in the society affected by it is positive
and the potential changes are damaging. However, it is a problem
when the change is required unless the religion, and hence the individual in the society, are to be adversely affected. Since religions are
fundamentally conservative and relatively unresponsive to change,
they are vulnerable in times when there is a rapid influx of new
knowledge.

Some former religions have been fragile because they included
practices or components which were unsound. Given time they might
have changed so as to exclude those unsound components. However,
when confronted with an alternative religion purveyed by a newly
encountered civilisation or an invader, they often died out. Strong
religions, which are likely to have changed in various ways during
their development, can still be greatly affected by new knowledge. It
will not be the key moral issues that the religion advocates which
will be threatened but rather the traditions of explanation and the
peripheral practices. The purveyors of every religion have felt it necessary to explain the origin of man and life in general, what happens after death and why dramatic natural events occur. Inevitably,
the explanation produced was very speculative but in some religions
it became a required belief for anyone who wished to be accepted
into the religious community. Gradually, as knowledge advanced,
certain beliefs had to be changed. For example, Ayala (1967) who
was a Dominican brother, pointed out that mankind could not have
been descended from a single human couple, Adam and Eve, because

a successful and diverse species could not go through a unique pair bottleneck. Ruse (2001) presents other criticisms of aspects of Christian doctrine.

Other components of religions which were speculative were those descriptions of the qualities of the deity which were designed to impress the hearers and convince them that they had better respect that deity and conform. Some powers which fall into this category are those concerned with ability to punish, and special powers are reported in parables which convey a useful message. As Dawkins (1993, 1995) and many other commentators have pointed out, Christian stories of the virgin birth of Jesus, the resurrection of Jesus after death, certain miracles such as Jesus walking on water, and some descriptions of Heaven and Hell were not credible to the average person in the 1990s. In the same way, the explanations in most religions of the origin of the world and of what happens after death are unlikely to be accepted by the educated (Hinde 1999, p. 33). Indeed the whole concept of a deity in human form is undermined by inability to explain the location of that deity. Hence statements made on behalf of religions can be so much at odds with current, widely accepted knowledge that people doubt the whole of the religious teaching. However, many people who adhere to religions do not feel it necessary to believe all of these statements.

The central moral elements of religions are the aspects which are least questioned with the advent of new knowledge. There are still difficult issues such as whether or when abortion can be justified but, for most people, these are not a reason for accepting or rejecting a whole religion. Customs concerning sexual behaviour may be presented as significant issues within religions but, as explained in Chapter 4, Section 4, many of these are not major moral issues. The deity or deities within religions are of central importance in religious structures and some of the explanations of their nature, qualities and abilities seem too unlikely for a significant proportion of people to accept. On the other hand, many individuals reject the less credible claims and have their own idea of the deity. Wilson (1978, p. 170) reported that 'According to a Gallup poll taken in 1977, 94% of Americans believe in God or some form of higher being'.

The most difficult problems for those who attempt to reconcile religious teaching with current knowledge concern explanations for physical phenomena. Some religious stories would be accepted in their entirety by few people, as elements of them are impossible according to present scientific knowledge, but they could all have been subject to human error in successive retellings. One response to this is that of Polkinghorne (1989, p. 87), who suggests that there can be divine direction in physical events without violation of the laws of physics. A God who created the universe is particularly difficult to imagine. God as the creator of life on Earth is also difficult to contemplate and there have been problems with such explanations for many authors who are aware of scientific knowledge. Rolston (1999) spends a lot of time discussing biological phenomena but there is then a considerable logical jump to his advocacy of creation. Ideas about the influence of non-human factors, and hence presumably of God, on genetic origins, or on how enzymes might have arisen during the initial appearance of living organisms are unconvincing to me. Creation ideas have proved to be a major obstacle to reconciling scientific knowledge and religion. 'Where did we come from?' is a big question but not one upon which religion should stand or fall. I consider other aspects of religious teaching to be much more important than these.

Some religious statements, which adherents to the religion may be reluctant to give up even though their foundation is not clear, cause other people to avoid the religion. Statements about the transformation of one individual into another, or the necessity for the subjugation of women, or the sending of a star to shine over a birth place, or the changing of water into wine or wine into blood are not credible to a high proportion of educated people. However, almost all of the statements which are most readily criticised are peripheral aspects of the religion. They are not needed for the moral code itself or for the principle support mechanism for that moral code. My views in this respect are not shared by the members of sects who believe that every word in their holy book is correct. For example the Jehovah's Witnesses (1996, p. 3) stated that 'The Bible tells us what we must do to please God' and 'Those who wrote the Bible were inspired by God. They wrote his thoughts, not their own'.

5.6   HARMS ASSOCIATED WITH RELIGIOUS PRACTICE

The greatest harms which have occurred as a result of the actions of those who would say that they are following religious teaching are the repression of individuals within societies and the initiation of conflicts between societies. Most of these actions could be described as being an aspect of tribalism but there are obvious links between religion and tribal attitudes. Most people do not, or do not wish to, recognise the great similarities among religions but concentrate on the differences. It is common for people to identify themselves with one religion whether or not they practise it. Religions often include practices, such as dietary regulation or circumcision, which tend to make their adherents identifiable and to make them feel distinct from others. Some of the teachings of religions emphasise their destructive qualities and explicitly or implicitly discourage fraternisation with unbelievers. Jews, Christians and Muslims are encouraged by some of their teaching to defend or fight for their faith, to actively try to convert others and to treat people of other faiths as outcasts. In a summary of the changing numbers of adherents to the world's major religions, Lloyd (1988, p. 52) says:

> It is clear from this picture that the Christian Church is very much on the march.

The militaristic analogy is clear. Such statements are especially strong in Islam, in particular in relation to unbelievers or persecutors of Muslims, for example (Qu'ran, Sura 22, 44):

> And how many cities which had been ungodly, and whose roofs are now laid low in ruin, have We destroyed! And wells have been abandoned and lofty castles.

Whilst 'religious' war or other conflicts are often about the greed of the initiators, the attitudes of those who lead the religion often reinforce such actions. In some societies the religious and secular leaders have been the same and the risk of conflict linked to religion is increased.

A fundamental problem for some religions concerns their statements about who is included in 'we' or 'us' and who is included in 'they' or 'them'. Alexander (1987, p. 254) points out the danger of a limited view of statements about what 'we' should do and of 'God bless us'. Us can easily be construed as meaning the people in this congregation, this community, this tribe, this nation or this religion rather than all people or all sentient beings. When saying the Nicene Creed 'we believe in one God', does a Christian include Allah? When saying 'we believe in one Holy Catholic and Apostolic Church' does the speaker think of the Church of England, or Christianity in general, or all people, or all sentient beings? There are occasions in many religious services where the words said about 'us' and 'them' could be interpreted narrowly. In some cases it is made quite clear that those who adhere to other religions are not included. On the other hand, each religion has clear statements about helping neighbours, who could be anybody, and about helping strangers, especially those in need of help. The divisive possibilities apparently allowed by religious statements are readily exploited by those seeking tribal gain, or personal gain at the expense of those who are not clearly of the same religious group.

Divisions within societies can also be perpetuated by religious teaching. Hinduism incorporates a system of castes within which individuals are expected to eat, socialise and marry. The principle is supposed to be that these are levels of holiness with the Brahmins at the top and the fifth class of untouchables at the bottom. The reality is that the levels are related much more to wealth than to holiness. The concept of a group of people who, because of their birth, are and will always be social outcasts, at least to some degree, is abhorrent to most non-Hindus. It is certainly my view that it is morally wrong and that it contrasts starkly with much other Hindu teaching which promotes moral behaviour. Christianity also combines teaching about charity to and responsibility for all, with statements which support ideas of strata in society and knowing your place. At a time when class distinctions within British society are seldom mentioned or considered, at least by more educated people, in Church of England services a hymn is still sung which includes:

> The rich man in his castle, The poor man at his gate, God made them high or lowly. . . .

Also, a frequently used prayer includes, as a significant part of it, requests to God to guide the leaders of the nation, the Queen and those who administer the law. This implies some order of precedence in society although it is much less hierarchical than the, now replaced, Catechism in *The Book of Common Prayer*, p. 197 which included:

> My duty . . . To honour and obey the King, and all that are put in authority under him: To submit myself to all my governors, teachers, spiritual pastors and masters: To order myself lowly and reverently to my betters.

There have always been some who condemned such statements as being against the fundamental tenets of Christianity. There is now a general decline in emphasis in religions on different sub-groups which are related to wealth or status in society.

Although racial tolerance has been preached within most well-developed religions, there are also examples of racism being promoted. In some cases it was a simple tribal or national competition situation in which the opponents happened to be from different races. In other cases, the two races were in the same nation but one was not discouraged from oppressing the other. Within various religions, slavery was permitted and some members of Christian Protestant churches in South Africa saw no problem in oppressing black people. However, there have been changes over time in moral attitudes to certain practices, such as slavery, and in decisions within religions about who are classified as us and as them. In general, those involved in promoting and organising religions have led society when changes to a more moral attitude have occurred.

A much more widespread suppression of minorities, within societies in which religions have played a significant role, has been the suppression of women. Women have played a significant role in Christian societies but, although they could be nuns, their role was mainly in teaching other women, and in mixed society none of the senior positions, and none of the influential positions at all were available to women. Christian teaching varied according to sect, with women having a higher profile in the Catholic than in the Protestant Church. Hindus have an important female deity and women often have significant senior roles in society but, on the other hand, the teaching of Islam is male-dominated to a high degree. Most of the Qu'ran appears to be addressed to men, whilst women are often spoken of as property or as rewards for good behaviour. In Sura 55, 40–56, among the rewards listed:

> for those who dread the majesty of their Lord shall be . . . damsels with retiring glances, whom nor man nor djinn hath touched before them.

Any society or religion in which women are substantially disadvantaged in comparison with men has a moral weakness in my view but the attitude which I espouse has appeared relatively recently in many societies and scarcely at all in some.

A harm in many societies is that resulting from the suppression or unreasonable restriction of sexual activity. Whilst Hindus glorify sexual activity between stable partners, some Christian sects have instilled guilt into even happily married individuals if they take pleasure in any sexual activity (see Chapter 4, Section 4). This attitude must have caused a very large number of personality disorders and may have led to poor quality parental behaviour on a large scale. The idea that celibacy is a desirable quality is also questionable on biological grounds. Forcing Catholic priests to remain unmarried seems to have resulted in far more problems than it has solved. I consider that a celibate priest, monk or nun is sometimes not in a good position to advise members of society in general. The monk or nun in a Christian, Buddhist or other religious order is deprived of more than just sexual activity. The average Buddhist is required to comply with five particular rules of conduct but monks and nuns must observe about two hundred training rules (Harvey 2000, p. 51). The permanent crushing of desire must have a very substantial cost and is entirely misguided in my view. A person who is involved in worldly activities can consider important moral issues and other important religious questions so it is not necessary to have a monastic existence in order to be helpful to others or creative. Investment in monastic life has been enormous over the centuries but, although some monks and nuns have made contributions to knowledge and philosophy, that contribution has been far less than might have been expected if the theory of monastic life were correct. Some individuals may be able to cope with life more easily in a monastic situation but they could be catered for without the necessity for all in their immediate community to live a celibate and relatively isolated life.

New religious sects often arise and their adherents can carry out acts and can have views which most in the world would condemn. Most of the sects might be called messianic in that the dominant figure in the sect either claims to be a saviour or messiah or claims to have effective contact with a messiah. Some of these individuals are fraudulent, some are deluded and few present as good a moral code as those of the established religions. As a consequence, most of these sects are short-lived but some do significant harm to their followers or to others. I see these sects as social phenomena which are not very relevant to established religion.

5.7   THE VALUE OF RELIGIONS AND THEIR FUTURE

The great value of religion is as a structure supporting and mechanism promoting moral codes. Societies are stabilised by moral systems. Individuals inside and outside the society can benefit from this stability and from the cooperation and altruistic acts, whether reciprocated or not, which moral systems promote. All major religions include moral codes as a central part of their teaching. The idea of God, or a god, who helps to reinforce moral codes is valuable, as are meetings and various rituals and methods of presenting and promoting the teaching.

Human society is very complex and it is difficult for individuals to appreciate and cope with its subtleties. There are other problems in life which can pose great problems for people and both social and non-social problems are easier to solve with social support in a stable and structured society. Religions generally facilitate such support, although examples of contrary effects have been given in Chapter 5, Section 6. The structure of the religions includes beliefs and practices which help people in various ways. Hinde (1999, p. 1) states:

> Religions have helped individuals to face injustice, suffering, pain and death. They have inculcated values of love and respect for others that have been fundamental for the smooth running of societies . . . But religions have also been used to perpetuate inequities, and religious differences have been used to justify torture and horrific religious wars.

In a general view of the effects of religious belief, Hood *et al.* (1996, p. 436) conclude that:

> faith buttresses people's sense of control and self-esteem, offers meanings that oppose anxiety, provides hope, sanctions socially facilitating behavior, enhances personal well-being, and promotes social integration.

People who have some social support and who feel that they are part of a community whose members have social relationships one with another are likely to be able to cope with problems in life better than those who do not have such support and relationships. Religions and some pseudo-religions (see Chapter 1, Section 8) can help in exactly the same way. Religions may give extra support because of the strength gained from belief and from a feeling of personal relationship with God, or with a god. Ways in which religion may help in coping with problems are reviewed by Pargament (1997). The benefit gained by people will vary from one individual to another, for example a person who lives alone may benefit more than one who lives in a family.

Those individuals whose welfare is better because of their direct involvement in religious practice are likely to feel happier, or more at peace, and will show less of other coping methods and less adverse effects. The likelihood of abnormal behaviour, abnormal physiological responses, depression, immunosuppression, clinical disease, injury and early death would be reduced. All of these effects are reviewed by Broom and Johnson (1993) and the effects of poor welfare on immune system functioning and disease are described in Broom and Johnson on pp. 121–128. People with high anxiety levels (Baker *et al.* 1985, Glaser *et al.* 1985) had reduced levels of T-helper lymphocytes in their blood; this suppression of immune system function was associated with increased plasma cortisol levels. Monkeys separated from their mothers (Coe *et al.* 1989), depressed human patients (Calabrese *et al.* 1986) and people who had been bereaved (Schleifer *et al.* 1983) showed reduced proliferation of lymphocytes which were stimulated with a chemical mitogen, also indicating immunosuppression. Similarly, human subjects showing depressive symptoms after bereavement had blood lymphocytes with lower activity of the natural killer cells which play a significant role in combating pathogens (Irwin *et al.* 1987). Such effects of poor welfare have also been demonstrated for a range of other animal species. Where the welfare of individuals is improved because of religious involvement, this may be evident as an improvement in health. Frequent religious practice was associated with better health in a study by Ferraro and Albrecht-Jensen (1991) and several other studies have produced evidence of this general kind. It is difficult to interpret such studies because the groups of people compared always vary in qualities other than extent of religious practice and because it is difficult to disentangle cause and effect. However, it seems very likely that the health of some people is improved by religious practice.

The general conclusion about the effects of belief and religious practice on individuals is that the welfare of some people is very greatly improved by it, whilst that of many others is somewhat improved. Much more important overall is that good behaviour is promoted and, for most of the time, the whole structure of society is stabilised, by religion. All long-lasting religions have these effects. There is some counterbalancing of this by the continuing adverse effects of intolerance and prejudice associated with some of the more peripheral aspects of religions. At times, tribal violence, which may be linked to religious differences, can lead to wars and can have very serious adverse effects on many individuals. As a consequence of substantial net benefits of religion to some people and some net benefit to most people, it is harmful for people to deride religion in all of its aspects. Balanced criticism of some peripheral aspects would not normally be harmful. Any critical comments should be tempered by giving credit to the positive aspects of religion.

What should those who have an organisational role in religions do to maximise the good done by religions and to minimise any harm? If religions do not change to take some account of currently accepted knowledge, the proportion of the populace who adhere to a religion is likely to continue to decline. For each religion the following should be done:

(1) Emphasise the moral aspects of its teaching.
(2) Point out to all that there are important common components of the moral code in the major religions of the world.
(3) Eliminate or minimise any practice or teaching which causes harm to individuals within or outside the religion.
(4) Eliminate or minimise any practice or teaching which is likely to encourage tribal or sectarian conflict now or in the future.
(5) Encourage interest in other religions and discourage efforts to magnify differences.
(6) Suppress or reduce in importance or modify any parables or traditional explanations of events which are clearly contradicted by widely accepted knowledge.

(7) Make the concept of God, or other deities, easier to comprehend and less imbued with qualities which elicit hostility or disbelief on grounds of widely accepted knowledge.

(8) Make other religious structures and practices which support the moral code and the essential elements of the religion more easy to understand and less repellent to people who are somewhat sceptical about some of their features.

(9) Make any statements which adherents are expected to say less prescriptive so as to allow more flexibility.

(10) Exclude nobody who shows an interest in important parts of the religion, even if they are not able to make some of the statements which are, at present, regarded as key aspects of faith.

Religions have always changed over time but, because of the explosion of new information, there is a need for much faster change if they are to survive and continue to have good influence. The changes proposed could result in a reversal of the current significant decline in involvement in religions, particularly among more educated people. I consider that societies need the support which religions provide and that there will always be religions of some kind. These may be the existing religions in modified form or they may be new structures for moral support which, whatever the intention of the initiators, will in essence be religions. Communications around the world are so effective now that it is very likely that there will be a more rapid blending or harmonising of religions. As in previous eras when this has happened, the result is often a better structure than that which existed before. However, it is also possible for extreme religious positions to arise. The more moderate and constructive religious philosophies should eventually come to be the most influential, but religious teachers and organisers should argue against those who espouse extreme positions and not ignore them. All should take a charitable view of the whole world when deciding on the reforms to be made to their religion.

6 Other views about the origins of morality and religion

6.1 MORALITY, RELIGION AND BIOLOGY AS MUTUALLY OPPOSED

The diatribes of nineteenth century theologians against evolutionary theory are well documented. The concern that the theory of evolution by natural selection would in some way invalidate or damage the Christian and other religions is frequently stated even now. Even in the last years of the twentieth century it was possible for the educational legislators of a State in the United States of America to propose the prohibition of the teaching of evolution in schools. However, although the view of man as having evolved from non-human ancestors is contrary to the concept of man held by many in the past, it does not contradict the important tenets of the Christian or other faiths, merely the stories which were contrived to explain the origin of humans. Even in 1870, many people did not take some parts of the Bible literally so the addition of another part which would not be viewed as correct was not as great a revolution as some people made out.

A much more long-lived and influential view which arose from the writings of Darwin and his followers about evolution was that processes in nature are just to do with competition. 'Nature red in tooth and claw' has been difficult to reconcile with codes of moral behaviour whether or not they were taught within a religious framework. The accumulated evidence against the view that all that goes on in animal life is calculated destruction of one individual by another, whenever this is possible, is presented in Chapter 2. Many kinds of animals survive and breed better if they collaborate than if they do not. 'Biological' and 'nature' do not refer to the dreadful origins against which we have to fight. However, many writers have assumed that this battle against our nature is the key to morality and civilisation. Hobbes (1651, Part I, Chapter 13) referred to morals as being invented by man. Moore (1903) argued that to pass from the factual 'is' to the normative 'ought' commits a basic error of logic which he called the 'naturalistic fallacy' so no scientific evidence can be relevant to understanding what is right or wrong and to speak of the evolution of morality is a contradiction in terms. A related position is that of existentialists such as Sartre (1943), who considered that morality requires free will so there is no nature or biological component. The cultural determinist view of White (1949) also excluded any biological contribution to civilisation e.g.:

> Culture may thus be considered a self-contained, self-determined process; one that can be explained only in terms of itself.

Even Rawls (1971), in his explanation of justice, makes no reference to any possible biological origins and does not see a knowledge of how the brain works as relevant to the questions which he considers.

Some biologists who have enthusiastically promoted Darwin's views and philosophers with an awareness of biological processes have argued that morality has not evolved. Dawkins (1976), as mentioned in Chapter 1, Section 3, took this view and Nagel (1970) said that he did not believe there could be a biological evolutionary explanation of ethics. Alexander (1979, p. 276) said that evolution has nothing to say about what people ought to be doing and Williams (1988, p. 438) went so far as to refer to morality as accidental and its production during evolution as stupid (see Chapter 1, Section 3). In quoting this, de Waal (1996, p. 2) calls it a startling statement and I agree with him, particularly because it seems to contradict Williams' other arguments. More recent statements include that of Feldman (1997, p. 49):

> With few exceptions, morality doesn't necessarily pay.

Whilst some moral actions might have a net cost, the case is presented here that moral behaviour does normally lead to benefits for the individual.

A different, or perhaps just more explicit, argument which would deny the evolution of morality is that of Fisher and Ravizza (1998, p. 1) that only persons can be morally responsible, so there could be no morality in non-humans. Rolston (1999, pp. 227–234) also argues against the evolution of morality, saying that a baboon cannot be a moral agent, but spends some time presenting the arguments for why a gene which promoted a tit-for-tat strategy would be success-ful and spread in a population. I believe that the case presented in this book counters all of these arguments and indicates that qualities which promote morality have evolved. I argue that morality develops in each individual as a result of interaction between a set of genes af-fecting a variety of functions in the brain and the information which results from the environment during development, including direct experience of the actions and instructions of others.

The link between evolutionary process and religion is ques-tioned by some authors but others have never considered the pos-sibility. My arguments relate in part to the core role of moral codes in religions. However Gert (1988, p. 256) considers that religion does not determine what is moral:

> People may fail to distinguish between a religion's support for morality and a religion's support for its own particular rules or ideals.

It is important to make that distinction but Gert does not seem to view religion as an important agent in promoting morality. Rolston (1999, pp. 292–307) refers to biological characteristics with links to re-ligion but makes no link via morality and concludes with the mystical statement (p. 308):

> Religion, we have been claiming, is a response to the prolific earth.

The arguments for an evolutionary basis for religion have been pre-sented in Chapter 5. These arguments, which may help to explain some of the human propensity for religion, do not in any way devalue religion. An increased knowledge of a subject has quite the reverse effect. This was a fundamental error of the objectors to Darwin's theory. Using the theory of the evolution of religion, I present the case for the current and future value of religion and make suggestions about how it could change so as to be even more valuable in its total effects.

6.2   THE 'SELFISH' GENE, SOCIOBIOLOGY, MORALITY AND RELIGION

6.2.1   Genes, selfishness and morals

Amongst the most important developments in knowledge in the last fifty years have been the substantial advances in our understanding of the ways in which social behaviour in general and altruistic behaviour in particular have evolved. These stem from the work of W. D. Hamilton (1963, 1964a, b). The concepts have been explained, popularised and extended by many authors including Wilson (1975, 1978), Dawkins (1976, 1986), Maynard Smith (1978, 1982) and Trivers (1971, 1985). However, in some of these writings, perhaps in order to shock with a clear point, statements are made which have wider connotations than their minimal scientific meaning. Some of these connotations are important far outside the academic argument and if widely quoted, especially out of context, may lead to false conclusions and do harm. For example, Wilson (1975, p. 3) says:

> the organism is only DNA's way of making more DNA.

However, although this statement has a true and dramatic message it is misleading in two ways. Firstly, the DNA depends on successive organisms for its existence so the implied separation of organism and DNA, phenotype and genotype, is false. Secondly, the use of the word 'only' belittles the importance of the organism. Organisms are very impressive and much more complex than their DNA. A similar kind of reductionist argument is presented by Dawkins (1976, p. ix):

> we are survival mechanisms – robot vehicles blindly programmed to preserve the selfish molecules known as genes.

It is misleading to use the word 'robot' because living organisms, including humans, are much more than robots. The word 'blindly' implies that the system is automatic and unseeing when there is much environmental influence in the development of every individual, and awareness is part of the capacity of individuals which itself develops as a consequence of interactions between genetic and environmental information. The use of the word 'selfish' is also questionable, see later. The key problem is that the words used have more than one meaning and it can be unclear which of these is relevant.

Statements such as those quoted above have been criticised by others, for example by Midgley (1994, p. 86). Sometimes the criticiser has a valid point but does not present a justifiably acceptable argument. Rodd (1990, pp. 203–211) says that Wilson (1975) writes as though the purpose of life is gene replication. She argues that he should distinguish in his arguments between function meaning selective value, and function referring to normal human purposive behaviour, and also says that we love our children because they are our children, not to preserve our genes. There is a valid point here but also a misunderstanding of the difference between proximal and ultimate arguments. The potential for human purposive behaviour and the potential for loving our children have evolved. There are genes that promote them which have spread in the population because their bearers were more likely to survive and reproduce than the bearers of alternative genes. It is important to discuss the genetic potential but it is also important to consider, at a different level, the human quality itself. The fact that you have genes which promote the loving of children does not mean that you have no responsibility yourself. Midgley (1985, pp. 122–131) argues for the importance of motive and Rodd (1990, p. 211) considers that:

> evolutionary theory and sociobiology cannot tell us anything about motives.

Whilst evolutionary theory could never tell us everything about motives, the evolution of the brain, hormonal systems, etc. does provide a propensity for having certain motives and taking certain decisions. A gene could promote charitable behaviour but each individual would develop in a different way in this respect because of variations in the environment of that gene. The actual decision to be charitable in a particular circumstance is under the control of the individual but influenced by the consequences of the action of that gene.

The use of the word 'selfish' by Dawkins (1976) and others to describe genes or molecules has caused many problems. The effect of a gene might be to bias meiosis in its own favour (Chapter 2 Section 4) or to promote reproductive output in an individual bearing it. Although Dawkins has often referred to it as a metaphor, the meaning taken by many people has been that: (1) genes are selfish and genes determine behaviour so behaviour is selfish, (2) humans are born selfish and cannot do much, if anything, about it, and (3) selfish behaviour is acceptable. Also, derived from such thinking, if genes are selfish and behaviour is selfish then morality could not have any evolutionary basis. Midgley (1994, p. 87) criticises Dawkins' usage of selfish, emphasising that only individuals can be selfish. Genes can have similar effects in many individuals so to refer to a selfish gene is misleading. de Waal (1996, p. 15) said:

> he borrowed a term from one domain, redefined it in a very
> narrow sense, then applied it in another domain to which it is
> completely alien.

Rolston (1999, p. 70) says that genes do not have a self so selfish is an inappropriate description of genes. He summarises (p. 47) the problem:

> 'The selfish gene' is vivid imagery. But imagery needs
> philosophical analysis, especially imagery that colors world views,
> even more if this seems to have a scientific sanction . . .
> scientists . . . borrow words from one domain of experience and
> transfer them to another. A careful analyst needs to be cautious
> about overtones also transferred . . . One must be careful not to let
> moral words, borrowed from nature, discolor nature.

A distinction between vernacular egoism, referring to the motivation and actions of individuals, and evolutionary egoism, which refers to genetic self-promotion, is proposed by Sober (1988). The latter term would apply to a plant. However, it is my view that terms such as selfish or egoism are best restricted to individuals. As explained in Chapter 2, Section 1, an individual is selfish if it is aware that its act is likely to confer benefits on itself and harm on others. If there was no such awareness but the act had these effects, this should be called harmful subject-benefit. The term 'selfish' should be used to refer to individual sentient beings only. The term 'harmful subject-benefit' could refer to genes or other entities or systems, whether living or not. It would not sound good in a book title!

The fact that competition between genes to get passed on to future generations of individuals does not mean that individuals must always show competitive behaviour has been explained many times in this book. Wilson tended to greatly emphasise competitive interactions between individuals but was clearly aware that successful strategies could involve collaboration (1978, p. 167):

> Human behaviour – like the deepest capacities for emotional response which drive and guide it – is the circuitous technique by which human genetic material has been and will be kept intact. Morality has no other demonstrable ultimate system.

Putting it in a more general way, Boyd and Richerson (1990) argued that the capacity for culture has evolved. Ridley (1996) and de Waal (1996) extended that argument to say that the basis for moral behaviour has evolved. A whole range of abilities in humans and other species are part of mechanisms for collaboration and altruism that are often more successful strategies than those which involve the individuals in more aggressive or selfish behaviour.

6.2.2   Whence religion?

Some scientists are strongly opposed to religion. Why is this when there is an obvious biological basis for many aspects of it? One reason may be a result of modern scientific philosophy. Part of the culture of scientific theory is that it should be defensible in its entirety. If there is a flaw in a part of a scientific theory, the whole structure of the theory falls. It is easy to find statements made by adherents to religions which are a result of attempts to explain phenomena for which no rational explanation is or was available. When scientists find arguments or statements presented from a religious viewpoint, which they cannot accept because of other kinds of evidence, they may dismiss the whole religion as nonsense. This is a logical error when a complex and heterogeneous system is being evaluated. The sound and useful parts of the religion should be accepted and the minor erroneous aspects ignored. Unfortunately, authorities within some religions have refused to acknowledge those who accept only part of the teaching, such as the sceptical scientist. This has enhanced the antagonism of those scientists. Perhaps, in part as a consequence of this, extreme statements have been made by some scientists such as likening religions to computer viruses.

The arguments presented in this book are that moral codes are the central part of each religion and a major stimulus encouraging the evolution of religion. A range of other biologically based propensities and predilections have become incorporated in religions. Hinde (1999) considers that the trigger for the initiation of religions was the desire to explain amazing events in the physical environment such as volcanic eruptions, storms and floods. Hinde also refers to the importance of the role of dreams (p. 81) and of meditation (p. 186) in the basic structure of religions. I see the explanation of dramatic natural events as insufficient to account for the long duration of religions. Dreams and meditation may produce ideas or comfort but are not of major importance.

The proposal by Reynolds and Turner (1983, p. 261) is that religions originated and persist because they are concerned with fertility enhancement. Reproductive success will be a consequence of having a moral code, with an effective structure supporting it such as that provided by religions. However, if the actual content of religion is considered, some include fertility rites but all long-lasting religions have much more substance than that. Hence fertility enhancement is just a small part of the selective advantage of having a religion.

The link between evolution, morality and religion is made by Wilson but in a rather scathing way. Wilson (1975, p. 120) said:

> When altruism is conceived of as the mechanism by which DNA multiplies itself through a network of relatives, spirituality becomes just one more Darwinian enabling device.

The reason for including the word 'just' here is probably to diminish the status of religion for it is not necessary for the argument. Wilson went into more detail (1978, p. 88) as follows:

> Beliefs are really enabling mechanisms for survival. Religions, like other human institutions, evolve so as to enhance the persistence and influence of their practitioners . . . All religions are probably oppressive to some degree.

The reference to 'other human institutions' implies that the individuals practising the religion are doing so in a selfish way and the oppression is more tribal than religious behaviour. Wilson also emphasises undesirable tribal aspects in (1975, p. 565) 'Xenophobia becomes a political virtue', i.e. love your neighbour but hate your enemies. These are valid criticisms of some actions but, in general, religion, as opposed to tribalism, acts in the other direction. Even the basis of altruistic acts is sometimes questioned, for example Rolston (1999, p. 318) says that religious acts, such as those of the good Samaritan, are pseudo-altruism because there is a selfish basis for the intention and the behaviour. This misunderstanding of altruism is discussed in Chapter 2. Despite such comments, my conclusion is that evolutionary processes make it likely that the development of religion in man will occur. As explained in Chapter 5, the criticisms of religious practices largely concern peripheral aspects or human qualities which are not principally to do with religion. The central moral aspects and their main supporting structure have effects which are beneficial.

In his more recent writings, Wilson (1998, pp. 265–296) argues for a difference between transcendentalists 'who think that moral guidelines exist outside the human mind, and empiricists who think them contrivances of the mind'. He firmly supports the empiricist view, criticises tribalism in religion (pp. 286–287) and points out, as does Hinde (1999), that much of religious behaviour could have arisen as a consequence of natural selection. However, he does not make the link between the evolution of morality, the evolution of the key aspects of religion and the consequences for his argument. Religions and the concept of God are important parts of the structure which has evolved as a consequence of the selective advantages of having stabilising moral codes which promote moral behaviour. Hence although moral guidelines are presented as a result of human thought, they have a basis in the propensities of the individual for moral action and information received from others with such propensities. The sum of the efforts of many individuals over many generations is outside the mind of individual humans now, but the final result in an individual is also, in part, a contrivance of the human mind.

7 Social and political consequences of this biological view of morality and religion

7.1 GOVERNMENT, FREE COMPETITION AND THE MAINTENANCE OF A MORAL SOCIETY

Ideas about the ways in which people should act, their attitudes, and especially their tolerance of other sentient individuals, may be altered by the views presented in this book. As explained by Broom (1981, p. 194):

> It is likely that reciprocal altruism is especially important and extensive in man because of our abilities to communicate and to recognise cheats . . . Many codes of conduct based on reciprocal altruism have been devised in human societies and these have been effective in promoting cohesion within the society which utilizes them. As communication improves, reciprocation is possible from more and more people so mankind becomes more like a single society with weaker and weaker barriers between previously discrete sections.

Given that moral codes in general are so important, how should societies be organised so that the greatest beneficial effect of such codes can be gained?

Hobbes (1651) described human beings as 'by their nature unrelentingly selfish'. This is clearly not correct. Another idea which is biologically untenable is that all of life is about competition and individuals should be: left to compete with no restriction, educated principally in methods of competing, or encouraged to compete whenever the opportunity presents itself. Preparedness for competition should be balanced with that for cooperation and assistance of others. Strategies for action which stabilise individual relationships and societies are, at least marginally, more successful than those which do not. There are implications of this for both individuals and governments. Some of these are relevant to personal conduct and some to political positions.

Crook (1980, p. 185) explained that reciprocation of favours can apply to governments as well as to individuals. A person can have a contract with a government in which the person does a favour to society, via the government, by paying tax or conforming with other rules and the government does a favour back by providing services such as deterring criminal action by others or maintaining conditions suitable for transport or communication. Gert (1988, p. 245) argued that governments should promote good welfare amongst individuals in the community. It is acceptable if, in order to do this, government sometimes carries out actions which would be unacceptable for any individual or non-governmental organisation within the society, for example imprisoning those whose behaviour is anti-social. Governments can act as a referee or mediator in disputes or promote systems which do so and can protect the weak against the strong.

A principle which is appealing to most people is that personal action, groups within society and government should promote some degree of equality within the society. However, as Sen (1992, p. 2) has emphasised, there is no common position as regards what should be equal, indeed:

> the judgement and measurement of inequality is thoroughly dependent on the choice of the variable.

The equality could be that of income, responsibilities, opportunities, utilities or something else of value such as health, power or honour. Sen proposes that it is the possibility to achieve 'functionings' that are of value which should be equal for each individual in a good society. These 'functionings' include sufficient food, good health and a reasonable life expectancy. The idea is similar to that of welfare, whether it refers to humans or to other animals (Broom 1996, 2001a).

Ridley (1996, p. 265), referring to countries, says:

> We must encourage social and material exchange between equals for that is the raw material of trust, and trust is the foundation of virtue.

He had previously argued that generous acts are done in expectation of some kind of reward but his reference to 'equals' seems very limiting. Brandt (1996, pp. 199–222) goes further, arguing that moral action by a government would involve some degree of aid to the needy and taxing of the rich. Hence resources would be given to poor people and poor countries. If a society includes within it people who are close to starvation, or are ill and unable to get treatment, or who have a substantially lower life expectancy than they could have, it is morally right for others who have spare resources to donate some of these resources. This would be done best via the government or could be done by other means. If people within a society perceive that there is great inequality within it and that no great effort is being made to rectify this situation, their concept of a moral system is challenged. Many of those who are disadvantaged in the society will continue to observe their moral code but anti-social actions, especially those directed against those with advantage in the society, are more likely than they would be if there was no perception of inequality. In extreme form, the disadvantaged cease to consider those with advantage as belonging to the same society.

As discussed in Chapter 2, Section 3 and Chapter 6, Section 1, human societies are not based principally on direct competitiveness but on the more successful strategies of cooperation and reciprocal altruism. Such factors are affecting larger and larger groups of individuals so it is not just the family or immediate social group who have to be treated in a civilised, moral way but it is all members of society, the nation and the world. Our concept of who is included in 'us' and who in 'them' has been changing fast (see Chapter 4) because of better communication and so possibilities for large-scale cooperation are increasing. As O'Neill (2000, p. 201 see also O'Neill 2002) put it:

Over the last fifty years boundaries have been becoming more porous. It has happened gradually, selectively and in faltering ways, and has transformed both political and economic life for countless people.

This view is being promoted more and more by religious leaders. The generalisation of small-group moral codes to the world as a whole is happening slowly with frequent examples of contrary actions. There are consequences of this extended moral structure for political systems and the distribution of power. If unlimited competition was biological and hence acceptable, a dictator could take over a community or country and oppress all within it. This is clearly unacceptable and most people believe that rebellion from within is reasonable in this situation and national or international action should be taken to prevent oppression by dictators. Similarly, unlimited competition can lead to oppression of individuals because they are female, old, children, a different race, weak, or poor, and most people would not only condemn such actions but be willing to vote against such a policy or pay to prevent it by extra taxes or making donations.

Individuals within societies will never be equal in all respects but who should be better rewarded? Some degree of provisioning for offspring is reasonable but enormous inequality in wealth at birth or a powerful hereditary aristocracy as the main order in society are unacceptable to many. A meritocracy, in which the more able are rewarded more than the less able, seems fairer but what ability should be rewarded? What if the ability is to be ruthless, to out compete others in illegal ways, or to profit from the exploitation or oppression of others? In these cases, or if it is to profit from the weakness of others, for example drug-taking or excessive consumption of alcohol, then this ability is not meritorious and the action runs contrary to the moral codes. The merit which leads to reward should be moral merit and action or use of ability which is constructive in society. Those who act in a way which promotes the stability of society or who invent or make something which is of long-term value should be rewarded. Those whose actions are immoral should not be rewarded at all. Rewards are not just financial but include status and general approbation. If a meritocracy is to function, rewards must be based on true merit, in particular moral merit. People should not be allowed to have substantial power unless they act in a moral way. Those elected to local or national office should receive no monetary benefit other than that agreed by the electorate and some crimes or truly immoral actions should disqualify people from office. Hence there should be mechanisms for checking on actions and performance and for removal of those who act in anti-social ways. The links between morality and law are discussed in Chapter 4, Section 6.

The most obvious contraventions of moral codes on a large scale occur when individuals with lower than average standards of morality become powerful or when groups within a society or even nations decide that another group is not within their moral framework. A leader of a group of bandits, gangsters, or Mafiosi or an individual who achieves power in a country may act in an oppressive way. Wherever this occurs and by whichever means the power was achieved, most people in the world would condemn the oppression. Rulers, or a ruling group, who kill people for arguing against them, suppress discussion or prevent freedom of movement or communication are acting in an immoral way. Group actions against other groups are universally condemned if they lead to extensive killing because it could not possibly be true that all of those people were themselves guilty of some great crime. The killing of many thousands or millions of people, such as that of Christian Armenians by Turks in 1915, of Jews by Germans in the 1940s, of educated Cambodians by Khmer Rouge Cambodians in the 1970s, of Tutsis by Hutus in Rwanda in the 1990s and of Bosnian Muslims by Serbs in the 1990s are now publicised and condemned rather than ignored. All killing or oppression during war is now being questioned as morality extends more and more to large groupings of people such as nations.

The arguments about how moral systems should be applied to the organisation of large groups of people, such as local and national government, are also relevant to the actions of commercial organisations. There is now considerable power in the hands of those who run large companies. Even those who run small commercial organisations have significant effects on society. The ideas that life is largely based on competition, that most practices are acceptable in the commercial world and that there should be a free market with few or no restrictions are at odds with moral codes and are incorrect. If each individual and company is financially rewarded according to ability and effectiveness at competing, even within the legal structures of the most organised countries, the result is that a substantial section of the populace loses out, being unable to compete effectively because of inability or misfortune. These individuals could die, be forced to leave the country, or become criminals. In the richest countries there might be as many as seventy percent living comfortably but, as a consequence, thirty percent are lacking in respect of food, health care and life expectancy. In poorer countries, the proportion of people in the seriously disadvantaged category where welfare is poor may make up ninety percent or an even greater proportion of the populace. Whether the ratio of successful to unsuccessful individuals is seven to three or one to nine, the whole system is unsatisfactory and should be changed. There is a moral obligation on the successful to help the unsuccessful within the country and for the more successful countries to help the weak in other countries. One way of improving the situation is for government to raise enough taxes from the successful to provide at least an adequate diet, health care and a reasonable quality of life for the unsuccessful. However, this will often still leave those who were unsuccessful in that particular competitive system feeling as if they are outcasts from society. At present in the affluent world there are differences in the philosophical positions of governments in the extent to which they pass legislation on moral issues and support both long-term initiatives for world preservation and the more impoverished sections of their communities. The more moral and civilised approaches tend to be supported by ever increasing proportions of the public but opposed by commercial companies whenever their activities might be restricted. In attempts to establish international agreements relevant to global warming and conservation, the organised opposition comes directly or indirectly from large companies. In the discussions at the World Trade Organisation, efforts to restrict trade to enforce legislation which has a moral objective is opposed by some influential companies and their lobbyists. Free trade in the world is presented as an ideal but it is obvious that open competition on the world market will prevent some morally based actions and will result in the strongest companies, and the countries in which they are based, becoming richer and the poorer countries becoming poorer. This has been happening very recently and the gap between rich and poor has been increasing within many countries and between the richer and poorer countries. World trade cannot be left to open competition. There must be a substantial governmental structure regulating it in such a way that at least the basic standards of living are promoted in all countries and high moral standards are promoted in the conduct of all organisations. The view that unlimited competition and free trade should be encouraged is a philosophical position and action that led to real harms for many people including the majority in whole societies. Hence this position will fail in the long-term. More efficient communication makes the speed of response greater now than in former times. Those who are harmed, or those acting on behalf of the underprivileged, will take drastic action to try to remedy the situation. Such actions may themselves be immoral and condemned by most people in the world, as in the case of the flying of hijacked airliners into the World Trade Center buildings. However, whilst in the short-term the perpetrators should be brought to justice if possible, the major response to the action should be to reconsider the basic philosophy which has led to the morally untenable situation and the alienation of people which triggered it. Great changes in the United States of America and in some other countries are clearly necessary.

With power in commercial organisations should go moral responsibility. If the leaders of large companies are perceived by the public as the new dictators, they will be hated in the same way that dictators in countries have been hated. In many cases, this will be associated with adverse effects on the sales of the company's products. Consumers are becoming more powerful in influencing what companies do by telling them of their views, threatening to withdraw their custom, or actually withdrawing it. Consumers can also lobby local and national government to curb a company's activities. A change in philosophy within companies is needed in order that there will be an end to the present situation in which, firstly, the morality within societies is being adversely affected by the actions of many commercial companies and, secondly, companies themselves are getting a bad name. Each organisation should have moral codes concerning what happens within the organisation and what effects the organisation has on others. A large company has responsibility to its employees, its customers and to all who might be affected by its activities. In particular, every company should consider, within an organised ethics committee, what harms might be done as a consequence of the company's activities and what good things could be done. Even if the company is not the subject of moral criticism by employees, customers or those directly affected by its activities, if much profit is being made, possibilities for using this to do good in the world should be investigated. Such actions should be accepted by shareholders. Governmental support or regulation can make this easier.

In a world in which there is much need, and concerted financial action can lead to projects which help to reduce the number of needy people, very high payments to some individuals seem entirely wrong to me. Whether the payments result from an investment return, performances such as singing, acting or playing sport, legal representation, damages following a legal action, holding some senior position in an organisation, or giving up such a position, payments of very large amounts of money are not justifiable. Wherever possible, systems should be changed so that the most excessive payments are prevented. If this cannot be achieved by other means, taxation should be used to prevent it, for example by limiting payments in different ways to some multiple of average national income. In the same way, governments should encourage companies to use, for good ends, part of any large profits which accrue, perhaps by specifying a proportion of profits on a sliding scale which must be used in this way. Profits above a certain level should not be given to shareholders or used for company expansion. Actions of this kind could have a significant effect in increasing the extent of morality in the larger scale components of society. By preventing harmful changes they could also reduce the extent of poor welfare in the world and increase the chances of a good quality of life for all in the future.

7.2 OUR VIEWS OF OTHER SPECIES

The broadening of the idea of 'us' to include more and more of humankind, as we have greater and greater contacts with all peoples, is tending increasingly to encompass animals of other species. This view was expressed by Singer (1981, p. 120):

> The circle of altruism has broadened from the family and tribe to the nation and race and we are beginning to recognise that our obligations extend to all human beings.

He went on to explain that other species are included, at least to some extent, within the extended family view of many people. The animals which people respect or have affection for, with the result that there is reluctance to kill them or cause their welfare to be poor, may be pets within the household, animals which are known as individuals, or particular kinds of animals such as primates, mammals or vertebrates. For many people the quality which counts is some threshold level of cognitive ability referred to as sentience.

Some people go further than having concern for sentient animals. Banner (1999, p. 174) says:

> Three commonly canvassed 'extensionist' alternatives to anthropocentrism take the higher animals (zoocentrism), living things (biocentrism), or ecosystems (ecocentrism), as proper objects for moral concern in addition to human beings.

As discussed in relation to concepts of right and wrong, Leopold (1949) and others have presented the view that there is something wrong about disrupting biotic communities. Wilson says (1984, p. 121):

> The one process now going on that will take millions of years to correct is the loss of genetic and species diversity by the destruction of natural habitats. This is the folly our descendants are least likely to forgive us.

And (1992, p. 303) 'Wilderness has virtue unto itself and needs no extraneous justification.' Johnson (1991, p. 5) also supports this view and argues that plants have interests and moral standing. I consider it important to distinguish among such values. The category of individuals with which we have an affinity, with which we identify because they are like us, is now often stretched to include sentient non-human animals. Some people also feel a link to non-sentient animals. The concern for plants, other living organisms such as fungi, bacteria and viruses and for ecosystems is real but different. We can speak of the welfare of animals but not of plants, or biological systems, or non-living objects. Hence the duties which we have to animals are not the same as those which we have to plants or ecosystems. Midgley (1995) suggests that candidates for moral consideration include works of art, buildings and geographical features as well as animals and other living organisms or systems including living organisms. However, whilst we have priorities concerning such entities, the nature of our moral obligation to individuals with which we identify is different. I support this view and consider that our perceived duty to humans and some other animals includes especially concern about their welfare. Banner (1999, pp. 179) also criticises the 'extensionism' argument which presents a smooth transition from concern about one's own close relatives to concern about ecosystems.

Similarity of functioning between man and a wide variety of animals is obvious to all and is a reason for feeling an affinity for and obligations to non-human animals. Epicurus (341–271 BC) considered that pain and pleasure were important determinants of what would be and what should be done in life and that other animals had such feelings. Arguing from a different viewpoint, Voltaire (1734) said that God gave animals organs of feeling and God does nothing in vain, therefore the animals are not simple machines. Darwin (1871, p. 123) described humanity to 'the lower animals' not only as a 'virtue' but as 'one of the noblest with which man is endowed'. To Darwin (p. 126) it seemed:

> 'extremely doubtful' that 'high mental powers, such as the formation of general concepts, self-consciousness, etc., were absolutely peculiar to man.'

Such similarities are discussed at length in Chapters 2 and 3. They have become very widely known because of television programmes, press articles and books which show how complex and clever many different kinds of animals are. As a consequence of such knowledge, people have feelings of conscience or moral outrage if animals are harmed. Such feelings are often greater if the animals look like juvenile humans and Coppinger and Smith (1983) propose that humans have selectively bred domestic animals so that they do have such neotenous characteristics. However, very many authors have stated that humans are completely different from other animals either without reference to evidence, or by striving to identify qualities which are not possessed by members of any other species. In doing this they may have been influenced by centuries of stories emphasising the need for the holy St George to slay the dragon, the epitome of beastliness. The decision as to whether non-human animals have the kinds of qualities which mean that they deserve to be treated well may hang on an assessment of something almost indeterminate, such as consciousness, but Bradshaw (1999), following the precautionary principle, argues that we should not demand absolute proof but assume that they have consciousness in case they do.

Although people may well always have had some conscience about what should be done to animals, most of the earlier writings showed little sign of sympathy for animals (see Johnson 1991, pp. 14–40). Aristotle (about 330 BC, 1254b and 1256b) said:

> Where there is such a difference as that between soul and body, or between men and animals . . . the lower sort are by nature slaves, and it is better for them as for all inferiors that they should be under the rule of a master.

The implication of this was that animals and less gifted people should serve their superiors. In the following century the Stoics believed that animals exist for the benefit of man and this was the view of most writers of the Old Testament of the Bible. St Thomas Aquinas (1259, book 3, part 2, chapter 12) was also entirely focused on man:

> other creatures . . . by divine providence they are intended for man's use in the natural order. Hence it is no wrong for man to make use of them, either by killing them or in any way whatever . . . And if any passages of Holy Writ seem to forbid as to be cruel to dumb animals . . . this is either to remove man's thoughts from being cruel to other men and lest through being cruel to animals one becomes cruel to human beings: or because injury to an animal leads to the temporal hurt of man.

The views of Descartes (1596–1650) were similar but as Midgley (1978, p. 231) points out, animals were not watched in detail at that time and little was known of the great apes. In fact, some people at that time were watching animals very carefully and using the information thus gained but these people were not able to write. Later in the seventeenth century, Locke (1690 paragraph 26) said that animals in their original state:

> belong to Mankind in common, as they are produced by the spontaneous hand of nature; and no body has originally a private Dominion exclusive of the rest of Mankind, in any of them.

Whilst humans could be enslaved and foreigners and savages were thought to have no moral code, few writers thought of animals as requiring much concern, exceptions being St Francis of Assisi and Bentham.

Some of the arguments used to deny that people had any obligation to treat animals well, except inasmuch as such treatment might encourage anti-social acts towards humans, seem unfounded or naïve now. The idea that, because animals cannot understand the Ten Commandments or Kant's arguments concerning moral principles, they could not themselves follow any moral rules and do not deserve good treatment is criticised in Chapter 4. The description of animals as wicked or immoral because they catch and kill prey or copulate in public seems as naïve as the conclusion that because of their wickedness, animals can be killed or tortured (Midgley 1978, p. 31). Kant (1780, p. 241) followed the arguments of Aquinas saying:

> If a man shoots his dog because the animal is no longer capable of service, he does not fail in his duty to the dog, for the dog cannot judge, but his act is inhuman and damages in himself that humanity which it is his duty to show towards mankind.

He did not acknowledge that the shooting of a baby or senile person would be subject to the same argument. Those people who considered that animals have some intrinsic natural value did not need to argue against cruelty or killing because of analogy to humans.

With increasing civilisation, there have been changes in ideas about how monarchs and other rulers should behave. In parallel with this, the term 'dominion over animals' has come to be interpreted as moral responsibility for animals rather than a right to use them. There has also been a reinterpretation of statements from various cultures and religions about the right way to manage the human environment in order to emphasise that there has always been concern for sustainability (Engel and Engel 1990).

Many relationships between humans and other animals have now been described which benefit both and which involve some friendship-type interactions. The shepherd and his dog are clearly interdependent and seem to value one another. The cattle which live with Fulani people in Africa may solicit grooming from humans and are generally very well treated. There is a large literature now on such interactions (see for example Rodd 1990, pp. 220) describing relationships of a type which must have existed for many thousands of years but which went largely unreported. The current ideas in most societies are moving very rapidly in the direction of condemnation of cruelty to animals or of any usage or action which results in poor welfare in the animals. As Banner (1999, p. 173) puts it:

> the boundaries of moral concern or obligation should be placed more widely.

Using a utilitarian argument, costs to animals should be balanced against benefits to humans or other animals when decisions are taken about whether particular procedures involving animals or uses of animals are acceptable. From a deontological perspective, some of the things which should never be done are actions where there is a severe adverse effect on a non-human animal. As described in Chapter 4, Section 2, the attitude of most people to questions about animal usage involve a combination of such deontological and utilitarian arguments. Whilst some actions which cause harms can never be justified by any benefit, most decisions should depend upon an assessment of cost and benefit which takes full account of costs to animals using our current knowledge of their functioning. Many dilemmas still remain.

7.3   MORALITY AND RELIGION IN OTHER SPECIES

7.3.1   Do other species require and have morality?

Much evidence is presented in Chapter 2 on the extent to which animals of a wide variety of species live in social groups, for most of the time in a friendly way, often cooperating with one another and sometimes showing reciprocal altruism. There are also conflicts and rivalries within social groups and it is possible for group members to kill one another. It is proposed in this book that individuals in stable, cooperative societies are more successful and hence that codes of behaviour which promote such societies and minimise anti-social behaviour are likely to have evolved in all social species. Various objections have been raised to using the term morality in relation to non-human species, some of which are discussed in Chapter 6, Section 1. Fisher and Ravizza (1998, p. 1) state that only persons have responsibility and hence only they can be moral. Bischof (1978) states that morality is 'apparently absent in animals, or specifically human' but refers to Lorenz's description of 'morally analogous behaviour'. Alexander (1987) describes the cooperation amongst workers within an ants' nest but says that they do not need morality because they are so closely related! It is argued in Chapter 2, Section 2.6 that they can show altruistic behaviour so this argument is wrong. Kummer (1978), as quoted in Chapter 1, Section 5, argues that morality involves the subject's appreciation of his own life and says that we cannot demonstrate in other species 'a symbolic representation of personal values'. This is an exacting demand and a high-level criterion for what constitutes moral behaviour. Rolston (1999, p. 212) says that:

> Ethics is distinctively a product of the human genius, a phenomenon in our social behaviour.

He goes on to quote de Waal (1996, p. 209):

> It is hard to believe that animals weigh their own interests against the rights of others, that they develop a vision of the greater good of society, or that they feel lifelong guilt about something they should not have done.

However, Rolston does not explain that de Waal is referring to the extremes of human abilities and moral actions and goes on to say that there is much more to morality than these extremes. He also refers to the conclusion of Singer (1994, p. 6) that we should 'abandon the assumption that ethics is uniquely human' but refers to Singer's examples of helping behaviour, etc. as 'pre ethical rather than ethical'. It would seem that, for Rolston, all moral behaviour must be present in order for the individual to be categorised as in any way moral, a curious position when there is such variety with age and amongst individuals in the extent of human moral behaviour. Even Ridley, who explains the importance of reciprocal altruism in various species, argues (1996, p. 38) that only humans 'Share a belief in pursuing the greater good' and hence have 'essential virtuousness'.

An important aspect of the arguments against morality in non-human species is that they involve the setting of a very high threshold or criterion. As explained in Chapter 3, Section 7, actions can still be moral if there is not full understanding of all issues involved in the action. However, the level of brain function which some other species have is quite sufficient for many moral actions. de Waal (1996, p. 210) argues that chimpanzees and bonobos have a significant degree of culture, language and politics and that the associated abilities are all that is needed for some aspects of morality. Other arguments about morality, or the lack of it, in non-human species centre on observations of behaviour which is considered to be immoral. For example, Hume (1739) points out that incest occurs in animals but these 'relations in animals have not the slightest moral turpitude and deformity'. Clark (1985) points out that inbreeding is harmful and that, in general, animals do have mechanisms to minimise its occurrence. Incest 'is indeed a natural evil'. Offspring are driven from the parental territory and siblings usually choose individuals with whom they have not grown up when selecting a mate. These actions and preferences generally prevent incest. Similar preferences exist in humans but there are examples of brothers and sisters who are reared apart not knowing one another becoming sexual partners. The basic mechanisms for avoiding inbreeding, and hence incest, are similar in humans in the efficiency of the system. Clark (1985) also argues that:

> A good mammal is one that cares for her young, gives deference where it is due, responds appropriately to her companions' signals of play, love and pride. It is reasonable to consider at least some of this behaviour as moral . . . The objectivity of morals can thus survive Hume's attack.

7.3.2 Empathy

Communication and the establishment of good relationships are enhanced if each individual makes some effort to see the other's view of the situation. O'Connell (1995) suggested that:

> empathy is the capacity to understand the experience of another person or an animal, cognitively and emotionally.

I should say that it is not correct to refer to the capacity to do so. Planalp (1999, p. 172) said that empathy is 'taking the other person's perspective'. This definition limits empathy to persons so it is better to refer to individuals. Hence my definition is: *empathy is the process of understanding the experience of another individual, cognitively and emotionally*. The concept existed as the single word 'Einfuhlung' in German but 'empathy' was not used until 1909. Examples of consolation and reconciliation behaviour are discussed in Chapter 2, Sections 2.7 and 2.8. de Waal (1996, p. 19) suggests that the attention paid to a chimpanzee about to give birth and the defence of that female by a friend shortly afterwards might involve empathy. de Waal and Aureli (1996) describe empathic distress spreading in groups of young chimpanzees. There are many occasions when humans show empathy for one another and many social interactions in mammals and birds are likely to involve some appreciation of the other as a functioning individual (e.g. Joubert 1991).

Some of the more striking examples of behaviour that indicates empathy are shown to animals of a different species. With reference to humans showing empathy, Serpell (1986) says that 'those animals that give us the most benefit evoke the greatest empathy, particularly farm animals and companion animals'. It has been suggested that empathy for other animals is greater in communities where humans rely more on animals for food (Curtis and Guither 1983) but as Phillips (in prep.) points out, there is little good evidence for this. The Buddhist concern not to harm animals certainly does not seem to fit, and are Inuit peoples the most caring about animals? Empathy, or at least great consideration, shown by other species is most extreme in symbiotic relationships such as that between cleaner fish and large reef fish. The alarm calls discussed in Chapter 2, Section 2.5 may involve empathy. Savage-Rumbaugh and Lewin (1994) describe an orang-utan with an amputated arm who investigated Savage-Rumbaugh's amputated finger and then put it against her own stump and looked at Savage-Rumbaugh with apparent empathy. The widely publicised records of dolphins and porpoises lifting towards the surface human swimmers who were actually or potentially in trouble seems to involve empathy. This array of anecdotes suggests that some degree of empathy can be shown by animals of various species.

7.3.3 Conclusions about morality and religion in other species

The term morality covers a wide range of actions. The simplest moral actions can be shown by many different kinds of animals whilst the most complex are shown only by humans. No individuals are moral all of the time and the occasional occurrence of moral actions may be of considerable significance in establishing relationships and stabilising a society. Hence it is wrong to conclude from the observation of one or several anti-social actions that the individual, or the members of the species, never show moral acts.

The moral codes of one species may well not coincide with those of another. For example, when parent coots have more chicks than they can possibly provide for, they kill the weakest one by drowning it. This action usually means that some chicks will be reared whereas if the parents had attempted to feed all of the chicks they might all have died. Hence it is not immoral in that species. In human society we consider the killing of young children as immoral although there have been circumstances when parents close to starvation have allowed children to die or have killed newborn babies. The coot is not social in the breeding season but humans and some other social species might be able to help one another to care for young in times of hardship. Some degree of morality exists in each animal which cares for its own young and morality is better developed in social species. When social groups are more complex and of long duration there is more moral behaviour. Humans live for a very long time and have many opportunities for reciprocal altruism and direct cooperation so morality is best developed in man. More elaborate brain function also makes possible a larger amount of moral behaviour.

Religions are structures underlying morality. Moral codes are communicated to young individuals to reinforce their natural dispositions to act in a moral way and the purveyors of religion help to do this. Since social animals other than man have feelings such as guilt, memories of past interactions and their consequences, relationships which are sometimes very long-lasting and elements of moral codes, they would benefit from some degree of structure to encourage the following of moral codes. This structure can be regarded as a precursor of religon. The idea of God as a spirit linking sentient beings is easily reconciled with such structures underlying moral codes. The empathy and respect felt by individuals of any species towards other individuals is a necessary link towards that common spirit. Hence some other species have the rudiments of religion and human attitudes towards other animals have a spiritual component.

8 Conclusions

Many animals, including man, live socially. There are various kinds of cooperation and the importance of these outweighs the importance of any disruptive competition which occurs so the individuals stay together. Some social interaction is altruistic. An altruistic act by an individual is one which involves some cost to that individual in terms of reduced fitness but increases the fitness of one or more other individuals. Altruistic thoughts are those which involve an intention to carry out an altruistic act or to reaffirm the value of an altruistic act which is being or has been carried out. Reciprocal altruism occurs when an altruistic act by A directed towards B is followed by some equivalent act by B directed towards A, or by an act directed towards A whose occurrence is made more likely by the presence or behaviour of B. Some altruistic acts have a high actual or potential cost but still occur. Such acts may be reciprocated. In many societies there is care for the weak. These and other altruistic acts may be noticed by others and result in some benefit to the altruist or may pass unnoticed. Where reciprocation of altruism occurs there must be mechanisms for detecting cheats. Harmful acts and their consequences may also be noticed and have consequences. The consequences of various possible strategies in social situations can be modelled but the strategies considered have generally been too simple. In biological systems, especially those concerning the brain, the assumption that the simplest explanations for observed events are correct is usually wrong.

The brains of many animals have great processing ability. In general, neither brain size, nor the possession of a similar distribution of brain regions to those which humans have, is a good indicator of intellectual ability. The ability to recognise other individuals and a high degree of awareness are present in a variety of animals, especially social animals. Feelings and emotions are valuable mechanisms which help individuals to cope with their environment and which have evolved. Feelings and cognitive processes are involved in dealing with moral issues and moral behaviour is described in many species.

It is proposed that the bases for the values which individuals have, and the ability to assess the best course of action, generally that which promotes cooperation and group stability, have evolved because those individuals which had such qualities were more likely to be successful. The moral structure is a set of values, feelings of obligation, desires to please and the utilisation of a capacity to analyse many of the consequences of actions for a range of individuals. Neither a wholly deontological approach nor a wholly utilitarian approach is adequate to further moral ends but elements of both approaches are necessary.

Moral acts are those which confer a benefit on other individuals which may or may not be closely related to the actor. This includes acts which support the structure of the society within which the actor lives and acts which, in addition to benefiting others, confer a short- or long-term benefit on the actor. Hence acts which are immoral are those which cause harm to other individuals, including those immediately affected and those which will be affected although they are distant or as yet unborn. Harms may involve poor welfare, either that involving difficulty in coping or that involving reduced fitness.

Most sexual behaviour is not a moral issue at all and, although some sexually motivated actions are immoral, in general the importance of sexual behaviour in morality has been greatly over-stated. The term 'sin' should be restricted to actions which are morally wrong in that they cause significant harm to others. Sexual codes and customs should be re-assessed to check the extent of truly harmful effects and particular attention should be paid to actions or rules whose real raison d'être is to help in male mate-guarding without conferring real benefits or preventing real harms.

Whilst some laws and their enforcement are of great moral value, others are not just. Morality and law can sometimes be at odds with one another.

It is argued that morality has a biological basis and has evolved. Reciprocal altruism has been important in the evolution of morality but it is not all of the biological basis as other mechanisms, such as feelings of empathy, compassion, love and guilt, are also involved. Human morality has, or had, parallels or antecedents in our immediate ancestors, other primates, other mammals and other vertebrate animals.

The emphasis placed on the evolution of morality does not in any way imply that moral actions are automatic or independent of environmental effects. Each behaviour of each individual is a consequence of interaction between genome and environment. Because of genes common to many individuals and similarities in many of the environmental factors affecting phenotype, many aspects of moral behaviour will be shown by most individuals. However, there will be differences in strategies and actions.

If the system underlying moral action has evolved, there are implications for the concept of free will because the individual does not have control of all aspects of the system. However, each individual still has to take decisions and how these are taken is far from predetermined. Free will is vital for the effective functioning of a system which involves many, partly predictable variables.

When the impacts of religions on people are thoroughly considered, the moral impact is so great in comparison with that of the more trivial, peripheral aspects of the religions that the similarities among religions are seen to be much greater than their differences. All human societies have a propensity for religion, in particular because religion provides a structure for the moral code which is valuable in all of those societies. If morality has evolved and morality is the cause of religions then the basis for religions has evolved.

Arguments for moral behaviour are relatively complex. The concept of a deity is helpful to support and simplify the arguments. The idea of someone whose behaviour is perfect, or of the person whom you can aspire to be or of someone who is aware of your transgressions, so you cannot do wrong without consequences, are helpful parts of religious structure for most people.

We know from scientific information and from personal knowledge that any society is more than the sum of its parts. Hence it might be said that there is a spirit within the society. The concept of God as a spirit linking all sentient individuals is reconcilable with the biological background and usable by all.

The meaning of God presented here is linked to existing and formerly existing sentient beings. Hence God cannot significantly alter the passage of the Sun, or the timing of the dawn, or the explosion of a volcano. God did not create the universe but started to have an impact after sentient beings had evolved and interacted significantly with one another. Hence it could be said that God was involved with the creation of the moral and social world.

Each religion would be expected to have change-resisting qualities. These qualities are valuable when the net effect of the religion on individuals in the society affected by it is positive and the potential changes are damaging. However, it is a problem when a change is required unless the religion and hence the individual in the society are to be adversely affected. Since religions are fundamentally conservative and relatively unresponsive to change, they are vulnerable in times when there is a rapid influx of new knowledge.

Statements made on behalf of religions can be so much at odds with current, widely accepted knowledge that people doubt the whole of the religious teaching. However, many people who adhere to religions do not feel it necessary to believe all of these statements. The central moral elements of religions are the aspects which are least questioned with the advent of new knowledge. The most difficult problems for those who attempt to reconcile religious teaching with current knowledge concern explanations for physical phenomena. Creation ideas have proved to be a major obstacle to reconciling scientific knowledge and religion. 'Where did we come from?' is a big question but not one upon which religion should stand or fall.

The greatest harms which have occurred as a result of the actions of those who would say that they are following religious teaching are the repression of individuals within societies and the initiation of conflicts between societies. Most of these actions could be described as being an aspect of tribalism. The divisive possibilities apparently allowed by religious statements are readily exploited by those seeking tribal gain, or personal gain at the expense of those who are not clearly of the same religious group.

Moral codes are the central part of each religion and a major stimulus encouraging the evolution of religion. The criticisms of religious practices and beliefs largely concern peripheral aspects, or human qualities which are not principally to do with religion.

The general conclusion about the effects of belief and religious practice on individuals is that the welfare of some people is very greatly improved by it, whilst that of many others is somewhat improved. Much more important overall is that good behaviour is promoted and, for most of the time, the whole structure of society is stabilised by religion.

If religions do not change to take some account of currently accepted knowledge, the proportion of the populace who adhere to a religion is likely to continue to decline. Ten recommendations for what should be done within religions in order that they survive and continue to have a good effect are made. The more moderate and constructive religious philosophies should eventually come to be the most influential but religious teachers and organisers should argue against those who espouse extreme positions and not ignore them. All should take a charitable view of the whole world when deciding on the reforms to be made to their religion.

The term 'selfish' is best restricted to individual sentient beings as its use to describe genes has been misleading. An individual is selfish if it is aware that its act is likely to confer benefits on itself and harm on others. Where there is no such awareness, the action could be called harmful self-benefit.

Human societies are not based principally on direct competitiveness but on the more successful strategies of cooperation and reciprocal altruism. This view is being promoted more and more by religious leaders. The generalisation of small-group moral codes to the world as a whole is happening slowly with frequent examples of contrary actions. However, unlimited competition is not biological and not acceptable.

Unlimited competition can lead to oppression of individuals because they are female, old, children, a different race, weak, or poor and most people would not only condemn such actions but be willing to vote against such a policy or pay to prevent it by extra taxes or making donations.

Who should be better rewarded in society? If a meritocracy is to work it must be based on moral merit, not on those who benefit themselves by means which harm other individuals or society in general. People should not be allowed to have substantial power unless they act in a moral way. Major crimes, including the killing of one group of people by another, should be publicised and prevented. National and international trade based on free competition leads to some consequences which are morally wrong. With an entirely free market economy, the weakest individuals in a country and the weakest countries will succumb. The system will fail, in part because criminality and terrorism will be encouraged whenever there are sections of the community with no hope of a reasonable life. The free market excesses must be curbed by government action.

There is now a widespread and increasing tendency, based on scientific knowledge, for people to think of animals of many species as sentient beings which have a value and are not just available for our unlimited use. Many of our ideas of moral obligation are extended to other sentient beings.

Many studies of a variety of species of animals indicate that they show moral behaviour, not just towards close kin but in the form of reciprocal altruism and altruistic behaviour which tends to stabilise their society. Many aspects of human morality have equivalents in the societies of other animals. There is evidence of empathy across species by humans and by other species. Morality need not be the same in different species. The feelings and cognitive functions which enable humans to have religions are present in other species of animals so some religion-like structure underlying moral codes could exist in them.

References

Ackroyd, P. 1998. *Life of Sir Thomas More*. London: Chatto and Windus.

Albright, J. L. 1978. Optimal group size for high-producing cows appears to be near 100. *Hoard's Dairyman*, 25 April 1978, pp. 534–535.

Alexander, R. D. 1978. Natural selection and societal laws. In *Morals, Science and Society*, Vol. 3. Ed. T. Engelhardt and D. Callahan. New York: Hastings Center.

 1979. *Darwinism and Human Affairs*. Pullman: University of Washington Press.

 1987. *The Biology of Moral Systems*. New York: Aldine de Gruyter.

Allee, W. C. 1938. *The Social Life of Animals*. New York: W. W. Norton.

Anil, M. H., Preston, J., McKinstry, J. L., Rodway, R. G. and Brown, S. N. 1996. An assessment of stress caused in sheep by watching slaughter of other sheep. *Animal Welfare*, **5**, 435–441.

Anil, M. H., McKinstry, J. L., Field, M. and Rodway, R. G. 1997. Lack of evidence for stress being caused to pigs by witnessing the slaughter of conspecifics. *Animal Welfare*, **6**, 3–8.

Anscombe, G. E. M. 1958. Modern moral philosophy. *Philosophy*, **33**, 1–19.

Aquinas, T. 1259. *Summa contra Gentiles*.

Aristotle. 330 BC (approx.) *Politics*.

 340 BC (approx.) *Nichomachean Ethics*.

Aureli, F. 1992. Post-conflict behaviour among wild long-tailed macaques (*Macaca fascicularis*). *Behavioral Ecology and Sociobiology*, **31**, 329–337.

Axelrod, R. 1984. *The Evolution of Cooperation*. New York: Basic Books.

 1997. *The Complexity of Cooperation*. Princeton: Princeton University Press.

Ayala, F. 1987. The biological roots of morality. *Biology and Philosophy*, pp. 235–252. Dordrecht: Kluwer.

Ayala, F. J. 1967. Man in evolution: a scientific statement and some theological and ethical implications. *The Thomist*, **31**, 1–20.

Baker, G. H. B., Irani, M. S. and Byrom, N. A. 1985. Stress, cortisol concentrations and lymphocyte subpopulations. *British Medical Journal*, **290**, 1393.

Banner, M. 1999. *Christian Ethics and Contemporary Moral Problems*. Cambridge: Cambridge University Press.

Barash, D. 1979. *Sociobiology: the Whisperings Within*. New York: Harper and Row.

Barton, R. A. and Dunbar, R. I. M. 1997. Evolution of the social brain. In *Machiavellian Intelligence II*. Ed. A. Whiten and R. W. Byrne, pp. 240–263. Cambridge: Cambridge University Press.

Bell, G. 1997. *Selection: the Mechanism of Evolution.* New York: Chapman and Hall.

Benham, P. F. J. 1984. Social organisation in groups of cattle and the interrelationship between social and grazing behaviours under different grazing management systems. PhD Thesis, University of Reading.

Bentham, J. 1781. *An Introduction to the Principles of Morals and Legislation.*

Bentham, J. 1984. An essay on pederasty. In *Philosophy and Sex.* Ed. R. Baker and F. Elliston. Buffalo: Prometheus.

Bercovitch, F. 1988. Coalitions, cooperation and reproductive success among adult male baboons. *Animal Behaviour,* **36,** 1198–1209.

Bertram, B. C. R. 1975. Social factors influencing reproduction in wild lions. *Journal of Zoology, London,* **177,** 463–82.

　1976. Kin selection in lions and in evolution. In *Growing Points in Ethology.* Ed. P. P. G. Bateson and R. A. Hinde. Cambridge: Cambridge University Press.

Binns, J. 2002. *An Introduction to the Christian Orthodox Churches.* Cambridge: Cambridge University Press.

Bischof, N. 1978. In *Morality as a Biological Phenomenon.* Ed. G. S. Stent. Berkeley and Los Angeles: University of California Press.

Blood, D. C. and Studdert, V. P. Ed. (1988). *Baillière's Comprehensive Veterinary Dictionary.* London: Baillière Tindall.

Blum, L. 1980. *Friendship, Altruism and Morality.* London: Routledge and Kegan Paul, pp. 234.

　1987. Particularity and responsiveness. In *The Emergence of Morality in Young Children.* Ed. J. Kagen and S. Lamb, pp. 306–337. Chicago: University of Chicago Press.

Blurton-Jones, N. G. 1987. Tolerated theft, suggestions about the ecology and evolution of sharing, hoarding and scrounging. *Social Science Information,* **26,** 31–54.

Blurton-Jones, N., Hawkes, K. and O'Connell, J. F. 1999. Some current ideas about the evolution of human life history. In *Comparative Primate Socioecology.* Ed. P. C. Lee, pp. 140–166. Cambridge: Cambridge University Press.

Box, H. O. 1978. Social behaviour in the common marmoset monkey (*Callithrix jacchus*). *Biology and Human Affairs,* **43,** 51–64.

Boyd, R. and Richerson, P. 1990. Culture and cooperation. In *Beyond Self-Interest.* Ed. J. J. Mansbridge. Chicago: Chicago University Press.

Bradshaw, R. H. 1999. Laboratory animal consciousness and feelings: adopting the precautionary principle. *Alternatives to Laboratory Animals,* **27,** 791–794.

Brambell, F. W. R. 1965. *Report on the Technical Committee to Enquire into the Welfare of Livestock Kept under Intensive Husbandry Conditions.* London: HMSO.

Brandt, R. B. 1979. *A Theory of the Good and Right.* Oxford: Clarendon Press.

　1996. *Facts Values and Morality.* Cambridge: Cambridge University Press.

Brody, J. F. 1998. *Healing the Moral Animal: Lessons from Evolution.* Unpublished.

Broom, D. M. 1975. Aggregation behaviour of the brittle-star *Ophiothrix fragilis*. *Journal of the Marine Biological Association of the United Kingdom*, **55**, 191–197.

1981. *Biology of Behaviour.* Cambridge: Cambridge University Press.

1996. Animal welfare defined in terms of attempts to cope with the environment. *Acta Agriculturae Scandinavica Section A. Animal Science Supplement*, **27**, 22–28.

1998. Welfare, stress and the evolution of feelings. *Advances in the Study of Behavior*, **27**, 371–403.

(Ed.) 2001a. *Coping with Challenge: Welfare in Animals Including Man, Dahlem Workshop Report.* Berlin: Dahlem Press.

2001b. Evolution of pain. In *Pain: its Nature and Management in Man and Animals*. Ed. Lord Soulsby and D. B. Morton. *Royal Society of Medicine International Congress Series*, **246**, 17–25.

Broom, D. M. and Johnson, K. G. 1993. *Stress and Animal Welfare*. London: Chapman and Hall.

Broom, D. M. and Leaver, J. D. 1978. The effects of group-housing or partial isolation on later social behaviour of calves. *Animal Behaviour*, **26**, 1255–1263.

Broom, D. M., Dick, W. J. A., Johnson, C. E., Sales, D. I. and Zahavi, A. 1976. Pied wagtail roosting and feeding behaviour. *Bird Study*, **23**, 267–279.

Brothers, L. 1990. The social brain: a project for integrating primate behavior and neurophysiology in a new domain. *Concepts in Neuroscience*, **1**, 27–51.

Bruce, S. 1995. The truth about religion in Britain. *Journal of the Scientific Study of Religion*, **34**, 417–430.

Budiansky, S. 1992. *The Covenant of the Wild.* New York: William Morrow.

Byrne, R. 1995. *The Thinking Ape: Evolutionary Origins of Intelligence.* Oxford: Oxford University Press.

Byrne, R. W. and Whiten, A. 1988. *Machiavellian Intelligence: Social Expertise and the Evolution of Intellect in Monkeys, Apes and Humans.* Oxford: Clarendon Press.

1997. Machiavellian intelligence. In *Machiavellian Intelligence II*. Ed. A. Whiten and R. W. Byrne, pp. 1–23. Cambridge: Cambridge University Press.

Cabanac, M. 1979. Sensory pleasure. *Quarterly Review of Biology*, **54**, 1–29.

Calabrese, J. R., Skwere, R. G., Barna, B., Gulledge, A. D., Valenzuela, R., Buktus, A., Subichin, S. and Krupp, N. E. 1986. Depression, immunocompetence and prostaglandins of the E series. *Psychiatry Research*, **17**, 41–47.

Cameron, J. and Abouchar, J. 1991. The precautionary principle: a fundamental principle of law and policy for the protection of the global environment. *Boston College International and Comparative Law Review*, **14**, 1–27.

1996. The status of the precautionary principle in international law. In *Interpreting the Precautionary Principle*. Ed. T. O'Riordan and J. Cameron. London: Cameron May.

Chance, M. R. A. and Mead, A. P. 1953. Social behaviour and primate evolution. *Symposium of the Society for Experimental Biology*, **7**, 395–439.

Cheney, D. L. and Seyfarth, R. M. 1986. The recognition of social alliances among vervet monkeys. *Animal Behaviour*, **34**, 1722–1731.

1990. *How Monkeys See the World*. Chicago: University of Chicago Press.

Chisholm, J. S. 1999. *Death, Hope and Sex: Steps to an Evolutionary Ecology of Mind and Morality*. Cambridge: Cambridge University Press.

Clark, S. R. L. 1985. Hume, animals and the objectivity of morals. *Philosophical Quarterly*, **25**, 117–133.

2000. *Biology and Christian Ethics*. Cambridge: Cambridge University Press.

Clayton, N. S. and Dickinson, A. D. 1999. Scrub jays (*Aphelocoma coerulescens*) remember when as well as where and what food items they cached. *Journal of Comparative Psychology*, **113**, 403–416.

Clutton-Brock, T. H. and Harvey, P. H. 1976. Evolutionary rules and primate societies. In *Growing Points in Ethology*. Ed. P. P. G. Bateson and R. A. Hinde. Cambridge: Cambridge University Press.

Cody, M. L. 1971. Finch flocks in the Mojave desert. *Theoretical Population Biology*, **2**, 142–158.

Coe, C. L., Lubach, G. R., Ershler, W. B. and Klopp, R. G. 1989. Influence of early rearing on lymphocyte proliferation responses in juvenile rhesus monkeys. *Brain Behaviour Immunology*, **3**, 47–60.

Colmenares, F. 1991. Greeting behaviour between male baboons: oestrous females, rivalry and negotiation. *Animal Behaviour*, **41**, 49–60.

Connor, R. L., Smolker, R. A. and Richards, A. F. 1992. Dolphin alliances and coalitions. In *Coalitions and Alliances in Humans and Other Animals*. Ed. A. H. Harcourt and F. B. M. de Waal. Oxford: Oxford University Press.

Coppinger, R. P. and Smith, C. K. 1983. The domestication of evolution. *Environmental Conservation*, **10**, 283–292.

Cords, M. 1992. Post-conflict reunions and reconciliation in long-tailed macaques. *Animal Behaviour*, **44**, 57–61.

1997. Friendships, alliances, reciprocity and repair. In *Machiavellian Intelligence II*. Ed. A. Whiten and R. W. Byrne, pp. 24–49. Cambridge: Cambridge University Press.

Crick, F. H. 1989. *What Mad Pursuit*. London: Penguin.

Crook, J. H. 1980. *The Evolution of Human Consciousness*. Oxford: Oxford University Press.

Curtis, S. E. and Gunther, H. D. 1983. Animal welfare, an international perspective. In *Beef Cattle Science Handbook*. Ed. F. D. Baker, pp. 1187–1191. Boulder: Westview Press.

Daly, M. and Wilson, M. 1988. *Homicide*. Hawthorne: Aldine de Gruyter.

Damon, W. 1983. *Social and Personality Development*. New York: Norton.

Dantzer, R. 2001. In *Coping with Challenge: Welfare in Animals Including Man*. Ed. D. M. Broom. Berlin: Dahlem University Press.

Darley, J. M. 1993. Research on morality: possible approaches, actual approaches. (Review of *Handbook of Moral Behavior and Development*). *Psychological Science*, **4**, 353–357.

Darwin, C. 1859. *The Origins of the Species*. London: Murray.

 1871. *The Descent of Man and Selection in Relation to Sex*. London: Murray.

Dasser, V. 1988. Mapping social concepts in monkeys. In *Machiavellian Intelligence: Social Expertise and the Evolution of Intellect in Monkeys, Apes and Humans*. Ed. R. W. Byrne and A. Whiten, pp. 85–93. Oxford: Clarendon Press.

Dawkins, M. 1977. Do hens suffer in battery cages? Environmental preferences and welfare. *Animal Behaviour*, **25**, 1034–1046.

 1993. *Through Our Eyes Only*. Oxford: Freeman.

Dawkins, R. 1976. *The Selfish Gene*. Oxford: Oxford University Press.

 1979. Twelve misunderstandings of kin selection. *Zeitschrift für Tierpsychologie*, **51**, 184–200.

 1982. *The Extended Phenotype*. San Francisco: Freeman.

 1986. *The Blind Watchmaker*. New York: Norton.

 1993. *Viruses of the Mind*. London: British Humanists Association.

 1995. Good and bad reasons for believing. In *How Things Are*. Ed. J. Brockman and K. Matson, pp. 17–26. London: Weidenfeld and Nicholson.

Dennett, D. C. 1984. *Elbow Room: the Varieties of Free Will Worth Wanting*. Cambridge, MA: MIT Press.

 1987. *The Intentional Stance*. Cambridge: MIT Press.

 1991. *Consciousness Explained*. New York: Little, Brown & Co.

 1995. *Darwin's Dangerous Idea: Evolution and the Meanings of Life*. New York: Simon and Schuster.

Devlin, P. 1965. *The Enforcement of Morals*. Oxford: Oxford University Press.

DeVore, I. 1965. Male dominance and mating behaviour in baboons. In *Sex and Behavior*. Ed. F. A. Beach. New York: Wiley.

Dittus, W. P. J. and Ratnayeke, S. M. 1989. Individual and social behavioral responses to injury in wild toque macaques (*Macaca sinica*). *International Journal of Primatology*, **10**, 215–234.

Dugatkin, L. A. 1997. *Cooperation Among Animals: an Evolutionary Perspective*. New York: Oxford University Press.

Dunbar, R. 1996. *Grooming, Gossip and the Evolution of Language*. London: Faber and Faber.

Dunbar, R. I. M. 1983. Structure of gelada baboon reproductive units: III. The male's relationship with his females. *Animal Behaviour*, **31**, 556–564.

 1988. *Primate Social Systems*. London: Croom Helm.

 1992. Neocortex size as a constraint on group size in primates. *Journal of Human Evolution*, **20**, 469–493.

Dunn, J. and Kendrick, C. 1979. Interactions between young siblings in the context of family relationships. In *The Child and the Family*. Ed. M. Lewis and L. A. Rosenblum, pp. 143–168. New York: Plenum.

Durkheim, E. 1894. *Les règles de la méthode sociologique*. Paris: Alcan.

Elgar, M. A. 1986. House sparrows establish foraging flocks by giving chirrup calls if the resources are divisible. *Animal Behaviour*, **34**, 169–174.

Eltringham, K. 1982. *Elephants*. Poole: Blandford Press.

Elzanowski, A. 1993. The moral career of vertebrate values. In M. Nitecki and D. Nitecki (Eds.) *Evolutionary Ethics*. Albany: State University of New York Press.

Emery, N. J. and Clayton N. S. 2001. Effects of experience and social context on prospective caching strategies by scrub jays. *Nature, London*, **414**, 443–446.

Emlen, J. M. 1973. *Ecology: an Evolutionary Approach*. Reading: Addison Wesley.

Emlen, S. T. 1970. Celestial rotation: its importance in the development of migratory orientation. *Science, New York*, **170**, 1198–1201.

Engel, J. R. and Engel, J. G. 1990. *Ethics of Environment and Development: Global Challenge and International Response*. London: Belhaven Press.

Fairbanks, L. A. 1988. Vervet monkey grandmothers: effects on mother-infant relationships. *Behaviour*, **104**, 176–188.

Falls, B. and Brooks, R. J. 1975. Individual recognition by song in white-throated sparrows: II. Effects of location. *Canadian Journal of Zoology*, **53**, 1412–1420.

Favre, J.-Y. 1975. *Comportement d'Ovins Gardés*. Paris: Ministères de l'Agriculture Ecole Nationale Supérieure Agronomique de Montpellier.

Feldman, F. 1975. World utilitarianism. In *Analysis and Metaphysics*. Ed. K. Lehner, pp. 255–271.

1980. The principle of moral harmony. *The Journal of Philosophy*, March 1980, 166–179.

1997. *Utilitarianism, Hedonism and Desert*. Cambridge: Cambridge University Press. pp. 220.

Ferraro, K. F. and Albrecht-Jensen, L. M. 1991. Does religion influence adult health. *Journal of the Scientific Study of Religion*, **30**, 193–202.

Firth, R. 1952. Ethical absolutism and the ideal observer. *Philosophy and Phenomenological Research*, **12**, 317–345.

Fischer, J. M. and Ravizza, M. 1998. *Responsibility and Control: a Theory of Moral Responsibility*. Cambridge: Cambridge University Press.

Francione, G. L. 1995. *Animals, Property and the Law*. Philadelphia: Temple University Press.

Fraser, A. F. and Broom, D. M. 1990. *Farm Animal Behaviour and Welfare*. Wallingford: C.A.B.I.

Freeman, D. 1983. *Margaret Mead and Samoa: the Making and Unmaking of an Anthropological Myth*. Cambridge: Harvard University Press.

Freud, S. 1930. *Civilisation and its Discontents*. New York: Norton.

Frisch, K. von 1946. Die Tänze der Bienen. *Österreichisches Zoologie*, **1**, 1–48.

Gallup, G. 1982. Self-awareness and the emergence of mind in primates. *American Journal of Psychology*, **2**, 237–248.

Gallup, G. G. 1983. Towards a comparative psychology of mind. In *Animal Cognition and Behaviour*. Ed. R. L. Mellgren, pp. 502–503. New York: North Holland Publishing.

Geist, V. 1971. *Mountain Sheep: a Study in Behavior and Evolution*. Chicago: University of Chicago Press.

Gert, B. 1988. *Morality: a New Justification of the Moral Rules*. New York: Oxford University Press.

Glaser, R., Kiecolt-Glaser, J. K., Stout, J. C., Tarr, K. L., Speicher, C. E. and Holliday, J. E. 1985. Stress-related impairments in cellular immunity. *Psychiatry Research*, **16**, 233–239.

Goldsmith, T. H. 1991. *The Biological Roots of Human Nature*. New York: Oxford University Press.

Goodall, J. 1986. *The Chimpanzees of Gombe: Patterns of Behavior.* Cambridge: Harvard University Press.

1990. *Through a Window*. Boston: Houghton Mifflin.

Gould, J. L. and Gould, C. G. 1988. *The Honey Bee*. New York: W. H. Freeman.

Grant, C. 2001. *Altruism and Christian Ethics*. Cambridge: Cambridge University Press.

Griffin, D. R. 1976. *The Question of Animal Awareness: Evolutionary Continuity of Mental Experience*. New York: Rockefeller University Press.

1981. *The Question of Animal Awareness*. 2nd edn. New York: Rockefellar University Press.

Griffin, J. 1986. *Well-being*. Oxford: Clarendon Press.

Groot, P. de 1980. Information transfer in a socially roosting weaver bird (*Quelea quelea*; Ploceinae): an experimental study. *Animal Behaviour I*, **28**, 1249–1254.

Guyer, P. 2000. *Kant on Freedom, Law and Happiness*. Cambridge: Cambridge University Press.

Hagen, K. and Broom, D. M. 2003. Cattle discrimination between familiar herd members in a learning experiment. *Applied Animal Behaviour Science*, **82**, 13–28.

Haig, D. 1993. Genetic conflicts in human pregnancy. *Quarterly Review of Biology*, **68**, 495–531.

Hamilton, W. D. 1963. The evolution of altruistic behaviour. *American Naturalist*, **97**, 354–356.

1964a. The genetical evolution of social behaviour. I. *Journal of Theoretical Biology*, **7**, 1–16.

1964b. The genetical evolution of social behaviour. II. *Journal of Theoretical Biology*, **7**, 17–32.

1971. Geometry for the selfish herd. *Journal of Theoretical Biology*, **31**, 295–311.

1975. Innate social aptitudes in man: an approach from evolutionary genetics. In *Biosocial Anthropology*. Ed. R. Fox, pp. 133–155. New York: John Wiley and Sons.

Harcourt, A. 1988. Alliances in contests and social intelligence. In *Machiavellian Intelligence: Social Expertise and the Evolution of Intelligence in Monkeys*. Ed. R. W. Byrne and A. Whiten, pp. 132–152. Oxford: Clarendon Press.

1992. Coalitions and alliances: are primates more complex than non-primates? In *Coalitions and Alliances in Primates and Other Animals*. Ed. A. H. Harcourt and F. B. M. de Waal, pp. 445–471. Oxford: Oxford University Press.

Hart, D. and Killen, M. 1995. Introduction: perspectives on morality in every day life. In *Morality in Everyday Life: Developmental Perspectives*. Ed. M. Killen and D. Hart pp. 1–20. Cambridge: Cambridge University Press.

Harvey, P. 2000. *An Introduction to Buddhist Ethics*. Cambridge: Cambridge University Press.

Harvey, P. H. and Krebs, J. R. 1990. Comparing brains. *Science, New York*, **249**, 140–146.

Harvey, P. H. and Pagel, M. D. 1988. The allometric approach to species differences in brain size. *Journal of Human Evolution*, **17**, 461–472.

Hay, D. F., Castle, J. and Jewett, J. 1994. Character development. In *Development through Life: a Handbook for Clinicians*. Ed. M. Rutter and D. F. Hay, pp. 319–349, Oxford: Blackwell.

Hediger, H. 1955. *Studies in the Psychology and Behaviour of Animals in Zoos and Circuses*. London: Butterworth.

Heinrich, B. 1989. *Ravens in Winter*. New York: Summit.

Heinsohn, R. and Packer, C. 1995. Complex cooperative strategies in group-territorial African lions. *Science, New York*, **269**, 1260–1262.

Hemelrijk, C. K. and Ek, A. 1991. Reciprocity and interchange of grooming and 'support' in captive chimpanzees. *Animal Behaviour*, **46**, 177–188.

Hemelrijk, C. K., Meier, C. and Martin, R. D. 1999. 'Friendship' for fitness in chimpanzees? *Animal Behaviour*, **58**, 1223–1229.

Heyes, C. and Huber, L. (Ed.) 2000. *The Evolution of Cognition*, Cambridge: MIT Press.

Hill, K. and Hurtado, A. M. 1991. The evolution of reproductive senescence and menopause in human females. *Human Nature*, **2**, 315–350.

Hill, K. and Kaplan, H. 1989. Population and dry-season subsistance strategies of the recently contacted Yora of Peru. *National Geographic Research*, **5**, 317–334.

Hinde, R. A. 1970. *Animal Behaviour: a Synthesis of Ethology and Comparative Psychology*. 2nd edn. New York: McGraw Hill.

1991. A biologist looks at anthropology. *Man*, **26**, 583–608.

1999. *Why Gods Persist: a Scientific Approach to Religion*. London: Routledge.

Hinde, R. A. and Stevenson-Hinde, J. (Ed.). 1973. *Constraints on Learning*. London: Academic Press.

Hinton, A. L. (Ed.) 1999. *Biocultural Approaches to the Emotions*. Cambridge: Cambridge University Press.

Hobbes, T. 1651. *Leviathan*.

1658. *De Homine*.

Hoffman, M. L. 1982. Is altruism part of human nature? *Journal of Personality and Social Psychology*, **40**, 121–137.

1984. Empathy, its limitations, and its role in a comprehensive moral theory. In *Morality, Moral Behavior and Moral Development*. Ed. W. Kurtines and J. Gewirtz, pp. 283–302. New York: Wiley.

1988. Moral development. In *Developmental Psychology*. Ed. M. Bornstein and M. Lamb, pp. 497–548. Hillsdale: Erlbaum.

Hood, R. W., Spilka, B., Hunsperger, B. and Gorsuch, R. 1996. *The Psychology of Religion*, New York: Guildford.

Hrdy, S. B. 1976. The care and exploitation of non-human primate infants by conspecifics other than the mother. *Advances in the Study of Behavior*, **6**, 101–158.

Hume, D. 1739. *A Treatise of Human Nature*.

1777. *An Inquiry Concerning the Principles of Morals.*

Humphrey, N. K. 1976. The social function of intellect. In *Growing Points in Ethology*. Ed. P. P. G. Bateson and R. A. Hinde, pp. 303–317. Cambridge: Cambridge University Press.

1986. *The Inner Eye*. London: Faber and Faber.

1992. *A History of Mind.* London: Chatto and Windus.

Hutchins, M. and Barash, D. 1976. Grooming in primates: implications for its utilitarian function. *Primates*, **17**, 145–50.

Huxley, T. H. 1893. *Evolution and Ethics*. London: Macmillan.

Irwin, M., Daniels, M. and Weiner, H. 1987. Immune and neuroendocrine changes during bereavement. *Psychiatry Clinical North America*, **10**, 449–465.

Jacobs, L. F., Gaulin, S. L., Sherry, D. F. and Hoffman, G. E. 1990. Evolution of spatial cognition: sex-specific patterns of spatial behaviour predict hippocampal size. *Proceedings of the National Academy of Sciences, USA*, **87**, 6349–6352.

Jehovah's Witnesses. 1996. *What Does God Require of Us?* Brooklyn: Bible and Tract Society.

Jerison, H. J. 1973. *Evolution of Brain and Intelligence.* New York: Academic Press.

Johnson, L. E. 1991. *A Morally Deep World.* Cambridge: Cambridge University Press.

Johnson, M. 1993. *Moral Imagination: Implications of Cognitive Science for Ethics.* Chicago: University of Chicago Press.

Jolly, A. 1966. Lemur social behaviour and primate intelligence. *Science, New York*, **153**, 501–506.

Joubert, D. 1991. Elephant wake. *National Geographic*, **179**, 39–42.

Kant, I. 1764. *An Inquiry Concerning the Directness of the Principles of Natural Theology and Morality* (in German). Berlin: Berlin Academy.

1780 (approx). *Lectures on Ethics* (translated L. Infield 1930). London: Methuen.

1781. *Critique of Pure Reason* (in German).

1785. *Groundwork for the Metaphysics of Morals* (in German).

1788. *Critique of Practical Reason* (in German).

Kawai, M. 1965. Newly acquired pre-cultural behavior of the natural troop of Japanese monkeys on Koshima island. *Primates*, **6**, 1–30.

Killen, M. and Nucci, L. P. 1995. Morality, autonomy and social conflict. In *Morality in Everyday Life: Developmental Perspectives*. Ed. M. Killen and D. Hart, pp. 52–86. Cambridge: Cambridge University Press.

Kitcher, P. 1993. The evolution of human altruism. *The Journal of Philosophy*, **90**, 497–516.

Kohlberg, L. 1969. Stage and sequence: the cognitive developmental approach to socialisation. In *Cognitive Development and Epistemology*. Ed. T. Mischel, pp. 151–235. New York: Academic Press.

Köhler, W. 1928. *The Mentality of Apes*. London: Routledge.

   1933. *Psychologische Probleme. Berlin: Springer.*

Krebs, J. R. 1974. Colonial nesting and social feeding as strategies for exploiting food resources in the great blue heron (*Ardea herodias*). *Behaviour*, **51**, 99–134.

   1990. Food-storing birds: adaptive specialisation in brain and behaviour. *Philosophical Transactions of the Royal Society B.*, **329**, 153–160.

Kropotkin, R. 1902. *Mutual Aid: a Factor in Evolution*. London: Allen Lane.

Kühme, W. 1965. Communal food distribution and division of labour in African hunting dogs. *Nature, London*, **205**, 443–444.

Kummer, H. 1968. *Social Organization of Hamadryas Baboons*. Chicago: University of Chicago Press.

   1978. Analogs of morality among non-human primates. In *Morality as a Biological Phenomenon*. Ed. G. S. Stent, pp. 31–47. Berkeley and Los Angeles: University of California Press.

Kummer, H., Goetz, W. and Angst, W. 1974. Triadic differentiation: an inhibitory process protecting pair bonds in baboons. *Behaviour*, **49**, 62–87.

Lazarus, J. 1978. Vigilance, flock size and domain of danger size in the white-fronted goose. *Wildfowl*, **29**, 135–145.

Leopold, A. 1949. *A Sand County Almanac*. London: Oxford University Press.

Lindauer, M. 1961. *Communication Among Social Bees*. Cambridge: Harvard University Press.

Lloyd Morgan, C. 1896. *Habit and Instinct*. London: Edward Arnold.

Lloyd, R. H. 1988. *A Pocket Guide to the Anglican Church*. Oxford: Mowbray.

Locke, J. 1690. *Two Treatises on Government Book II*.

Lüscher, M. 1961. Air-conditioned termite nests. *Scientific American*, **205**, 138–145.

Luther, M. 1525. *De servo Arbitrio*.

Macphail, E. M. 1982. *Brain and Intelligence in Vertebrates*. Oxford: Clarendon Press.

Marler, P., Dufty, A. and Pickert, R. 1986. Vocal communication in the domestic chicken. *Animal Behaviour*, **34**, 188–193.

Massey, A. 1977. Agonistic aids and kinship in a group of pigtail macaques. *Behavioral Ecology and Sociobiology*, **2**, 31–40.

Maynard Smith, J. 1978. *The Evolution of Sex*. Cambridge: Cambridge University Press.

   1982. *Evolution and the Theory of Games*. Cambridge: Cambridge University Press.

McFarland, D. 1985. *Animal Behaviour*, London: Pitman.

Mead, M. 1928. *Coming of Age in Samoa*. New York: Morrow.

Mech, L. D. 1970. *The Wolf: the Ecology and Behavior of an Endangered Species.* Garden City: Doubleday.

Menzel, E. W. 1974. A group of young chimpanzees in a one-acre field. In *Behaviour of Nonhuman Primates*, Vol. 5. Ed. A. M. Schrier and F. Stollnitz.

Messenger, J. B. 2001. Cephalopod chromatophores: neurobiology and natural history. *Biological Reviews*, **76**, 473–528.

Midgley, M. 1978. *Beast and Man: the Roots of Human Nature.* Hassocks: Harvester Press.

    1985. *Evolution as a Religion.* London: Methuen.

    1992. *Science as Salvation*. London: Routledge.

    1994. *The Ethical Primate.* London: Routledge.

Mill, J. S. 1843. *System of Logic, Deductive and Inductive*. London: Longman.

    1863. *Utilitarianism*. London: Longman.

Moore, G. E. 1903. *Principia Ethica.* Cambridge: Cambridge University Press.

More, T. 1516. *Utopia.*

Moss, C. 1988. *Elephant Memories: Thirteen Years in the Life of an Elephant Family.* New York: Fawcett Columbine.

Moss, C. J. and Poole, J. H. 1983. Relationships and social structure of African elephants. In *Primate Social Relationships: an Integrated Approach.* Ed. R. A. Hinde, pp. 315–325. Oxford: Blackwell.

Murdoch, I. 1970. *The Sovereignty of Good.* New York: Schocken.

Nagel, T. 1970. *The Possibility of Altruism.* Oxford: The Clarendon Press.

Noe, R. 1986. Lasting alliances among adult male savannah baboons. In *Primate Ontogeny, Cognition and Social Behavior.* Ed. J. Else and P. C. Lee. Cambridge: Cambridge University Press.

Nozick, R. 1974. *Anarchy, State and Utopia.* Oxford: Blackwell.

O'Connell, S. M. 1995. Empathy in chimpanzees – evidence for theory of mind. *Primates*, **36**, 397–410.

O'Neill, O. 2000. *Bounds of Justice.* Cambridge: Cambridge University Press.

    2002. *A Question of Trust.* Cambridge: Cambridge University Press.

Packer, C. 1977. Reciprocal altruism in *Papio anubis. Nature, London*, **265**, 441–443.

Pargament, K. I. 1997. *The Psychology of Religion and Coping.* New York: Guildford.

Pepperberg, I. 1990. Conceptual abilities of some non-primate species with an emphasis on an African grey parrot. In *Language and Intelligence in Monkeys and Apes.* Ed. S. T. Parker and K. R. Gilson, pp. 469–507. Cambridge: Cambridge University Press.

Petrinovich, L. 1998. *Human Evolution, Reproduction and Morality.* Cambridge: MIT Press.

Phillips, C. J. C. in prep. The evolution of empathic feelings for animals of other species and the implications for our attention to animal welfare.

Piaget, J. 1932. *The Moral Judgement of the Child.* London: Kegan Paul, Trench, Trubner & Co.

Pitcher, T. J. 1979. Sensory information and the organisation of behavior in a shoaling cyprinid fish. *Animal Behaviour*, **27**, 126–149.

Planalp, S. 1999. *Communicating Emotion: Social, Moral and Cultural Processes.* Cambridge: Cambridge University Press, and Paris: Maisons des Sciences de l'Homme.

Plato 380 BC (approx.) *Protagoras.*

370 BC (approx.) *Republic.*

Polkinghorne, J. 1989. *Science and Providence: God's Interaction with the World.* Boston: Shambhala.

Porter, J. 1995. *Moral Action and Christian Ethics.* Cambridge: Cambridge University Press.

Rasa, O. A. E. 1979. The effects of crowding on the social relationships and behaviour of the dwarf mongoose (*Helogale undulata vufula*). *Zeitschrift für Tierpsychologie*, **49**, 317–329.

Rawls, J. 1971. *A Theory of Justice.* Cambridge: Harvard University Press.

Reynolds, V. E. and Turner, R. 1983. *The Biology of Religion.* London: Longman.

Rheingold, H. L. and Hay, D. F. 1978. Prosocial behavior of the very young. In *Morality as a Biological Phenomenon.* Ed. G. S. Stent, pp. 93–108. Berkeley and Los Angeles: University of California Press.

Richards, R. J. 1993. Birth, death and resurrection of evolutionary ethics. In *Evolutionary Ethics.* Ed. M. H. Nitecki and D. V. Nitecki, pp. 113–131. Albany: State University of New York Press.

Ridley, M. 1996. *The Origins of Virtue.* London: Viking.

Riolo, R. L., Cohen, M. D. and Axelrod, R. 2001. Evolution of cooperation without reciprocity. *Nature, London*, **414**, 441–443.

Rodd, R. 1990. *Biology, Ethics, and Animals.* Oxford: Clarendon Press.

Rolston, H. 1999. *Genes, Genesis and God: Values and their Origins in Natural and Human History.* Cambridge: Cambridge University Press.

Rosenthal, D. 1990. A theory of consciousness. *Report No. 40 Research Group on Mind and Brain Perspectives in Theoretical Psychology and the Philosophy of Mind.* Bielefeld: Universität Bielefeld.

Ross, W. D. 1930. *The Right and the Good.* Oxford: Oxford University Press.

Rottschaefer, W. A. 1998. *The Biology and Psychology of Moral Agency.* Cambridge: Cambridge University Press.

Rousseau, J-J. 1755. *Discourse on the Origin and Foundation of Inequality Among Mankind.*

Ruse, M. 1982. *Darwinism Defended: a Guide to the Evolutionary Controversies.* Reading, Mass.: Addison-Wesley.

Ruse, M. 1986. *Taking Darwin Seriously: a Naturalistic Approach to Philosophy.* Oxford: Blackwell.

2001. *Can a Darwinian be a Christian?* Cambridge: Cambridge University Press.

Sahlins, M. D. 1965. On the sociology of primitive exchange. In *The Relevance of Models for Social Anthropology*. Ed. M. Barton, pp. 139–236. London: Tavistock.

Sartre, J-P. 1943. *L'être et le néant*. Paris: Gallimard.

Savage-Rumbaugh, S. and Lewin, R. 1994. *Kanzi: the Ape at the Brink of the Human Mind*. London: Doubleday.

Sawaguchi, T. and Kudo, H. 1990. Neocortical development and social structure in primates. *Primates*, **31**, 283–290.

Schaik, C. P. van. 1983. Why are diurnal primates living in groups? *Behaviour*, **87**, 120–144.

Schaik, C. P. van and Noordwijk, M. A. van. 1985. Evolutionary effect of the absence of felids on the social organisation of the macaques on the island of Simeulue (*Macaca fascicularis fusion*, Miller 1903). *Folia Primatologica*, **44**, 138–147.

Schaik, C. P. van, Noordwijk, M. A. van and Nurn, C. L. 1999. Sex and social evolution in primates. In *Comparative Primate Socioecology*. Ed. P. C. Lee, pp. 204–240. Cambridge: Cambridge University Press.

Schleifer, S. J., Keller, S. E. and Camerino, M. 1983. Suppression of lymphocyte stimulation following bereavement. *Journal of American Medical Association*, **250**, 374–377.

Schopenhauer, A. 1818. *The World as Will and Representation*.

Sechenov, I. M. 1863. *The Reflexes of the Brain* (in Russian). Moscow: National Academy of Sciences.

Sellars, W. 1963. *Science, Perception and Reality*. New York: Humanities Press.

Sen, A. 1992. *Inequality Re-examined*. New York: Russell Sage Foundation.

Sen, A. K. 1977. Rational fools: a critique of the behavioral foundations of economic theory. *Philosophy and Public Affairs*, **6**, 317–344.

Serpell, J. 1986. *In the Company of Animals*. Oxford: Blackwell.

Seyfarth, R. M. and Cheney, D. L. 1984. Grooming alliances and reciprocal altruism in vervet monkeys. *Nature, London*, **308**, 341–343.

Sherman, P. W. 1977. Nepotism and the evolution of alarm calls. *Science, New York*, **197**, 1246–1253.

Simonds, P. E. 1965. The bonnet macaque in South India. In *Primate Behavior*. Ed. I. DeVore. New York: Holt, Rinehart and Winston.

Singer, P. 1981. *The Expanding Circle: Ethics and Sociobiology*. New York: Farrar, Strauss and Giroux.

1994. *Ethics*. Oxford: Oxford University Press.

Skinner, B. F. 1973. *Beyond Freedom and Dignity*. London: Penguin.

1974. *About Behaviourism*. London: Jonathan Cape.

1978. *Reflections on Behaviorism and Society*. Eaglewood Cliffs: Prentice Hall.

Smart, N. 1998. *The World's Religions*. 2nd Edn. Cambridge: Cambridge University Press.

Smith, A. 1759. *A Theory of Moral Sentiments*.

1776. *An Inquiry into the Nature and Causes of the Wealth of Nations*.

Smuts, B. B. 1985. *Sex and Friendship in Baboons*. New York: Aldine.

Sober, E. 1988. What is evolutionary altruism? *Canadian Journal of Philosophy*, **14**, 75–99.

Sober, E. and Wilson, D. S. 1998. *Unto Others: the Evolution and Psychology of Unselfish Behavior*. Cambridge: Harvard University Press.

Sommerville, B. A. and Broom, D. M. 1998. Olfactory awareness. *Applied Animal Behaviour Science*, **57**, 269–286.

Spencer-Booth, Y. 1970. The relationships between mammalian young and conspecifics other than mothers and peers: a review. *Advances in the Study of Behavior*, **3**, 120–194.

Stammbach, E. 1988. Group responses to specially skilled individuals in a *Macaca fascicularis* group. *Behaviour*, **107**, 241–266.

Stanford, C. B., Wallis, J., Mpongo, E. and Goodall, J. 1994. Hunting decisions in wild chimpanzees. *Behaviour*, **131**, 1–18.

Stent, G. S. 1978. Introduction. In *Morality as a Biological Phenomenon*. Ed. G. S. Stent, pp. 1–18. Berkeley and Los Angeles: University of California Press.

Strier, K. B. 1992. Causes and consequences of non aggression in the woolly monkey, or muriqui (*Brachyteles arachnoides*). In *Aggression and Peacefulness in Humans and Other Species*. Ed. J. Silverberg and J. P. Gray, pp. 100–116. New York: Oxford University Press.

Struhsaker, T. T. 1967a. Social structure among vervet monkeys (*Cercopithecus aethiops*). *Behaviour*, **29**, 83–121.

1967b. Auditory communications among vervet monkeys (*Cercopithecus aethiops*). In *Social Communication Among Primates*. Ed. S. A. Altmann. Chicago: University of Chicago Press.

Struhsaker, T. T. and Leland, L. 1979. Ecology of five sympatric monkey species in the Kibale forest, Uganda. *Advances in the Study of Behavior*, **9**, 159–228.

Strum, S. C., Forster, D. and Hutchings, E. 1997. Why Machiavellian intelligence might not be Machiavellian. In: *Machiavellian Intelligence II: Extensions and Evaluations*. Ed. A. Whiten and R. W. Byrne, pp. 50–85. Cambridge: Cambridge University Press.

Sykes, S. 1984. *The Identity of Christianity*, London: SPCK.

Temerlin, M. K. 1975. *Lucy: Growing up Human*. Palo Alto: Science and Behavior Books.

Thompson, N. 1976. My descent from the monkey. In *Perspectives in Ethology*. Ed. P. Bateson and P. Klopfer, pp. 221–230. New York: Plenum.

Thompson, P. (Ed.) 1995. *Issues in Evolutionary Ethics*. Albany: State University of New York Press.

Thorpe, W. H. 1974. *Animal Nature and Human Nature*. London: Methuen.

Timothy, H. 1991. *The Biological Roots of Human Nature*. New York: Oxford University Press.

Trivers, R. 1985. *Social Evolution*. Menlo Park: Benjamin Cummings.

Trivers, R. L. 1971. The evolution of reciprocal altruism. *Quarterly Review of Biology*, **46**, 35–57.

1974. Parent-offspring conflict. *American Zoologist*, **14**, 249–264.

Tu, W. 1978. The moral universal from the perspectives of East Asian thought. In *Morality as a Biological Phenomenon*. Ed. G. S. Stent, pp. 167–189. Berkeley and Los Angeles: University of California Press.

Turnbull, C. M. 1972. *The Mountain People*. Touchstone: New York.

Voltaire, F-M. A. 1734. *Philosophical Letters*.

Waal, F. B. M. de 1982. *Chimpanzee Politics: Power and Sex among Apes*. London: Jonathan Cape.

1984. Sex differences in the formation of coalitions among chimpanzees. *Ethology and Sociobiology*, **5**, 239–255.

1989. Food sharing and reciprocal obligations among chimpanzees. *Journal of Human Evolution*, **18**, 433–459.

1996. *Good Natured*. Cambridge: Harvard University Press.

Waal, F. B. M. de and Aureli, F. 1996. Consolation, reconciliation and a possible cognitive difference between macaques and chimpanzees. In *Reaching into Thought: the Minds of the Great Apes*. Ed. A. E. Russon, K. A. Bard and S. T. Parker, pp. 80–110. Cambridge: Cambridge University Press.

Waal, F. M. B. de and Luttrell, L. 1988. Mechanisms of social reciprocity in three primate species: symmetrical relationship characteristics or cognition. *Ethology and Sociobiology*, **9**, 101–118.

Ward, P. 1965. Feeding ecology of the black-faced dioch *Quelea quelea* in Nigeria. *Ibis*, **107**, 173–214.

1972. The functional significance of mass drinking flights by Sandgrouse: Pteroclididae. *Ibis*, **114**, 533–536.

Ward, P. and Zahavi, A. 1973. The importance of certain assemblages of birds as 'information centres' for food-finding. *Ibis*, **115**, 517–534.

Warner, G. F. 1971. On the ecology of a dense bed of the brittle-star *Ophiothrix fragilis*. *Journal of the Marine Biological Association of the United Kingdom*, **51**, 267–282.

Watts, D. P. 1994. Social relationships of immigrant and resident female mountain gorillas, II. Relatedness, residence, and relationships between females. *American Journal of Primatology*, **32**, 13–20.

Weiskrantz, L. 1997. *Consciousness Lost and Found: a Neuropsychological Exploration*. Oxford: Oxford University Press.

Westermarck, E. 1906. *The Origin and Development of the Moral Ideas*. New York: Macmillan.

White, L. A. 1949. *The Science of Culture: a Study of Man and Civilisation*. New York: Farrar, Strauss and Giroux.

Wiepkema, P. R. 1985. Abnormal behaviour in farm animals: ethological implications. *Netherlands Journal of Zoology*, **35**, 279–289.

Wilkinson, G. S. 1984. Reciprocal food sharing in the vampire bat. *Nature, London*, **308**, 181–184.

1990. Food sharing in vampire bats. *Science, New York*, **262**, 76–82.

Williams, B. 1972. *Morality: an Introduction to Ethics*. Harmondsworth: Penguin.

1981. *Moral Luck*. Cambridge: Cambridge University Press.

1985. *Ethics and the Limits of Philosophy*. Cambridge: Harvard University Press.

Williams, G. C. 1988. Reply to comments on 'Huxley's evolution and ethics in sociobiological perspective'. *Zygon*, **23**, 437–438.

1989. A sociobiological expansion of 'Evolution and Ethics'. In *Evolution and Ethics*. Princeton: Princeton University Press, pp. 179–214.

Wilson, E. O. 1971. *The Insect Societies*. Cambridge: Harvard University Press.

1975. *Sociobiology. The New Synthesis*. Cambridge: Harvard University Press.

1978. *On Human Nature*. Cambridge: Harvard University Press.

1992. *The Diversity of Life*, Cambridge: Harvard University Press.

1998. *Consilience: the Unity of Knowledge*. London: Little, Brown & Co.

Wilson, J. Q. 1993. *The Moral Sense*. New York: Free Press.

Wilson, M. 1995. Duties concerning islands. In *Environmental Ethics*. Ed. R. Elliot, pp. 89–103. Oxford: Oxford University Press.

Wolff, P. H. 1978. The biology of morals from a psychological perspective. In *Morality as a Biological Phenomenon*. Ed. G. S. Stent, pp. 83–92. Berkeley and Los Angeles: University of California Press.

Wrangham, R., McGrew, W., Waal, F. de and Heltne, P. (Eds). 1994. *Chimpanzee Cultures*. Cambridge: Harvard University Press.

Wright, R. 1994. *The Moral Animal: the New Science of Evolutionary Psychology*. New York: Pantheon.

Wynne-Edwards, V. C. 1962. *Animal Dispersion in Relation to Social Behaviour*. Edinburgh: Oliver and Boyd.

Zahavi, A. 1974. Communal nesting by the Arabian babbler. A case of individual selection. *Ibis*, **116**, 84–87.

Zahn-Waxler, C. and Radke-Yarrow, M. 1982. The development of altruism: alternative research strategies. In *The Development of Prosocial Behavior*. Ed. N. Eisenberg, pp. 109–138. New York: Academic Press.

Species list

ani	*Crotophaga* spp.
ant, e.g.	*Pogonomyrmex* spp.
ant, e.g.	*Solenopsis* spp.
babbler, e.g.	*Turdoides squamiceps*
baboon, gelada	*Theropithecus gelada*
baboon, hamadryas	*Papio hamadryas*
baboon, anubis, savannah, yellow	*Papio cynocephalus*
bat, frugivorous, e.g.	*Phyllostomus discolor*
bat, vampire	*Desmodus rotundus*
bee-eater, white-fronted	*Merops bullockoides*
bonobo	*Pan paniscus*
brittle stars, e.g.	*Ophiothrix fragilis*
cat, golden	*Profelis aurata*
chimpanzee	*Pan troglodytes*
chimpanzee, pigmy	*Pan paniscus*
cleaner fish, e.g.	*Labroides dimidiatus*
coot	*Fulica atra*
dolphin, striated	*Lagenorhynchus obliquidens*
eland	*Taurotragus oryx*
elephant, African	*Loxodonta africana*
fairy wren, e.g.	*Malurus* sp.
fieldfare	*Turdus pilares*
gazelle, Thompson's	*Gazella thompsoni*
grasshopper, e.g.	*Melanoplus femor-rubrum*
hawk, Harris'	*Parabuteo unicinctus*
honeyguide	*Indicator indicator*
huia	*Heterolochia acutirostris*
hunting dog, painted	*Lycaon pictus*
jay, scrub	*Aphelocoma coerulescens*
kookaburra	*Dacelo gigas*
ladybird (beetle), e.g.	*Adalia* spp.
lemur, ring-tailed	*Lemur catta*
leopard	*Panthera pardus*
macaque, Japanese	*Macaca fuscata*
macaque, long-tailed	*Macaca fascicularis*
macaque, pig-tailed	*Macaca nemestrina*
macaque, rhesus	*Macaca mulatta*
macaque, stump-tailed	*Macaca arctoides*
macaque, toque	*Macaca sinica*
man	*Homo sapiens*
mole-rat, naked	*Heterocephalus glaber*

mongoose, dwarf	*Helogale undulata*
monkey, blue	*Cercopithecus mitis*
monkey, capuchin	*Cebus capucinus*
monkey, colobus, e.g.	*Colobus guereza*
monkey, vervet	*Cercopithecus aethiops*
monkey, woolly	*Brachyteles arachnoides*
monkey, *see also* baboon, macaque	
muriqui	*Brachyteles arachnoides*
native hen, Tasmanian	*Tribonyx mortierii*
orang-utan	*Pongo pygmaeus*
ox-pecker	*Buphagus africanus*
peccary	*Peccari ongulatus*
pike	*Esox* spp.
Portuguese man-of-war	*Physalia* spp.
prairie dog	*Cynomys ludovicianus*
ratel	*Mellivora capensis*
red deer	*Cervus elaphus*
reindeer	*Rangifer tarandus*
sea urchin, e.g.	*Paracentrotus lividus*
sheep, big-horn	*Ovis canadensis*
sparrow, white-throated	*Zonotrichia albicollis*
squid, e.g.	*Loligo* spp.
squirrel, ground, e.g.	*Spermophilus beldingii*
termite, e.g.	*Globitermes sulfureus*
tern, arctic	*Sterna paradisaea*
blue tit	*Parus caeruleus*
vicuña	*Vicugna vicugna*
weaver bird, e.g.	*Philetarius* sp.
whale, pilot	*Globicephala macrorhynchus*
wren, superb blue	*Malurus cyaneus*

Author index

Subject index